ADOBE PREMIERE PRO MASTERY 2025

Advanced Strategies for Stunning Video Content for Beginners and Experts

Sloane Delaney

TABLE OF CONTENTS

INTRODUCTION

Adobe Premiere Pro 2025 is currently recognized as a nonlinear editing application that leads in the film, broadcasting, journalism, and content creation industries for professionals and students alike. Its user-friendly interface harmoniously combines with precision-oriented tools that empower users to handle everything from basic edits to intricate compositing with ease. Whether you are starting from scratch or picking up where you may have left off, Premiere Pro offers unparalleled flexibility in your edits. Begin a new project effortlessly by selecting "New Project" (Windows: Ctrl+Alt+N, macOS: Opt+Cmd+N) or dive back into your work with "Open Project" (Windows: Ctrl+O, macOS: Cmd+O). Plus, if you've begun editing in Adobe Premiere Rush (a mobile-friendly, lightweight companion app), you can effortlessly transition your work to Premiere Pro for more advanced developments, ensuring continuity and creative freedom.

Importing media into Premiere Pro 2025 is quick and effortless, with a couple of different ways to get video, audio, and other assets into your workspace. Whether via the Media Browser (Windows: Ctrl+Alt+I, macOS: Opt+Cmd+I) or through Adobe's dynamic linking feature, users can integrate elements directly from After Effects, Photoshop, and Illustrator into their projects. Once the media is imported, the Timeline and Source Monitor become the main creative tools for crafting a sequence. These features allow for frame-accurate in-and-out point settings, smooth reordering of clips, and fine-tuned adjustments to get every frame just right. This ease of work is intended to help editors of all skill levels make video creation accessible and professional.

Premiere Pro 2025 doesn't stop at basic editing but empowers users to give these projects some stunning developments. Everything from creating customized titles using the Type tool and saving them as reusable Motion

Graphics templates, down to finessing the visuals in the Lumetri Color panel, which accommodates a suite of tools to add polish, that is, adding transition effects, audio adjustments, and even advanced sound mixing with Adobe Audition. When ready, share your work using the Adobe Media Encoder options to ensure great, smooth playback on any platform. And that's why this all-around suite makes Premiere Pro the ultimate choice for editors producing outstanding content.

Looking ahead, more features coming into Premiere Pro 2025 will continue breaking the creative barriers. But the latest developments, now in beta and available via the Adobe Creative Cloud desktop app, are all about innovative workflow improvements and powerful new tools. It's all about saving time, simplifying your processes, and giving editors unparalleled creative flexibility. Whether one is making a documentary, editing social media content, or producing a feature film, these developments may mean a complete redefinition of how one approaches a project.

Boost your video production workflows, that is, the features coming first in Premiere Pro 2025. Envision intuitive templates that smartly adjust to your unique needs, tools that streamline even the most complex jobs into intuitive processes, and a workspace designed to put your creative vision first. Give them a try today share your input with Adobe, and get an early understanding of how they can help boost your editing process. Put together, all these developments, combined with your imagination, will continue to reshape the future of video editing and ensure that every story you tell is realized with exactness and flair.

CHAPTER ONE

GETTING STARTED

What's new in Premiere Pro?

Adobe Premiere Pro 25.0 boasts a long list of improvements to help both the beginning and advanced video editor. First and foremost, it's the completely new, context-sensitive **Properties Panel**. It automatically switches and shows the most appropriate tools for any given moment. An interface with the minimum number of tabs for a beginner will reduce the learning curve while working with Premiere Pro. Advanced users, on the other hand, will appreciate the efficiency it brings to their workflow: getting things done quicker and in fewer clicks.

Another improvement with the Premiere Pro's is the redesigned interface which is sleek and modern. Users have various options to customize the look and feel of the software as per their tastes and requirements. It allows options such as two dark modes for a low-light environment, a light mode, and even an optimized high-contrast mode for accessibility. This range of choice therefore provides a more personalized and comfortable experience in which users may prefer the setting that best suits their editing environment and visual needs.

The creation process for projects has also been significantly improved. The new **Creation dialog** simplifies the preliminary setup by making some basic settings like naming, storage location, template selection, and project parameters easily accessible. An innovative "skip import mode" will let you start editing immediately for an even smoother workflow. This makes new projects easier and faster to start, and that way, users can save valuable time from administrative work on creative processes.

More recently, Premiere Pro has further increased the support for Canon cameras and notably includes Canon EOS C80 files. With extended compatibility, users are allowed to import Canon EOS C80 source files and begin editing straight away without necessarily having to transcode the footage. Native support allows high-quality playback, thus efficient editing, paving the way for a less cumbersome process of editing high-end footage.

Best practices for updating to the latest Premiere Pro

Keeping Adobe Premiere Pro updated is one of the best ways to ensure optimal performance by benefiting from bug fixes, new features, and stability improvements.

When to Update

Like with all professional software, we recommend that you update during less busy periods in your projects. For instance, the best time is between projects or when you've got little work.

This way, you can be sure that the risks of interruptions are at their lowest. Auto-update settings can be set in the Adobe Creative Cloud Desktop app. If you prefer having a bit more control over your updates, consider disabling auto-updates for Premiere Pro.

Understanding the Update Cycle

Premiere Pro gets around six planned updates each year. They are frequently "dot releases" (such as 25.1 or 25.2), which are partial releases of the same major release. Dot releases are intended to be compatible with other dot releases of the same major release backward; projects created in 25.0 can open in any other 23. x version.

Also, there is usually one major Adobe release every year, identified by its version number, which changes-for example, 24. x or 25.x. Major releases contain more dramatic changes, that is, new tools and improvements are often introduced with major releases.

Scheduled Updates: Recommended Routine Maintenance

- **Check for System Drivers**: Often, one of the most basic reasons behind the laggy performance is drivers that aren't updated. You can check your drivers by opening Premiere Pro and heading to the **Help menu**. After that, click on **System Compatibility Report**.
- **Clear Media Cache**: Clearing your media cache from time to time will clear up storage space and increase responsiveness. This can be done through reset options when launching Premiere Pro.
- **Rebuilding the Plugin Cache**: If you feel things are running slow, you can reset the plugin cache. You get to this within reset options by holding down Cmd (macOS) or Ctrl (Windows) as you launch Premiere Pro.

Major Releases: Full Maintenance Checklist

For major updates, like from 24.6 to 25.0, we highly recommend deeper maintenance to ensure that the integration of the new version is glitch-free. Besides the steps described above, the following are other things you could look at:

- **Third-Party Plugins:** First of all, make sure that all third-party plugins are updated and compatible with the new major version. Older plugins may give you surprises.
- **Save Your Presets:** Sometimes, big updates mess with or even reset certain settings. Because of this, you'll want to export your preferences, keyboard shortcuts, and workspace layouts, so you don't lose your customization.

These practices will keep your workflow lean and get you the most out of Premiere Pro's latest capabilities with as little interruption as possible.

Keyboard shortcuts in Premiere Pro

In this in-depth section, learn how to use and customize keyboard shortcuts in Adobe Premiere Pro 2025.

Interactive Keyboard Layout for Shortcut Customization

This visual representation of the keyboard layout shows you which keys have already been assigned to a command and which are free to be customized. Hovering over a key shows its assigned command's name, and clicking a modifier key will highlight all the shortcuts that use the modifier. You can also click modifier keys directly on your hardware keyboard for the same effect.

Clicking a key in the layout shows you all the commands assigned to that key across various modifier combinations. Premiere Pro recognizes your keyboard type and changes the display accordingly. If Premiere does not support your keyboard, it defaults to U.S. English. If you edit any shortcuts, the preset changes to "Custom" and you can then save that as a new set of shortcuts.

Color Coding for easier navigation

- Purple: Application-wide shortcut
- Green: Panel-specific shortcut

- Purple & Green: Panel commands assigned to keys that also have application commands

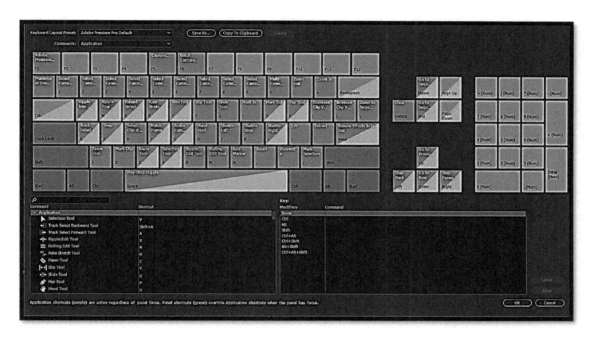

Application vs. Panel Shortcuts

Premiere Pro supports application-wide and panel-specific shortcuts. Application shortcuts (but a few oddities) work whatever the active panel is, but panel-specific shortcuts work only when that panel has focus. If a panel shortcut conflicts with an application shortcut, the panel-specific shortcut overrides it when that panel is forward. You can also pop up a window that shows a listing of shortcuts for a specific panel, such as the timeline.

Use the Command List to find commands and define new shortcuts by highlighting the command and pressing the key combination you'd like to use. You are warned if:

- An application shortcut is already defined for another application command.
- A panel shortcut conflicts with another command of the same panel.

- A panel shortcut overrides an application shortcut when that panel is active.

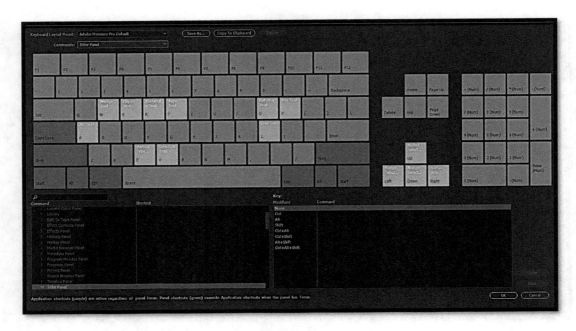

Drag-and-Drop Shortcut Assignment

Assign shortcuts by simply dragging the commands from the Command List onto keys in the Keyboard Layout or to modifier combinations shown in the Key Modifier List. To add modifiers, hold the desired modifiers down while dragging.

Easy Conflict Resolution

If a shortcut conflict occurs, a warning is given and the conflicting commands turn blue. The active state of the Undo and Clear buttons allow for easy editing or clearing of conflicting assignments.

Premiere Pro Default Keyboard Shortcuts

Many commands in Premiere Pro have keyboard shortcut equivalents, allowing you to complete tasks with minimal mouse use. You can also create or edit keyboard shortcuts.

A. File Commands

Project...

- Windows: Ctrl + Alt + N
- macOS: Opt + Cmd + N

Sequence...

- Windows: Ctrl + N
- macOS: Cmd + N

Bin

- Windows: Ctrl + /
- macOS: Cmd + /

Open Project...

- Windows: Ctrl + O
- macOS: Cmd + O

Close Project

- Windows: Ctrl + Shift + W
- macOS: Shift + Cmd + W

Close

- Windows: Ctrl + W
- macOS: Cmd + W

Save

- Windows: Ctrl + S
- macOS: Cmd + S

Save As...

- Windows: Ctrl + Shift + S
- macOS: Shift + Cmd + S

Save a Copy...

- Windows: Ctrl + Alt + S

- macOS: Opt + Cmd + S

Import from Media Browser

- Windows: Ctrl + Alt + I
- macOS: Opt + Cmd + I

Import...

- Windows: Ctrl + I
- macOS: Cmd + I

Export Media

- Windows: Ctrl + M
- macOS: Cmd + M

Get Properties for Selection...

- Windows: Ctrl + Shift + H
- macOS: Shift + Cmd + H

Exit

- Windows: Ctrl + Q
- macOS: Cmd + Q

B.   **Edit Commands**

Undo

- Windows: Ctrl + Z
- macOS: Cmd + Z

Redo

- Windows: Ctrl + Shift + Z
- macOS: Shift + Cmd + Z

Cut

- Windows: Ctrl + X
- macOS: Cmd + X

Copy

- Windows: Ctrl + C

- macOS: Cmd + C

Paste

- Windows: Ctrl + V
- macOS: Cmd + V

Paste and Insert

- Windows: Ctrl + Shift + V
- macOS: Shift + Cmd + V

Paste Attributes

- Windows: Ctrl + Alt + V
- macOS: Opt + Cmd + V

Clear

- Windows: Delete
- macOS: Forward Delete

Ripple Delete

- Windows: Shift + Delete
- macOS: Shift + Forward Delete

Duplicate

- Windows: Ctrl + Shift + /
- macOS: Shift + Cmd + /

Select All

- Windows: Ctrl + A
- macOS: Cmd + A

Deselect All

- Windows: Ctrl + Shift + A
- macOS: Shift + Cmd + A

Find...

- Windows: Ctrl + F
- macOS: Cmd + F

Edit Original

- Windows: Ctrl + E
- macOS: Cmd + E

Keyboard Shortcuts

- Windows: Ctrl + Alt + K
- macOS: Cmd + Opt + K

C. Clip Commands

Make Subclip...

- Windows: Ctrl + U
- macOS: Cmd + U

Audio Channels...

- Windows: Shift + G
- macOS: Shift + G

Audio Gain

- Windows: G
- macOS: G

Speed/Duration...

- Windows: Ctrl + R
- macOS: Cmd + R

Enable

- Windows: Shift + E
- macOS: Shift + Cmd + E

Link

- Windows: Ctrl + L
- macOS: Cmd + L

Group

- Windows: Ctrl + G
- macOS: Cmd + G

Ungroup

- Windows: Ctrl + Shift + G
- macOS: Shift + Cmd + G

D.   Sequence Commands

Render Effects in Work Area

- Windows: Enter
- macOS: Enter

Match Frame

- Windows: F
- macOS: F

Reverse Match Frame

- Windows: Shift + R
- macOS: Shift + R

Add Edit

- Windows: Ctrl + K
- macOS: Cmd + K

Add Edit to All Tracks

- Windows: Ctrl + Shift + K
- macOS: Shift + Cmd + K

Trim Edit

- Windows: Shift + T
- macOS: Cmd + T

Extend Selected Edit to Playhead

- Windows: E
- macOS: E

Apply Video Transition

- Windows: Ctrl + D
- macOS: Cmd + D

Apply Audio Transition

- Windows: Ctrl + Shift + D

- macOS: Shift + Cmd + D

Apply Default Transitions to Selection

- Windows: Shift + D

- macOS: Shift + D

E. **Markers Commands**

Mark In

- Windows: I

- macOS: I

Mark Out

- Windows: O

- macOS: O

Mark Clip

- Windows: X

- macOS: X

Mark Selection

- Windows: /

- macOS: /

Go to In

- Windows: Shift + I

- macOS: Shift + I

Go to Out

- Windows: Shift + O

- macOS: Shift + O

Clear In

- Windows: Ctrl + Shift + I

- macOS: Opt + I

Clear Out

- Windows: Ctrl + Shift + O
- macOS: Opt + O

Clear In and Out

- Windows: Ctrl + Shift + X
- macOS: Opt + X

Add Marker

- Windows: M
- macOS: M

Go to Next Marker

- Windows: Shift + M
- macOS: Shift + M

Go to Previous Marker

- Windows: Ctrl + Shift + M
- macOS: Shift + Cmd + M

Clear Selected Marker

- Windows: Ctrl + Alt + M
- macOS: Opt + M

Clear All Markers

- Windows: Ctrl + Alt + Shift + M
- macOS: Opt + Cmd + M

F. **Graphics and Titles Commands**

New Layer - Text

- Windows: Ctrl + T
- macOS: Cmd + T

New Layer - Rectangle

- Windows: Ctrl + Alt + R
- macOS: Opt + Cmd + R

New Layer - Ellipse

- Windows: Ctrl + Alt + E
- macOS: Opt + Cmd + E

Bring to Front

- Windows: Ctrl + Shift +]
- macOS: Shift + Cmd +]

Bring Forward

- Windows: Ctrl +]
- macOS: Cmd +]

Send Backward

- Windows: Ctrl + [
- macOS: Cmd + [

Send to Back

- Windows: Ctrl + Shift + [
- macOS: Shift + Cmd + [

G. Window Commands

Reset to Saved Layout

- Windows: Alt + Shift + 0
- macOS: Opt + Shift + 0

Audio Clip Mixer

- Windows: Shift + 9
- macOS: Shift + 9

Audio Track Mixer

- Windows: Shift + 6
- macOS: Shift + 6

Effect Controls

- Windows: Shift + 5
- macOS: Shift + 5

Effects

- Windows: Shift + 7
- macOS: Shift + 7

Media Browser

- Windows: Shift + 8
- macOS: Shift + 8

Program Monitor

- Windows: Shift + 4
- macOS: Shift + 4

Projects

- Windows: Shift + 1
- macOS: Shift + 1

Source Monitor

- Windows: Shift + 2
- macOS: Shift + 2

Timelines

- Windows: Shift + 3
- macOS: Shift + 3

H. Help Commands

Premiere Pro Help...

- Windows: F1
- macOS: F1

I. Audio Track Mixer Panel Commands

Show/Hide Tracks

- Windows: Ctrl + Alt + T
- macOS: Opt + Cmd + T

Loop

- Windows: Ctrl + L
- macOS: Cmd + L

Meter Input(s) Only

- Windows: Ctrl + Shift + I
- Ma   cOS: Ctrl + Shift + I

J.   Effect Controls Panel Commands

Remove Selected Effect

- Windows: Backspace
- macOS: Delete

Loop During Audio-Only Playback

- Windows: Ctrl + L
- macOS: Cmd + L

K.   Effects Panel Commands

New Custom Bin

- Windows: Ctrl + /
- macOS: Cmd + /

Delete Custom Item

- Windows: Backspace
- macOS: Delete

L.   Essential Graphics Panel Commands

Text Layer

- Windows: Ctrl + T
- macOS: Cmd + T

Rectangle

- Windows: Ctrl + Alt + R
- macOS: Opt + Cmd + R

Ellipse

- Windows: Ctrl + Alt + E
- macOS: Opt + Cmd + E

Bring to Front

- Windows: Ctrl + Shift +]

- macOS: Cmd + Shift +]

Bring Forward

- Windows: Ctrl +]

- macOS: Cmd +]

Send Backward

- Windows: Ctrl + [

- macOS: Cmd + [

Send to Back

- Windows: Ctrl + Shift + [

- macOS: Cmd + Shift + [

Select Next Layer

- Windows: Ctrl + Alt +]

- macOS: Cmd + Opt +]

Select Previous Layer

- Windows: Ctrl + Alt + [

- macOS: Cmd + Opt + [

Clear Selection

- Windows: Backspace

- macOS: Delete

Increase Leading by One Unit

- Windows: Alt + Up

- macOS: Opt + Up

Decrease Leading by One Unit

- Windows: Alt + Down

- macOS: Opt + Down

Increase Leading by Five Units

- Windows: Alt + Shift + Up

- macOS: Opt + Shift + Up

Decrease Leading by Five Units

- Windows: Alt + Shift + Down
- macOS: Opt + Shift + Down

Increase Font Size by One Unit

- Windows: Ctrl + Alt + Right
- macOS: Opt + Cmd + Right

Decrease Font Size by One Unit

- Windows: Ctrl + Alt + Left
- macOS: Opt + Cmd + Left

Increase Font Size by Five Units

- Windows: Ctrl + Alt + Shift + Right
- macOS: Opt + Shift + Cmd + Right

Decrease Font Size by Five Units

- Windows: Ctrl + Alt + Shift + Left
- macOS: Opt + Shift + Cmd + Left

M. History Panel Commands

Step Backward

- Windows: Left
- macOS: Left

Step Forward

- Windows: Right
- macOS: Right

Delete

- Windows: Backspace
- macOS: Delete

N. Media Browser Panel Commands

Open in Source Monitor

- Windows: Shift + O
- macOS: Shift + O

Select Directory List

- Windows: Shift + Left
- macOS: Shift + Left

Select Media List

- Windows: Shift + Right
- macOS: Shift + Right

O. Metadata Panel Commands

Loop

- Windows: Ctrl + L
- macOS: Cmd + L

Play

- Windows: Space
- macOS: Space

P. Multi-Camera Commands

Go to the Next Edit Point

- Windows: Down
- macOS: Down

Go to the Next Edit Point on Any Track

- Windows: Shift + Down
- macOS: Shift + Down

Go to Previous Edit Point

- Windows: Up
- macOS: Up

Go to Previous Edit Point on Any Track

- Windows: Shift + Up
- macOS: Shift + Up

Go to Selected Clip End

- Windows: Shift + End
- macOS: Shift + End

Go to Selected Clip Start

- Windows: Shift + Home
- macOS: Shift + Home

Go to Sequence-Clip End

- Windows: End
- macOS: End

Go to Sequence-Clip Start

- Windows: Home
- macOS: Home

Increase Clip Volume

- Windows:]
- macOS:]

Increase Clip Volume Many

- Windows: Shift +]
- macOS: Shift +]

Maximize or Restore Active Frame

- Windows: Shift + `
- macOS: Shift + `

Minimize All Tracks

- Windows: Shift + -
- macOS: Shift + -

Play Around

- Windows: Shift + K
- macOS: Shift + K

Play In to Out

- Windows: Ctrl + Shift + Space
- macOS: Opt + K

Play In to Out with Preroll/Postroll

- Windows: Shift + Space

- macOS: Shift + Space

Play from Playhead to Out Point

- Windows: Ctrl + Space

- macOS: Ctrl + Space

Play-Stop Toggle

- Windows: Space

- macOS: Space

Reveal Nested Sequence

- Windows: Ctrl + Shift + F

- macOS: Ctrl + Shift + F

Ripple Trim Next Edit To Playhead

- Windows: W

- macOS: W

Ripple Trim Previous Edit to Playhead

- Windows: Q

- macOS: Q

Select Camera 1

- Windows: 1

- macOS: 1

Select Camera 2

- Windows: 2

- macOS: 2

Select Camera 3

- Windows: 3

- macOS: 3

Select Camera 4

- Windows: 4

- macOS: 4

Select Camera 5

- Windows: 5
- macOS: 5

Select Camera 6

- Windows: 6
- macOS: 6

Select Camera 7

- Windows: 7
- macOS: 7

Select Camera 8

- Windows: 8
- macOS: 8

Select Camera 9

- Windows: 9
- macOS: 9

Select/Find Box

- Windows: Shift + F
- macOS: Shift + F

Select Clip at Playhead

- Windows: D
- macOS: D

Select Next Clip

- Windows: Ctrl + Down
- macOS: Cmd + Down

Select Next Panel

- Windows: Ctrl + Shift +.
- macOS: Ctrl + Shift +.

Select Previous Clip

- Windows: Ctrl + Up
- macOS: Cmd + Up

Select Previous Panel

- Windows: Ctrl + Shift +
- macOS: Ctrl + Shift +

Set Poster Frame

- Windows: Shift + P
- macOS: Cmd + P

Shuttle Left

- Windows: J
- macOS: J

Shuttle Right

- Windows: L
- macOS: L

Shuttle Slow Left

- Windows: Shift + J
- macOS: Shift + J

Shuttle Slow Right

- Windows: Shift + L
- macOS: Shift + L

Shuttle Stop

- Windows: K
- macOS: K

Step Back

- Windows: Left
- macOS: Left

Step Back Five Frames - Units

- Windows: Shift + Left

- macOS: Shift + Left

Step Forward

- Windows: Right

- macOS: Right

Step Forward Five Frames - Units

- Windows: Shift + Right

- macOS: Shift + Right

Toggle All Audio Targets

- Windows: Ctrl + 9

- macOS: Cmd + 9

Toggle All Source Audio

- Windows: Ctrl + Alt + 9

- macOS: Opt + Cmd + 9

Toggle All Source Video

- Windows: Ctrl + Alt + 0

- macOS: Opt + Cmd + 0

Toggle All Video Targets

- Windows: Ctrl + 0

- macOS: Cmd + 0

Toggle Audio during Scrubbing

- Windows: Shift + S

- macOS: Shift + S

Toggle Full Screen

- Windows: Ctrl +

- macOS: Ctrl +

Viewing and Finding Keyboard Shortcuts

There are a few ways to view and find keyboard shortcuts to help you work more efficiently in Premiere Pro. Here are ways to access and view them.

1. **Tool and Button Shortcuts**: Rest your pointer on a tool or button to see its tooltip. Its keyboard shortcut shows up after the tool description if any.

2. **Menu Commands:** All menu commands that have a keyboard shortcut have the key displayed next to the command in the menu.

3. **Shortcut list:** For other commonly used shortcuts that don't appear in tooltips, or the menus, refer to the shortcut list seen above. To display all default and current keys use the following:

   a) On Windows: Click the **Edit menu.** After that, click on the **Keyboard Shortcuts.**

   b) **On** Mac OS: Click on **Premiere Pro** before clicking on the **Keyboard Shortcuts.**

4. **Search Field under Keyboard Customization**: In the Keyboard Customization dialogue, the search field is used in locating certain commands rather quickly.

Modifying Shortcuts and Loading Them

Premiere Pro allows modification of keyboard shortcuts to more closely resemble other applications one might deal with, allowing flexibility in customizing your editing experience. To adjust or load keyboard shortcuts:

1. **Launch the Keyboard Customization Dialogue**:

   • On Windows: Click the **Edit menu.** After that, click on the **Keyboard Shortcuts.**

   • **On** Mac OS: Click on **Premiere Pro** before clicking on the **Keyboard Shortcuts.**

2. **Selecting Shortcut Types:**

   • Application Commands: Lists your commands organized by category under the menu bar.

- Panel Commands: Displays commands assigned to panels and menus.
- Tool Commands: Lists all your tool icons.

3. **Creating New Shortcuts:**
   - Locate the command for which you want to create a shortcut, and select its shortcut field.
   - In the field, type your new shortcut. If that shortcut has already been used, you'll get an alert.
   - If you wish to clear that shortcut or update it, you'll have to click "Undo," "Go To," "Clear," or "Redo."

4. **Save Your Key Set:**
   - Once satisfied with your changes, click **Save As**, name your Key Set and save for later use.

Important Notes: The reserved keys can't be reassigned in Premiere Pro on some operating systems. Some keys, such as the plus (+) and minus (-) keys on the numeric keypad can't be reassigned because they are used to enter timecode values.

Syncing/Copying Keyboard Shortcuts to Other Computers

You can easily transfer your edited shortcuts between computers for identical editing environments:

1. **Using Creative Cloud Sync:**

   Premiere Pro allows you to share your shortcuts with Creative Cloud for easy maintenance of identical shortcuts across different computers.

   Note: The shortcuts will sync only across the same operating system - Windows to Windows, Mac OS to Mac OS.

2. **Manual Transferring of Shortcut Files:**

   Locate your .kys file with your customized shortcuts and copy it to another computer, if you like.

File paths:

Creative Cloud Sync:

- Windows: Users\[username]\Documents\Adobe\Premiere Pro\[version]\Profile-CreativeCloud-\Win\

- Mac OS: Users/[username]/Documents/ Adobe /Premiere Pro/[version]/Profile-CreativeCloud-/Mac/

No Sync:

- Windows: Users\[username]\Documents\Adobe\Premiere Pro\[version]\Profile-username\Win\

- Mac OS: Users/[username]/Documents/ Adobe /Premiere Pro/[version]/Profile-username/Mac/

- Copy the .kys file onto a removable drive then copy it into the new computer in the same folder.

Append Multiple Keys to a Single Command

Premiere Pro allows you to attach multiple keys to a single command:

- **Adding Shortcuts:** To add another shortcut, click next to an existing shortcut. To create a new shortcut button, click on the **Shortcut** column.

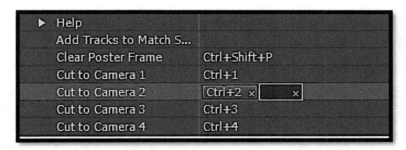

- **Edit shortcuts:** To edit or delete shortcuts, click directly on a shortcut text to replace it, or select 'x' to delete an assigned shortcut.

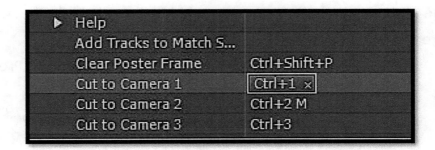

- **Delete Shortcuts**: To delete shortcuts, open the Keyboard Customization dialog via; On

- Windows: Click the **Edit menu.** After that, click on the **Keyboard Shortcuts.**

- **On** Mac OS: Click on **Premiere Pro** before clicking on the **Keyboard Shortcuts.**

3. **Clear a single shortcut:** From the Key list, select the key from which you want to clear an assignment and click the **Clear button.**

4. **Delete a set of shortcuts:** Choose a key set from the Set menu and click the **Delete button**; then click **Yes** in the warning dialog that appears.

Printing Keyboard Shortcuts

You can print out the list of keyboard shortcuts for yourself to use as a reference document.

1. **Export into a document:**
   - Press Ctrl + Shift (Windows) or Command + Shift (Mac OS) to open the Keyboard Shortcuts dialog.
   - Click the Clipboard button, open a text editor or spreadsheet, paste, and save the document.

2. **Printing Shortcut Documentation:** This document can be printed directly or saved as a PDF for later use, so you can review and integrate these shortcuts seamlessly into your workflow.

Accessibility in Premiere Pro

Accessibility involves designing and developing products to make them usable by people with a wide range of disabilities related to vision, hearing, motor control, and cognition. That is to say, it means making it possible for every user to use technology conveniently.

Accessibility Features

A variety of accessibility features make software highly usable. Following are a few examples:

- **Screen Reader Support:** Software that provides a means of communicating on-screen text and non-text elements, like buttons and images, to users who are visually disabled.
- **Text Equivalents:** It is a method of presenting information without relying on graphics, images, and multimedia by giving text descriptions.
- **Keyboard Navigation:** This means allowing users to navigate through software using other interfaces than a mouse, due to their condition of impairment in mobility.
- **High Contrast Displays**: It provides ways of altering color schemes to improve readability for users who have visual sensitivities.

Premiere Pro's Commitment to Accessibility

Adobe Premiere Pro leads the way in providing an accessible platform for video editing. It has several facilities that will be able to assist the video editors with certain needs in their workflow process:

- **Screen Magnifier Support:** Enables a user to zoom in to view selected areas of the interface.
- **Keyboard Navigation**: Enables keyboard shortcuts so that through keys, one can navigate an application to perform tasks, hence avoiding the use of a mouse.

- **OS Compatibility:** Integrates with the operating system's accessibility features such as macOS to provide a consistent experience.

Creating Accessible Content with Premiere Pro

In addition to the user interface accessibility, Premiere Pro has resources that will enable editors to make content accessible to all audiences, following established accessibility guidelines to provide this much-needed access. This includes:

- **Static Content**: Videos do not include anything that flashes, blinks, moves, scrolls, or auto-updates in a way that is known or likely to cause seizures or physical reactions. This also keeps viewers from becoming distracted or disoriented.
- **Text Contrast:** Text is implemented that is easily read against its background to improve readability.
- **Captions:** Providing captions for videos, ensuring that content is accessible by individuals who may have hearing disabilities.
- **Audio Descriptions:** Audio descriptions inform blind and low-vision users about important visual information happening within a video.

Assistive Technology Support

Premiere Pro has partial support for assistive technologies such as screen readers and screen magnifiers with improved use for people using such tools.

1. **Using the Keyboard to Navigate Premiere Pro**

    You can access almost everything within Premiere Pro by using a keyboard:

    - **Panel Navigation:** Users can rotate through panels using keyboard shortcuts (e.g., Ctrl+Shift+. on Windows or Control+Shift+. on Mac) and focus on panels indicated by a blue outline. This facilitates quick access to various editing tools.

- **Playback Control**: Common tasks such as starting and stopping playback, or stepping through frames, can be accomplished with simple keyboard shortcuts.

- **Dialog Box Navigation:** Users can traverse dialog boxes using the Tab key and arrow keys, allowing for efficient interaction with various settings and options.

Even though most of the functions are controllable with the keyboard, there are various limitations, for example, around specific dialogues or panels in which there is no navigation without the mouse.

2. Visual Preferences for Accessibility

Premiere Pro has options to toggle visual preferences according to the needs of accessibility. You can switch between high and low contrast modes using the **Appearance preference** according to how visible or focused you want your content to be.

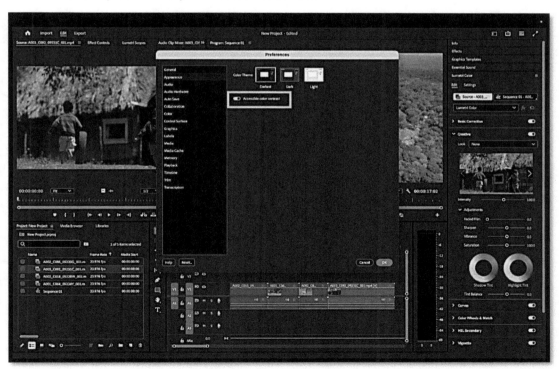

The integration of the **Spectrum design system** is meant to provide harmony across different Adobe applications by considering inclusive, scalable, and user-centered design principles. This way, it will ensure that all users can use and interact with the tools they need to perform their tasks in an effective manner to evoke equity in the digital space.

CHAPTER TWO
HARDWARE AND OPERATING SYSTEM REQUIREMENTS

System requirements

To take full advantage of Adobe Premiere Pro 2025, your computer should meet the technical requirements outlined below. Minimum system requirements differ depending on what you are doing in editing. Recommended specifications are the best for a smooth experience.

The applicable Versions is simply the Premiere Pro version 25.0 and later.

1. **Windows System Requirements**

Minimum Specifications HD Editing

- Processor: Intel® 6th Gen CPU or AMD Ryzen™ 1000 Series, with support for AVX2.
- Memory: 8 GB of RAM
- Network: 1 Gigabit Ethernet for HD
- GPU: 2 GB of GPU memory
- Display: 1920 x 1080
- Storage: 8 GB of available hard-disk space for installation; additional free space required during product installation. Not compatible with removable flash storage.
- Sound: ASIO compatible or Microsoft Windows Driver Model
- Operating System: Windows 10 (64-bit) v22H2 or later

Recommended Specifications 4K and Higher Editing

- Processor: Intel® 11th Gen CPU with Quick Sync or AMD Ryzen™ 3000 Series / Threadripper 3000 Series or later.
- Network: 10 Gigabit Ethernet for shared 4K network workflows.

- Storage: Fast internal SSD for app installation and cache, plus additional high-speed drives for media.
- Memory: 16 GB RAM for HD; 32 GB or more for 4K and higher
- GPU: 8 GB or more of GPU memory
- Display: 1920 x 1080 or higher, DisplayHDR 1000 for HDR workflows.
- Operating System: Windows 10 (64-bit) v22H2 or later, or Windows 11

2. **macOS System Requirements**

Minimum Specifications (HD Editing)

- Processor: Intel® 6th Gen CPU or Apple silicon M1.
- Network: 1 Gigabit Ethernet (for HD workflows)
- Memory: 8 GB of RAM; 16 GB unified memory for Apple silicon.
- Display: 1920 x 1080
- GPU: 2 GB of GPU memory for Intel; 8 GB of unified memory for Apple silicon.
- Storage: 8 GB of available disk space for installation; additional free space required for media files; SSD recommended; removable flash storage not supported.
- Operating System: macOS Monterey (v12) or later.

Recommended Specifications (4K and Higher Editing)

- Processor: Apple silicon M1 Pro, M1 Max, M1 Ultra, or later processor
- Network: 10 Gigabit Ethernet for shared 4K network workflows.
- Memory: 16 GB of unified memory for Apple silicon
- GPU: 16 GB of unified memory for Apple silicon.
- Storage: Fast internal SSD for app installation and cache, plus additional high-speed drives for media.

- Display: 1920 x 1080 or greater, DisplayHDR 1000 for HDR workflows.
- Operating System: macOS Monterey (v12) or later

Additional Requirements and Information

- **Internet Access:** Required for activation, subscription validation, and online service access.
- **Age Requirement:** Adobe services are available only to users aged 13 and older.
- **Language Support:** English, Spanish, French, German, Italian, Portuguese (Brazil), Russian, Japanese, Korean, and Simplified Chinese; text composition is also available in Middle Eastern and Indic scripts.

Premiere Pro performs best when systems meet or exceed the recommended requirements to provide an efficient editing experience for HD and high-resolution projects.

GPU and GPU Driver requirements

In upgrading to Adobe Premiere Pro, driver compatibility is one of the most important things to consider for the smooth running of the program and to avoid a lot of problems. Below are the most important driver updates and recommendations to follow through, but mainly for NVIDIA, Intel, and Apple GPUs.

Recommended Driver Updates for Adobe Premiere Pro

Adobe recommends the use of the latest Studio drivers for supported NVIDIA GPUs to reduce problems. What this entails is summarily broken down into:

- **NVIDIA GeForce GTX/RTX (Desktop and Notebook)**: Use the Studio drivers.

- **NVIDIA RTX/Quadro (desktop and notebook):** It is also recommended to use the Studio drivers for these models.
- **Legacy NVIDIA GPUs (900 series and below**): These models no longer receive Studio Driver updates. On those GPUs, it is recommended to use the latest available Game Ready drivers.
- **NVIDIA Kepler Mobile:** No driver update is available for this series. When you launch Premiere Pro, there is a compatibility warning notice. Updates are impossible to create for these models.

Common Driver-Related Issues

Incompatible drivers may give rise to several performance problems in Premiere Pro. A few examples of these problems include:

- **Color Streaks:** Green, pink, or purple color streaks may appear in imported or exported video files.
- **Renderer Unavailability:** The renderer option may be grayed out by heading to the **File menu**. After that, select the **Project Settings** before clicking on **General.**
- **Unexpected Crashes:** Crashes may occur at edits randomly.
- **Playback and Preview Problems**: Inability to view any previews, distorted or slow previews, lost frames, and numerous performance issues. Smooth Playback and editing will be affected.

CUDA graphics acceleration is supported with the recommendation of drivers compatible with CUDA 11.8 or later (version 522.25 or later). Even though it is not necessary to use most of the Adobe applications, it is nice to have regarding the performance.

Updating NVIDIA Drivers on Windows

Make sure your drivers are current as NVIDIA is releasing updates pretty frequently. Go to the NVIDIA website and verify you have the most recent version compatible with your hardware.

Apple Metal GPU Acceleration

Adobe supports only versions of macOS that Apple supports actively - generally the last three versions of macOS. For macOS Mojave 10.14 and later, CUDA is not supported. To see if any GPU-related updates on macOS follow these steps:

- Go to the Apple logo
- After that, click on **About This Mac.**
- In the Overview tab, click **Software Update.**
- Run available software updates.

Intel GPU Driver Updates

For optimal compatibility and performance, Premiere Pro requires an Intel driver dated 27.20.100.8476 or later. For stability and performance, ensure that your Intel drivers are at least at this version. If updated drivers cause any compatibility problems with Adobe applications, Adobe recommend that you get an updated driver from your computer manufacturer. If your manufacturer has not posted a newer driver, do not update past 100.6286 for legacy drivers.

Premiere Pro in Dual-GPU System

In multi-GPU configurations, Premiere Pro communicates with one of the GPU drivers depending on the type of rendering in use:

- **OpenCL Acceleration**: Premiere Pro prioritizes the Intel/AMD GPU driver.
- **CUDA Acceleration:** The NVIDIA GPU driver is prioritized.

  Remember, Adobe always recommends making a backup of your system before performing any update to a driver.

Hardware recommendations

Adobe Premiere Pro and **After Effects** are optimized for both macOS and Windows, ensuring a high-performance experience across platforms. While individual setups might vary, a well-configured system with some basic understanding of formats, editing workflows, and hardware requirements will go a long way in smoothly producing video and motion graphics content.

- **Highlights for macOS**

  In the Apple ecosystem, things are seamless in terms of hardware-to-software integration. For video editing, a system with 16 GB or more of memory, SSD storage, and an Apple silicon or high-performance Intel CPU paired with an AMD GPU is recommended.

- **Highlights for Windows**

  Windows systems are flexible, easily upgradable, and even more economical sometimes. It is possible for users to have their setup according to their specific needs or just choose tested configurations provided by Dell, Lenovo, HP, amongst others, while custom workstation Puget Systems. Upgrades in general are easier, therefore extending the systems' life.

How to Choose Between a Desktop and a Laptop

Both desktops and laptops can handle video editing configurations. Generally, desktops offer better value, configuration options, and upgrade paths. Laptops are often a lot more expensive but offer portability, and with external monitors, storage, or eGPUs, they can achieve very powerful editing setups.

- **Apple Desktops**

  Systems on Apple desktops such as Mac Pro, M1 iMac, iMac Pro, and Mac Mini can handle video workflows provided they are configured with at least 16GB of RAM and SSD storage.

- **Apple Laptops**

  The MacBook Pros, with at least 16GB RAM and SSD storage, are perfect for a portable solution with immense power for HD and 4K editing.

- **Windows Desktops**

  For Windows desktops, this could be a recommended specification, that is, the multi-core CPU, AMD or NVIDIA GPU, SSD storage, and 32GB RAM will provide powerful video editing capability.

- **Windows Laptops**

  Alternatively, Windows laptops can similarly be configured to powerful mobile workstations.

Storage Requirements for Video Editing

Video files take up a lot of space. You'll want at least one external SSD or NVMe for active editing, and several more as completed projects with high-capacity storage and fast onboard storage.

- **Resolution and File Size**

  HD files (1920 x 1080) are more manageable when it comes to storage and processing, while 4K files (3840 x 2160) provide much higher detail, but require more storage and computing power.

- **Bit Depth**

  8-bit video files are the norm for most workflows, while 10-bit files have more color detail for advanced color grading but also need more processing power.

Key Components of the System for Video Editing

- **Processor (CPU)**

  Premiere Pro drool over high-clock-speed CPUs above 3.2 GHz, whereas on many-core CPUs, their performance is not excellent. This partially changes with the Multi-Frame Rendering in versions 22.0 and later.

The sweet spot should be Intel Core i7/i9 or AMD Ryzen 7/9, but for heavy projects, check the prices of AMD Threadripper and Intel Xeon series.

- **RAM (Memory)**

  For Windows and Intel-based Mac systems, 32GB is best. For Apple silicon, 16GB works well.

- **Graphics Card (GPU**)

  Premiere Pro use your computer's graphics card to enhance performance. Premiere Pro can get by with as little as 4GB VRAM, but After Effects 22.0 and later should have at least 8GB VRAM. Since Apple silicon systems use 'Unified Memory', at least 16GB is a good minimum for video editing.

- **Storage**

  Fast SSD or NVMe drives are required to make the production smooth. Theoretically speaking, a system should employ three drives: one for OS and applications, another for media cache files, and the remaining one for media assets. If shared setups, a fast network-attached storage is recommended with local storage of media cache.

Upgrade Your System for Better Performance

For Premiere Pro:

- RAM: Upgrade up to 128GB if possible for longer content.
- GPU: Faster rendering basically means adding or updating more of those GPUs.
- Storage: Add faster or add more SSD/NVMe drives.
- CPU: A faster clock speed will be preferable.

GPU Accelerated Rendering & Hardware Encoding/Decoding

Hardware acceleration in Adobe Premiere Pro gives a great increase in performance in video export and playback, especially when working with H.264 and H.265 [HEVC] formats. Hardware accelerated encoding speeds up export times, while hardware accelerated decoding improves timeline playback to allow smoother and faster video editing. The enabling of this capability requires that the users have a GPU that supports hardware-accelerated encoding and decoding.

Hardware and Software Compatibility

To determine whether your GPU supports hardware accelerated encoding and decoding, consult your computer's hardware specification. Premiere Pro supports the following major platforms for this feature:

- AMD
- NVIDIA
- Intel
- Apple Silicon: Apple silicon (M1 and onwards) supports hardware-accelerated H.264 and H.265 decoding and encoding, including 10-bit 4:2:2 decoding. For HEVC HLG 4:2:0 10-bit encoding, it's still software-based.

Activate Hardware-Accelerated Encoding

Hardware-accelerated encoding operates most effectively when exported in H.264 and HEVC format. To activate:

- In the **Export Settings window**, choose **H.264/HEVC** from the Format menu.
- From the **Video tab menu,** choose **Encode Settings**. After that, set Performance to Hardware Encoding

Supported codecs include:

- H.264/AVC (8 bit)
- HEVC 4:2:0 (8 and 10-bit), Up to 4096x4096 res minimum, Up to 8192x8192 on 10th Generation Intel Core and later

Enable Hardware-Accelerated Decoding

The hardware-accelerated decoding option will improve playback such as H.264 and HEVC. To activate:

- Select **Preference** before choosing **Media.**
- Then, select **Enable hardware-accelerated decoding** (requires restart).

- Restart Premiere Pro.

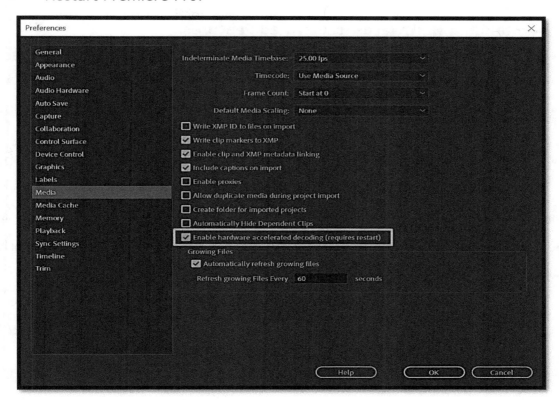

Supported codecs include:

- H.264/AVC
- HEVC (4:2:2 10-bit), for Adobe Premiere Pro, Adobe Media Encoder, and After Effects (version 22.0 or later).

Note: The M2TS format (MPEG-2 Transport Stream) is unsupported. For better performance with 4K M2TS media, transcode to a supported MP4 codec, which receives hardware-accelerated decoding.

System Recommendations

Intel® integrated GPUs: Systems with 16GB or more RAM are recommended, since Intel-integrated GPUs share system memory, performance on lower-RAM systems can be impacted.

Understanding Hardware-Accelerated Features

- **Mercury Playback Engine (GPU Acceleration**): Improves playback and effects rendering by using the GPU

- **Hardware-accelerated Encoding**: Speeds export in H.264/AVC and HEVC codecs

- **Hardware-accelerated Decoding:** Improves real-time playback by decoding H.264/AVC and HEVC media in real-time.

With the right setup and correct hardware, these features go a long way in making Premiere Pro a powerful encoding and playback tool that is particularly suited to smoothing the workflow when it comes to video editing.

CHAPTER THREE
HOW TO CREATE PROJECTS

How to start a new project

Import Mode in Premiere Pro features an impressively intuitive and sleek interface that allows users to kick-start their projects by reworking previous ideas, selecting and arranging media, and constructing video sequences that can then be edited.

By enabling the Import Mode, it becomes much easier for users to navigate, preview, and gather its host of media from various sources, each of a different type, be it video footage, audio files, or pictures. As these assets are selected, they are automatically gathered in a tray always available at the bottom of the window, providing a truly interactive and visual interpretation of your ever-growing project.

A. **Creating a New Project**

On the home screen, click **New Project.** This opens a New Project dialogue where you can define the following:

- **Project Name**: This is a unique name you give to your project.
- **Location:** This is where you want your files to be stored.
- **Template:** You may use one of the many project templates or load one from your system if it already has one set up.

You can bypass **Import Mode** to go directly to the workflow by skipping this step and opening it directly in the Project panel by selecting **Skip Import Mode**. This preference will be followed unless changed.

B. **Modify Project Setting**

The **Settings icon** opens the Project Settings, which has options for Color, General, Scratch Disks, and Ingest Settings. You can adjust important parameters according to the needs of your project here.

C. **Selecting and Organizing Media**

Use **Import Mode** to select and preview your media assets before they enter the project. Premiere Pro offers tools such as hover scrubbing for quick reviews and a list view to reveal detailed information about each file. Star frequently-used storage locations to add them to your Favorites for easy access.

As you choose media, the assets will start filling up your **Selection Tray**. To whittle down a selection right-click on any selected item in the tray to remove it, or clear the tray if you want to begin anew.

D. **Import Settings**

The following are some of the ways you might import media into Adobe Premiere Pro 2025:

- **Organize Media:** Organize the assets of your project by sorting them into new bins. This does not duplicate the files of your project.

- **Copy Media**: Allow copying for those temporary sources, such as camera cards. Premiere Pro automatically copies the files in the background as you begin editing. For extra security, create MD5 checksum verification to prevent file corruption.

- **Create New Sequence:** Simplifies sequence creation by having Premiere Pro set the sequence parameters for you, based on the first asset that you select. When enabled, selected media is added as a new sequence. If disabled, media is added to the Project panel.

Click **Create** to complete your project setup and begin importing media.

E. **Importing Media into an Existing Project**

Import media into an existing project by clicking the **Import option** from the top-left of the header bar. All the highlighted assets will be pulled into the active project. Depending on the setting for **Create New Sequence**, the new media may start a new sequence, or it may only show up in the Project panel.

F. **Additional Import Options**

Premiere Pro has several ways to import:

- Click the **File menu.**

- After that, click the **Import tab** from the menu bar.

- Use the Media Browser in **Edit mode** to browse your files within a more organized structure.

- Double-click in the Project panel to open a Finder/Mac or Explorer/Windows directly to where you can access your files.

- Drag files or folders directly onto the Project panel from your computer's file system.

How to launch projects

With Premiere Pro for Windows, you can open project files that were created in earlier versions, offering more compatibility among multiple releases. You can open only one project at a time in Premiere Pro; however, you can import content from other projects using the **Import command.**

Auto Save in Premiere Pro automatically saves copies of your project to the Auto-Save project folder a regular intervals, so your work will be automatically backed up in case of an unexpected problem.

If some files get lost during editing, you can always use offline files as placeholders, which helps you smoothly continue with your edit. Offline files let you go through the work process uninterruptedly; however, you will have to bring your original files back online to render your final output. For reconnecting lost files, directly use the **Link Media command** inside the project, instead of closing or restarting Premiere Pro.

- Open an existing project by going to the **File menu**

- After that, click on **Open Project** or use the keyboard shortcut Ctrl+O (Windows) Cmd+O (Mac).

- Then, browse the project file and select.

The **Where Is The File dialog** may appear. If this is so, find the missing file in the **Look In** field or select from:

- **Find:** Bring up Windows Explorer (Windows) or Finder (Mac OS) to find the missing file.
- **Skip:** Temporarily replaces the missing file with an offline clip. It will ask for the location of the file the next time you open the project.
- **Skip All:** Similar to Skip, it will replace all missing files temporarily with offline files.
- **Skip Previews:** It won't search for pre-rendered preview files; generally, this makes the opening of a project faster, but some re-rendering will be required for playback.
- **Offline**: Replaces missing files with a persistent offline clip, remembering all references to the file from session to session so you do not have to search each time you open a project.
- **Offline All:** This works like **Offline** but persists across sessions for all missing files.

When you choose **Skip or Skip All,** keep in mind that these temporary placeholders will need to be replaced if the file is crucial. In contrast, **Offline options** create permanent placeholders. References to the missing files are available from session to session within a project.

Note: Unless source files used in your project are recapturable files, such as those captured using device control, do not delete source files. Source files can safely be deleted, if necessary after the final movie has been delivered.

How to move and delete projects

Moving a project to another computer, especially where you will continue editing involves transferring all of the project's assets with the main project file. You should ensure these assets retain the exact same naming and folder structure on the second computer, so that the editing application can find them and automatically relink them with their respective clips within the project.

Also ensure that any necessary codecs used in the original project computer have been loaded into the second computer. This will prevent playback or edit issues with specific file formats.

To delete a Project File;

- Navigate to your project's location in File Explorer for Windows, or Finder for Mac OS. The Premiere Pro project files have a file extension of .prproj.
- Now, select the file and press **Delete** to get rid of it from your system.

How to work with multiple open projects

Adobe Premiere Pro 2025 provides good flexibility in using an application for multiple projects. You can open several projects at one time, view them, and manage them in one session.

A. Opening and Managing Multiple Projects

You can open multiple projects in Premiere Pro. You would be able to work across different timelines and assets all within that session. You can also easily open an existing project or create a new one even when you're actively working on another project.

This is extremely useful when you have to copy assets, media or sequences from one project to another. Just click and drag elements between project panels, or copy and paste items as needed.

B. Viewing all Open Projects

- To view a complete list of all opened projects, go to Premiere Pro.
- Then, click on **Projects** before selecting the **Menu**.

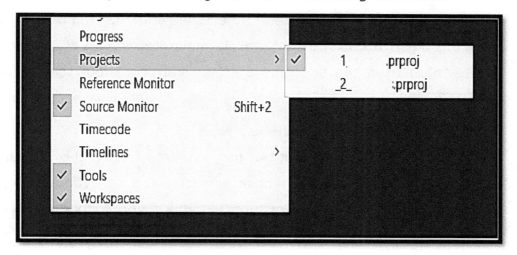

There, you will see a complete list of all opened projects and the associated panels that are opened for each project. If you click on any project's content panel such as the Timeline Panel, Project Panel, Program Monitor or Source Monitor, that project becomes the "active project" and you can quickly toggle between projects you are working on.

C. Closing Projects

When you are finished with a project and would like to close it;

- Simply head over to the **File menu.**
- After that, click on **Close Project**. Also, you can choose to close a project by using the shortcuts on Windows: Ctrl+Shift+W or on Mac: Shift+Cmd+W.

If you wish to quit Premiere Pro all altogether, be prepared to save changes for each of the projects currently open. You'll be prompted for each that needs saving, that way, all of your edits are maintained.

D.   Transferring Assets between Projects

Moving media or sequences from one project to another in Premiere Pro is relatively easy to perform. It automatically creates copies by dragging and dropping them into a new project, leaving the originals in their source project. If you want to entirely move items, you will be able to delete them from the source project by copying them to the target project.

E.   Customizing and Saving Workspaces

When you are working on a lot of projects, you frequently will want to have a workspace setup for those projects. You can choose **Import Workspace** from Projects to ensure that your favored workspace opens when opening new projects.

If you are ending work on a project for the day, it's best to save the workspace but clear the project and timeline panels associated with that project before closing. This keeps to a minimum the amount of panels reopening when you next open up to work in Premiere, so it can stay clean and relevant.

Note

By default, Premiere Pro does not save your workspace settings unless you go into Projects and select **Import Workspace**. It keeps your workspace consistent from session to session and from project to project for ease of editing.

Using these tools and techniques, you are going to be able to command control over your workflow, keep your assets organized, and set up your workspace, so that the interface in Premiere Pro is clean, organized, and ready for use on every new project.

How to work with Project Shortcuts

With Project Shortcuts, you have the option to add other projects so that you can have them quick, right in your workspace for access. It allows the addition of more projects as accessible links, hence making it simpler for you to manage and work on different files.

Importing Projects as Shortcuts

- **Access the Import Option**: Go to **File menu** before clicking on **Import**. After that, select the project file (.prproj) that you want to import.
- **Enable the Option for Project Shortcut Import**: In the Import Project dialog box, check the option that says **Import as Project Shortcut** and click **OK.**

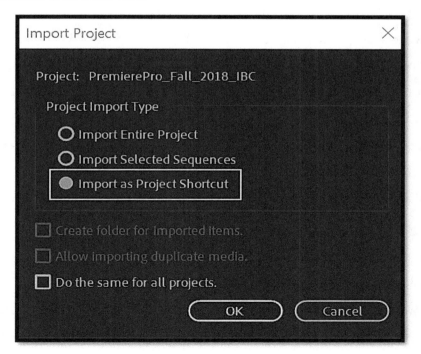

Access and Work with Your Project Shortcuts

This distinctive link icon, which you get when you import your project into the **Project panel**, shows that it acts like a quick-access link to that original project.

How to open and edit Premiere Rush projects in Premiere Pro

Take your projects to the next level by moving your projects from Adobe Premiere Rush to advanced editing in Adobe Premiere Pro. Thanks to unified cloud-based integration, all your synced Rush projects that are saved in the cloud can be opened natively and further refined in Premiere Pro.

Before You Start

- **Enable Project Syncing in Premiere Rush:** Make sure project syncing is turned on. It's turned on by default, but if it's turned off, the project will not show up in Premiere Pro.

- **Check your Version of Premiere Pro:** Make sure you are on the latest Premiere Pro version. If you are working with an earlier version, remember that projects created in Rush are unsupported in those earlier versions.

- **One-Way Workflow Notice**: Once a project is opened in Premiere Pro, it cannot be re-edited in Premiere Rush. Complete all your edits and publish directly from Premiere Pro.

Opening a Premiere Rush Project in Premiere Pro

- Select **Open Premiere Rush Project** in Premiere Pro's start screen.

- Browse through your synced projects and select the Rush project that you want to open. This feature enables you to have access and continue with any cloud-synced project from Rush in an instant.

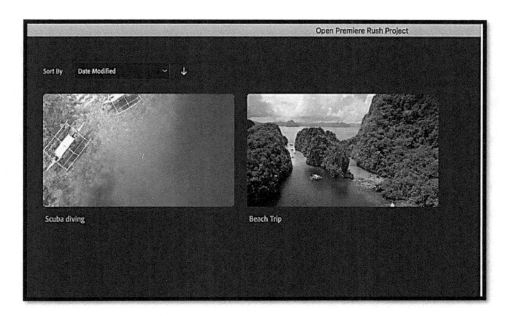

Editing and Saving Your Project in Premiere Pro

With the project opened, one can deeply exploit all the powerful editing options provided by Premiere Pro: adding more advanced effects, transitions, and any other creative touch one would need.

After editing:

- **Save Your Project:** The default action will save the file to a "Converted Rush Projects" folder on your computer. You can choose to also go to the **File menu** before clicking on **Save As** to save to another location.

How to create your project templates

Video production is a multi-process, staged event that requires organization and precision for its completion. One of the major keys to managing and scaling your projects is setting up an efficient workflow from the very beginning. Using project templates in Adobe Premiere Pro, sets up a standardized project structure that is organized, saves you time from the get-go, and continually streamlines your process throughout production.

Templates improve your pipeline, minimize errors, and provide a foundation for future projects.

Why Use Project Templates?

Project templates go beyond simple organization. They give you a solid framework, that is, a preconfigured with media bins, timeline layouts, track names, labels, effects, and many more that you can adapt and reuse. This foundational structure provides benefits for all types of users:

- **New Users** gain insight into the editing workflow and Premiere Pro's interface.
- **Experienced Editors** can use templates to maintain consistency, plan projects, and optimize work time.
- **Collaborative Teams** can standardize setups for easier collaboration, especially on large projects.

Key Elements of Premiere Pro Project Templates

A template can include everything the normal project would need; however, it is fully customizable to meet your specific needs.

- **Organized Bins and Media Folders**: Your template can pre-build bins for the organization of different kinds of content, including video, audio, graphics, and more, which allows easy access to media without wasting too much time in search.
- **Timeline and Track Layouts:** Templates can be blueprinted with named tracks, color-coded labels, and organized timelines. This saves time by applying uniformity to both the editing and review processes.
- **Search Bins:** You can create them to rapidly find specific media-like music or behind-the-scenes footage with your pre-set search criteria, so you could view only relevant media without having to navigate all the bins.

- **Graphics, Music, and SFX**: Templates can include some general-used graphics, like logos, backgrounds, and an organized audio library so that one doesn't have to spend a lot of time setting up things that aren't unique. In the same vein, being able to save useful timelines and revisit or revise them at will is also very helpful.

Practical Uses of Project Templates

Project templates are a great, flexible guide for your creativity. Here are some of the typical ways these can be pre-arranged for maximum efficiency:

- **Variations in Timeline Configurations:** Templates may include a range of timeline configurations for standard 1080p sequences, social media formats, and multichannel audio configurations with sub-mixes for dialogue, effects, and music.
- **Track-Based Audio Effects**: Add hard limiter and loudness radar effects to a master track for broadcast or high-quality audio to ensure your audio meets some sort of industry standard.
- **Multichannel Output:** Multichannel timelines for multilingual or international releases will include separate mixes for dialog, effects, and music to facilitate the localization process easier.

How to Use Project Templates

To begin using any project template, follow these steps;

1. First and foremost, download the template folder to a drive, and extract the folder.
2. To create a new folder for each new project, copy the project file, and rename the file. If you open the project in Premiere Pro, you will see:
   - **Organized Bins:** Labeled but empty bins are created for multiple media types; text notes are added to describe how to use them.

- **Preset Timelines:** Duplication of the tracks and settings by using the timeline that best suits the format of the project to have increased speed in editing.

You can include **search bins** in a template as a part of your advanced organization to reflect media that contains certain criteria to save time in searching your bins. You are also able to set search bins for things like sound effects, stock footage, or interview clips, editing as necessary to customize to your project's needs.

How to work with a sample project template

1. Download Template

Download the **project template zip file** onto your computer. Save this in a folder that you use to house all your project resources, so it's easy to access for future projects.

2. Setup Your Working Folder

Extract the downloaded zip file, and duplicate the template folder. Rename the duplicated folder to your current project name or focus, then relocate it to your media drive - your main storage point where you save all of the media and project files while editing.

Name
▶ 📁 00_Scratch disk - optional scratch disk location for caches or previews
▶ 📁 05_Other Project files - Adobe After Effect...udition, Photoshop and other project files
▶ 📁 10_Raw footage - Copy of media
▶ 📁 20 Graphic sources - copy graphics here before importing
▶ 📁 30 Music and SFX sources - place here before importing
▶ 📁 80 Stock elements
▶ 📁 85 Common stock elements (elements tha...mmon among multiple projects like logos)
▶ 📁 99_Exported files - Client exports
▶ 📁 100_Production paperwork - SCRIPTS, BUDGETS, ETC
📄 READ ME about project templates.txt

What's Included in the Project Template

The root folder of the template includes:

- **A Premiere Pro Project File**: This is the central file with which you will be working inside Premiere Pro, pre-set with an organized bin structure.

- **A Set of Folders**: These folders mirror the bins in your Premiere Pro project and are meant to organize your media files and project assets. Each folder comes with a placeholder text file containing notes about its intended purpose.

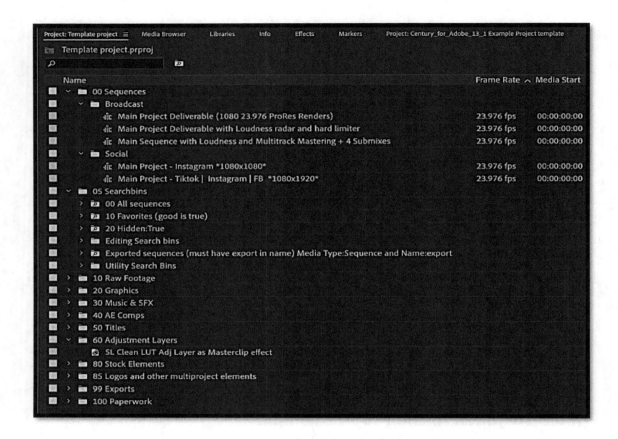

The image above shows the Project panel with the following structure:

Project: Template project — Media Browser — Libraries — Info — Effects — Markers — Project: Century_for_Adobe_13_1 Example Project template

Template project.prproj

Name	Frame Rate ^	Media Start
∨ 00 Sequences		
∨ Broadcast		
Main Project Deliverable (1080 23.976 ProRes Renders)	23.976 fps	00:00:00:00
Main Project Deliverable with Loudness radar and hard limiter	23.976 fps	00:00:00:00
Main Sequence with Loudness and Multitrack Mastering + 4 Submixes	23.976 fps	00:00:00:00
∨ Social		
Main Project - Instagram *1080x1080*	23.976 fps	00:00:00:00
Main Project - Tiktok | Instagram | FB *1080x1920*	23.976 fps	00:00:00:00
∨ 05 Searchbins		
> 00 All sequences		
> 10 Favorites (good is true)		
> 20 Hidden:True		
> Editing Search bins		
> Exported sequences (must have export in name) Media Type:Sequence and Name:export		
> Utility Search Bins		
> 10 Raw Footage		
> 20 Graphics		
> 30 Music & SFX		
> 40 AE Comps		
> 50 Titles		
∨ 60 Adjustment Layers		
SL Clean LUT Adj Layer as Masterclip effect		
> 80 Stock Elements		
> 85 Logos and other multiproject elements		
> 99 Exports		
> 100 Paperwork		

3. **Using the Folder Structure and Customization**

Also, notice that, in most templates, the folders have a specific order, often numbered, to help you keep consistency throughout projects. You can use this template as a guide, where:

- Intros, graphics, background audio, and other reusable content go into the appropriately-named folders.

- You appropriately name and create new folders or even rename some of these to better fit your project and don't worry, there's plenty of room for customizing.

4. **Opening and Using the Template in Premiere Pro**

Open this project in Premiere Pro, and you'll notice that the Project panel has been organized into bins reflecting the structure of the folder inside the main folder. This is perfect for keeping everything neat so that you have quick access to media, effects, and assets.

Add media to the template by following these steps;

- Drag your raw source media files into the "10 Raw Footage" folder.

- Open up the corresponding bin in Premiere Pro and start importing your media directly into it. The advantage of this is that you set yourself up for a well-organized and smooth workflow right from the beginning.

5. **Find Media Easily Using Search Bins**

Search bins in Premiere Pro are dynamic bins that will automatically show their contents based on specific search criteria you set. This can be a huge timesaver for your workflow as this enables you to easily find clips or media with certain metadata. For example, all clips are tagged with "BTS" for behind-the-scenes content.

- **Creating a Search Bin**: To create a search bin, go to the **File menu**. After that, click on **New** before accessing the **Search Bin** to open this search dialog.

- **Defining Search Criteria**: In the dialog box, choose your desired search criteria, that is, a keyword, or a specific kind of metadata, such as file type or camera model. You are able to create up to two criteria to refine your search.

- **Saving and Managing Search Bins:** Click **OK** after you have established your criteria. The new search bin will appear in the Project panel and automatically update when new media that matches the criteria is added.

To refine or otherwise modify your search bin, right-click it and choose **Edit Search Bin** to modify the search criteria.

Search Bins within the Sample Project Template

Within the sample project template, a range of default search bins is available to suit multiple needs and preferences for adding or creating search bins. Below is an advanced instruction that contains basic search terms to make the editor's task simple and transparent in an advanced time organization and track type consideration.

A. Project Organization Overview

Good organization is vital in editing workflows so that clarity and efficiency could be maintained. In the sample project template, a variety of search bins are already set up for you, but you can add to those to extend the functionality for your particular project. The whole point is that logical and intuitive categorization of assets will go a long way in smoothly navigating and retrieving files faster.

B. Editorial Organization: How to Improve Efficiency in Workflow

This will go a long way in keeping the editorial process organized and efficient, right from the very start of a sequence that has pre-named tracks. Also, through naming conventions and structuring of tracks, editors can work flawlessly especially on big projects with many contributors. By having the track names already set up, you won't get confused, and everyone will be on the same page.

If several editors are working together on the project, standardized and organized tracks will go a long way in sharing work, collaborating on editing tasks, and maintaining continuity throughout the project.

C. **Common Timeline Track Types**

Following are some common names and types of tracks for both video and audio elements that will further simplify your editorial task:

Video Track Names:

- Main: This is the main track that contains the primary footage.
- Alternate Versions: One track for housing the different versions of the sequence, such as cuts and edits.
- B-Roll: Additional footage added apart from the main visuals.
- VFX: One dedicated track for the visual effects layers.
- Graphics: A track for overlaying titles, lower thirds, and other graphics.

Audio Track Names:

- Dialog: This is a track for the main spoken dialogue in your project.
- SFX: Track for ambient sounds or whatever is not dialogue.
- VO: This is a separate voiceover track for any narration or other secondary voiceovers.
- Ambiance: Tracks recording the background or ambient soundscapes.
- Music: The audio tracks exclusively assigned for all the musical pieces or scores.

Audio Submixes:

Audio submix tracks do an important job in compiling a number of audio tracks into one track for easy management. The tracks themselves don't contain clips but serve as a destination for audio output from other tracks.

By submixing a number of audio tracks, you are easily able to apply audio effects en masse across these tracks, which can save time and provide consistency. In such a way, you have more effective control over complex audio arrangements with only a single set of effect controls.

Visual Treatment with Adjustment Layers

The use of adjustment layers is very effective when it comes to the application of global color grading or looks, or even visual effects, which may enhance the overall aesthetic feel of a sequence. This allows one to pre-establish easily a "Look" on an adjustment layer and apply color treatments to footage throughout the editorial process.

Ease of toggling on/off: These color adjustments can easily be turned on/off with a click, allowing a preview of the footage with or without the treatment applied. With visual tone and color in constant flux for editors on projects, such flexibility is important.

Exporting with Multichannel Setup

Templates can also be applied to export settings for multichannel audio projects, that is, a format used in content delivery when separate audio elements are needed, such as a music-and-effects mix. An **M&E** mix ensures you are compatible with multilingual or international formats and still maintain control over certain audio elements.

How to Create Your Own Project Template

- First and foremost, make a copy of the sample.
- After that, adapt it to suit your needs, and save it in a project folder of its own.

- Make a neat workflow, easy to back up and restore, by keeping the assets well away from Premiere Pro and using metadata views showing which paths against the project file are currently in use.

  By structuring based on a template, you will be free to concentrate on the creative aspect without the aggravation of repeated setup and allow your project to grow with you while keeping things efficient and scalable.

Organize Your Assets outside Premiere Pro

For the best practice for keeping projects organized and future backups or restores hassle-free, structure your project folders in a system outside Premiere Pro. You will want to create a clear folder hierarchy where all of the project assets are housed in one location to be easily found and backed up.

Consider using numbered folders to control order and allow ease when adding new folders without disturbing your organizational flow. Example:
- Project Files: Place Premiere Pro project files here.
- Raw Footage: Store all original video footage in this folder.
- Audio: Organize music, sound effects, and voiceovers here.
- Graphics: Save logos, lower thirds, and other graphical elements.
- Exports: Keep all exported sequences in one spot for ease of tracking.

With Premiere Pro's **File Path Metadata View**, you can quickly check to make sure all of the media in your project is pointing at the correct locations. This is super helpful for larger projects or archiving older projects.

Advanced Techniques: Creating/Customizing your Project Template

One of the powerful things about working with Premiere Pro 2025 is that you can create project templates for a range of different project types. Here are some advanced ways to improve your templates:
- **Custom Track Layout for Different Deliverables:** Depending on the project, be it commercial, documentary, or social media, there is often

a different setup on the timeline. Create templates that have different layouts and different export settings, like 4K for high-resolution work, or square timelines for social media.

- **Integrate After Effects Compositions:** Place live After Effects compositions right into your Premiere Pro template, if you work in animated graphics or motion design elements on a regular basis. By linking up editable compositions, you are able to make changes in **After Effects** that immediately update in Premiere, thereby smoothing the process of making edits.

- **Consistency in Visuals with the Use of Adjustment Layers**: Keep color and other effects consistent throughout sequences by adding adjustment layers with LUTs or filters directly in your template. These can be adjusted for each project while still having a consistent look.

- **Develop a Library of Pre-Built Sequences and Templates for Common Edits**: Recurring elements, such as title screens, lower thirds, or split screens, can be set up in a dedicated **Templates bin**. This makes adding them to new projects a matter of dragging and dropping.

- **Track Changes with Version Control**: A good project template sets up the collaborating team to use bins that are version controlled. For example, one folder would be labeled "In Progress" and another "Final". Clearly explain to the team where work-in-progress segments should be saved versus completed segments so that it would be easy for them to revert to earlier edits if needed.

Keep It Simple, Adapt as Needed

Premiere Pro project templates should be looked at as flexible starting points. They give you the structure that you will then adapt to your specific needs as projects unfold. By making a template which is general yet extendable, you should be able to take on larger more complicated projects without losing track of important assets, or on redundant setup tasks.

A good template makes your workflow repeatable and scalable, supports creative work, and is productive and less prone to errors. Be it solo content creation or with a team, having an organized workflow through Premiere Pro templates is going to give you ongoing rewards by having you work on producing quality video content, rather than having to start from scratch over and over again.

CHAPTER FOUR

IMPORT MEDIA

How to import media

The three ways you can import media with Adobe Premiere Pro 2025 is by;

- Transferring files
- Importing Still images and,
- Importing digital audio.

A. Transferring files

The following are steps to properly manage and organize project files and assets while transferring projects in Adobe Premiere Pro from one computer to another in a streamlined, consistent manner.

How to Transfer Projects across Computers

Transferring projects across computers in Adobe Premiere Pro 2025 is facilitated with the **Project Manager tool:**

1. Access the Project Manager dialog via the **File menu**
2. After that, click on **Project Manager.**

3. In the Sequence section, select the sequences you want to transfer.

4. In **Resulting Project**, select from the following:

    • **Collect Files and Copy to New Location:** This will copy all needed files to a new location.

    • **Consolidate and Transcode:** This will transcode source media to one format using a specific codec and copy all to a new location for uniformity.

5. In **Destination Path,** click the **Browser** to open File Explorer (Windows) or Finder (macOS), then choose a destination folder.

6. Under **Options,** place check marks in any options you would like to use like exclude unused clips, or preserve effects.

7. Click **Calculate** to confirm how much disk space the transfer will require.

8. When ready, click **Run** to begin the copying of files.

Tips for Transferring Projects Successfully

• Make sure all project assets and media files transfer and are in folders that have the same directory structure as on the computer where the project originated.

• Keeping file paths intact insures you won't have issues with files having to be relinked, if you open the project on another computer.

Transfer Assets from File-Based Media

You should always copy media files from their source like a SxS card, P2 card, or DVD, to a local drive for best editing performance. To do so, you can follow these steps:

- Transfer the entire folder and all of its subfolders from the file-based media using **File Explorer** on Windows or **Finder** on macOS to the hard drive.
- In Premiere Pro, import those transferred files from the hard drive into your project.

Note: Folder structure should not be broken, as that will introduce errors in the file path. Also, ensure that the video files at the media are moved to a folder that is assigned based on project scratch disk setting.

Edit While Ingesting Media

To save time with workflow, Premiere Pro can edit even when media files are being ingested in the background:

- In the Media Browser panel, click the **Ingest checkbox** to turn on the background ingestion.
- To set ingest options, click **the settings icon** to open the **Project Settings dialog**.

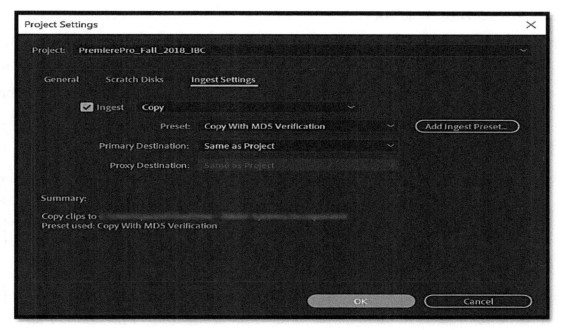

Ingest Settings

The Ingest Settings dialog provides four options:

- **Copy:** Copies media to a selected destination, usually from removable media to a hard drive.

- **Transcode:** Transcodes media to a selected format, which is great for matching post formats.

- **Create Proxies:** Creates lower-resolution proxies to aid in smoother editing. Full resolution may be switched to for final output.

- **Copy and Create Proxies**: This copies the media and at the same time creates proxies for editing.

All of these have default destinations. The default is "Same as Project." You can also set it to a custom location or use **Adobe Creative Cloud Files** for automatic cloud synchronization. If that is not good enough, **Adobe Media Encoder** allows you to make custom ingest presets.

B. **Importing Still Images**

With Adobe Premiere Pro 2025, you can import a single file of still images or you can import them as sequences. The import options extend to files from Adobe applications like Photoshop and Illustrator, offering smooth integration in terms of designs and assets.

Importing a still image into Premiere Pro automatically sets a default duration for that clip, which can later be changed in the sequence settings. The maximum frame size for imported images is 256 megapixels, or 32,768 pixels in any direction.

Preparing Images for Import

To save time rendering in Premiere Pro, consider fully preparing your image file before importing:

- **Verify File Compatibility**: Ensure the format is compatible with your operating system.

- **Set Pixel Dimension**: Resize the image to the resolution of the project with no quality loss in case of upscale. Upscaling it 200% for example requires that you will need to double the size of the frame of the project.

- **Crop Unwanted Areas**: The areas of the image which are not visible within it should be cropped.

- **Transparency:** Set alpha or work in transparency in Photoshop or Illustrator to set areas transparent.

- **Avoid Thin Horizontal Lines:** To minimize the occurrence of flickering on interlaced displays, avoid 1-pixel horizontal lines or give it some blur in order to make it look more handsome on a normal television.

- **File Naming For Windows:** Three-character extensions are recommended.

- **Color Space Management:** To ensure color consistency among applications, video-friendly color space is recommended i.e. sRGB or NTSC RGB.

Importing Adobe Photoshop and Illustrator Files

To begin, Premiere Pro itself can support Photoshop and Illustrator files, including transparency, blending modes, and alpha channels that may have been established within those images. Premiere Pro can import Photoshop files as layered compositions so the user has some flexibility with layer manipulation:

- **Layered Import Options:** When you import Photoshop files, there are a few options to do so, such as "Merge All Layers" or "Individual Layers" to bring in layering into the timeline.

- **Compatibility Tips**: Some advanced Photoshop layer effects, like special blending modes, might not work fully in Premiere Pro. Try to stick to basic settings for transparency and opacity settings for optimum results.

- **Working with Animations:** You are able to import a Photoshop document that contains animations. Some adjustment may need to be taken but because length set for a still image can make animation speed seem off from your project's frame rate.

Premiere Pro rasterizes and anti-aliases the art upon import of Illustrator images. Clear areas import as transparency. To import images at specific dimensions, place crop marks in Illustrator before import.

Image Sequences

With animations, you may import a series of single still images in which each still represents a video frame. Before importing:

- **Set the Frame-rate:** Before you import ensure that the correct timing occurs by first setting the frame-rate via heading to the **Preferences section** and thereafter, clicking on **Media**.

- **Use Consistent Filenames**: All filenames should contain the same number of digits so that the sequence can be recognized correctly.

To import a sequence, find the first numbered file and, holding down **Image Sequence,** open it. Each file will be interpreted by Premiere Pro as a single frame.

Resizing Imported Images

High-resolution images may show up cropped in the Timeline. This is where you'll be using the **Set to Frame Size command** to scale the image without quality loss:

- Right-click (Windows) or Control-click (Mac OS) the image in the Timeline.

- Select **Set to Frame Size** to have the image fit within the sequence frame. This command preserves the image-native resolution so that the image will be at optimal quality when you zoom in on it.

When you disable **Scale to Frame Size**, playback performance will be improved.

C.   Importing digital audio.

Digital audio integration within Premiere Pro is solid and flexible, offering support for a range of file types, configurations, and sources for optimal quality and editing flexibility.

How to Import Digital Audio Files

Audio can be purely digital, including standalone audio files, but also those embedded in video files, sourced from hard drives, audio CDs, DATs, and other digital formats. When you want the best fidelity, it is best to transfer audio into your computer digitally rather than capture the analog signal through a sound card.

- To capture audio-only content from a digital video source, select **Audio** from the Capture menu. The Capture menu is located in the **Logging section** of the Capture panel.

- Note that not all formats, including HDV, support audio-only capture in Premiere Pro.

Capturing Audio from CDs

To be able to import the CDA files into Premiere Pro, these need to be converted into a format compatible with Premiere Pro, either WAV or

AIFF. You can perform the conversion using some audio software such as Adobe Audition.

Ensure that you have the copyright to any audio tracks to use in your project.

Working with Compressed Audio

Compressed formats like MP3 and WMA sacrifice some data in favor of fidelity. When you import these files into your project, Premiere Pro decompresses them and resamples them, if necessary. For optimal sound quality, try to use uncompressed formats or CD-quality versions of audio files whenever possible.

Audio Editing with Adobe Audition

Adobe Audition offers advanced audio editing features, and any audio files exported from Audition in a compatible format can be directly imported into Premiere Pro for further integration and editing.

Supported Sample Rates

The following are the Audio Sample rates supported by Premiere Pro:

- 96000 Hz
- 48000 Hz
- 44100 Hz
- 32000 Hz
- 22050 Hz
- 11025 Hz
- 8000 Hz

Conforming Audio for a Smooth Playback

To ensure high-quality playback, all audio is processed in Premiere Pro at 32-bit floating-point depth and the sequence's designated sample rate. Some audio files require this process, called conforming, especially if they are compressed or have different sample rates. These CFA preview files, which Premiere Pro creates during this process of conforming, can be stored in a specified location using the Scratch Disk settings.

Note: It's possible to apply effects to audio at any time, even when it hasn't fully conformed. Only those parts that have conformed will preview with audio during playback.

Audio Conforming Rules

*   **Uncompressed Audio:** Premiere Pro does not conform uncompressed audio of matching sample rates. If it is used in sequences with non-matching rates, it does conform upon export or when generating audio previews.
*   **Compressed Audio:** Premiere Pro always conforms to the media of compressed formats - for example, MP3, WMA - at the source file sample rate. If used in a sequence that has a different sample rate, it plays back at the sequence rate.

Additional Information about Media Cache Files

To smoothly manage a project, Premiere Pro creates PEK files to represent waveform displays of all audio files in the Timeline. The **Media Cache Files** location, as specified in the Preferences dialog of the Media pane, stores the **PEK files** along with the conformed audio files.

How to import from Avid or Final Cut

A. **Importing projects from Avid Media Composer to Adobe Premiere Pro**

This process of transferring projects from Avid Media Composer to Adobe Premiere Pro is necessary due to the compatibility limitations between the native project formats of these two platforms. Native Avid

Media Composer (.avp) project files are, by nature, not supported in Adobe Premiere Pro, which requires the exportation of an Advanced Authoring Format file from Avid and then importation into Premiere.

Understanding AAF Files

The Advanced Authoring Format, or AAF for short, refers to the interchange file format that was created to make collaboration between different video editing and post-production software packages as smooth as possible. It fills a need by allowing formats that are not directly compatible with each other, such as .prproj files in Premiere and .avp files in Avid Media Composer. Essential elements such as clips, timelines, and some effects can be transferred using AAF and it creates bigger project flexibility.

Preparing for Export

You will want to ideally prepare your sequence and simplify it within Avid Media Composer before exporting an AAF file. Also, have each type of media asset on its own track to ease the process of exportation for smoother importation. You will also want to export a **Reference Movie** to help identify and rebuild any effects that may not transfer in Premiere.

Steps on how to export from Avid Media Composer

To export an AAF from Avid Media Composer:

1. **Open the Project:** Open your Avid project, and open the project bin where you have stored the sequence you wish to export.
2. **Select the Sequence:** Highlight the sequence in the bin.
3. **Initiate Export**: Go to the **File menu** before clicking on **Export.**
4. **Configure Export Settings**: In the Export Settings dialog, make the following selections:
   - Set "AAF Edit Protocol."

- Choose to include all video, data, and audio tracks of the sequence.
- If required, restrict export to selected parts of the timeline using **In/Out points.**

5. **Media Linking:**
   - In the Video / Data Details tab, select "Link to [Don't Export] Media."
   - In the Audio Details tab, also checkmark "Link to [Don't Export] Media" and if you want, rendered audio effects too.

6. **Save:** After setting your options, save your AAF file

Importing AAF Files into Premiere Pro

With the AAF file exported, now you are ready to import it into Adobe Premiere Pro:

1. Open or Create a Project in Premiere Pro.
2. Import the AAF File:
   - In the Project panel go to the **File menu** before clicking on **Import**.
   - Navigate where the AAF file was saved and select **Import**.
3. **Sequence Creation**: Premiere will automatically create a new sequence named after the AAF file, along with a bin containing the media used in the sequence.
4. **Translation Report**: If there is some sort of compatibility issue, an FCP Translation Results file will be generated in the main bin that details how unsupported effects, titles, or transitions were translated.

Post-Import Adjustments

After import, verify the translation and edit accordingly:

Supported Elements:

- Comments and custom metadata fields will translate
- Markers will indicate where unsupported effects were present
- Dissolves, speed changes, audio levels, and keyframes often translate well
- LUT metadata applied to master clips should translate correctly

Unsupported or Partially Supported Elements:

- Complex animations, some motion parameters, and multi-cam sequences may require adjustments.
- Certain color filters and LUTs applied as effects in Avid do not carry over.
- Matte keys may lose alpha channel data, which may need re-creation.

This workflow will be able to facilitate editors easily moving back and forth between Avid and Premiere Pro while maintaining core sequence elements and metadata for easier collaboration between systems and flexibility in the workflows.

B. **Importing Projects from Final Cut Pro to Adobe Premiere Pro**

This section serves as a guide for those who wish to import projects, selected clips, or sequences exported from FCP 7 and FCP X into Adobe Premiere Pro. It shall delve into conversion needs, and recommended tools, and outline in detail on an element-by-element basis what translates well and what you may need to adjust.

Importing from Final Cut Pro X into Adobe Premiere Pro

1. **Background on FCP X Exports:**

   Final Cut Pro X exports projects as .fcpxml files, which are not natively supported by Adobe Premiere Pro. In that respect, a need for a bridging process via a third-party converter would make it possible to support Premiere Pro's standard .xml import capabilities.

2. **Conversion Tool:**

   The recommended tool for conversion by Adobe is XtoCC, which can convert a .fcpxml file into a standard .xml format readable by Premiere Pro.

   Step-by-Step Migration Process

   - **Export from FCP X**: Export the project in .fcpxml format.
   - **Convert with XtoCC:** Take the .fcpxml file and use the XtoCC utility to translate it into a Premiere Pro-friendly .xml file.

- **Import into Premiere Pro**: In Premiere Pro, select the **File menu** before clicking on **Import.** After that, select the translated .xml file and click **Open.**

3. **Translation Limitations:**

    While XtoCC can translate the majority of FCP X elements, not all will import perfectly. Here's a high-level overview of what will and won't transfer:

    - **Event Clips**: Imported into organized bins
    - **Gap Clips:** Come in as empty spaces
    - **Compound Clips:** Translated as nested sequences
    - **Synchronized Clips**: Translated as merged clips
    - **Multi-cam Clips**: Become collapsed clips with the active angle preserved.

4. **Specific Elements Converted**

    - **Projects**: The video and still clips in the main storyline come in as track V1 in Premiere Pro. Audio clips stay in their main storyline positions on track A1.
    - **Timecode:** The source project's time code set-up and start times are preserved.
    - **Markers:** To-do markers, chapter markers, and completed to-dos are color-coded in Premiere Pro.
    - **Audio:** Volume, pan settings, and fade transitions are applied across imported audio tracks.
    - **Effects and Transitions:** The default transitions including **Cross Dissolve** and some blend mode-specific settings such as Multiply, and Screen are supported in Premiere Pro. Any unsupported settings are defaulted to similar options.

5. **Importing XML Files from Final Cut Pro 7**

Premiere Pro 2025 allows the direct import of XML files exported from Final Cut Pro 7, retaining much of the original project structure and metadata.

Import Workflow

- **Export XML out of Final Cut Pro 7**: In Final Cut Pro 7, export the project, clips, or sequences to an XML file.

- **Close the Source Project**: To prevent conflicts with source files, ensure the source project has been closed in FCP.

- **Import into Premiere Pro:** To import into Premiere Pro, go to the **File menu** before clicking on **Impor**t. After that, select the XML file to open it.

Key Translated Elements

- **Clip Metadata:** Data fields such as the Description, Scene, ShotTake, and LogNote are preserved.

- **Sequence and Track Structure:** Premiere Pro recreates your original track structure including locked tracks, markers, and timecodes.

- **Text and Titles:** Final Cut Pro Text generator data is translated as Premiere Pro titles.

- **Effects, Transitions, and Composite Modes:** Premiere Pro preserves the basic motion and opacity effects. FCP-compatible transitions, audio effects, and composite modes are translated to their closest equivalent in Premiere Pro.

6. **Summary of Converted Effects, Transitions, and Composite Modes**

- **Video Effects**: Effects such as Crop and Gaussian Blur are directly translated.
- **Transitions:** All regular transitions, such as **Dip To White** and **Cross Dissolve**, have a corresponding Premiere Pro transition.
- **Audio Effects:** The Volume, pan values, and filters (Low Pass, High Pass) will be preserved within Premiere Pro.
- **Composite Modes**: The most used modes like Overlay, Screen, and Multiply map have similar options.

Multicam Support: Premiere Pro supports the Multiclips in Final Cut Pro. The un-collapsed Multiclips can be imported as multi-camera sequences of up to four inputs. If there are more than four inputs on a project, it will give a warning.

File formats

Some filename extensions such as MOV, AVI, and MXF indicate container formats, rather than specific types of audio, video, or image data. These containers are just versatile wrappers that can contain data encoded with a variety of different compression and encoding methods. Adobe Premiere Pro can import files in these container formats, but the ability to import the data within the container file depends on the specific codecs installed on the system.

Supported File Dimensions in Premiere Pro

- **Sequence Size Limits**

  Projects impose a maximum size for video and still image files. Sequences have a maximum frame size limit of 10,240 x 8,192 pixels. If, in the Sequence Settings, a frame dimension is set higher than the maximum limit, then Premiere Pro will automatically reset it to the maximum size allowed.

- **Import Size Limits for Still Images and Movies**

    Premiere Pro accepts still images and video files for import at a maximum of 256 megapixels. The maximum dimension of a side can be 32,768 pixels; therefore, while images sized at 16,000 x 16,000 pixels or 32,000 x 8,000 pixels can be imported, larger dimensions such as 35,000 x 10,000 pixels exceed the import limits.

Supported Native Audio and Video Formats

Adobe Premiere Pro ensures compatibility with the largest number of various audio and video formats to make workflows easier and to support the latest broadcast formats.

Supported Formats

- **3GP, 3G2 (.3gp)**: Multimedia container format
- **AAC**: Advanced Audio Coding
- **Apple ProRes:** High-quality compression format with broad support for acquisition, production, and delivery; macOS and Windows can work with it.
- **GIF:** Animated GIF
- **HEIF and HEVC (H.265**): High Efficiency Image Format with up to 8K resolution support; HEVC is supported for 8192 x 4320 media.
- **AIFF, AIF:** Audio Interchange File Format
- **ASND**: Adobe Sound Document
- **AVI (.avi):** DV-AVI, Microsoft AVI Type 1 and Type 2 formats supported
- **BWF**: Broadcast WAVE format
- **Canon CRM**: Cinema RAW Light format
- **DNxHD and DNxHR**: Supported as MXF and QuickTime wrapper formats, offer high-quality editing codecs.

- **ASF:** NetShow (support on Windows only)
- **H.264 AVC**: Supports variety of H.264 encoded media

Specialized Formats and Professional Codecs

- **MPEG Variants**: MPEG-1, MPEG-2, and formats such as M2V for DVD-compliant MPEG-2, and MP4 for high-quality QuickTime movie formats.
- **R3D:** RED RAW format for high-resolution footage.
- **OpenEXR:** High-dynamic-range image files often used in compositing workflows.
- **MXF**: Container format for a large number of broadcast and professional codecs, including but not limited to ARRIRAW, AVC-Intra, X-OCN, XAVC, and IMX, among others, with specific compatibility for Panasonic and Sony formats.
- **Other Formats**: This includes the WAV (Windows Waveform), VOB (DVD container format), and other formats that might employ third-party components so that specific QuickTime codecs are enabled outright.

These supported formats give extensive options in regards to video and audio import, covering most bases in a wide range of production needs.

Still-Image and Image Sequence File Formats

Premiere Pro provides extensive support for still-image and still-image sequence formats, including both 8bpc and 16bpc (4 bytes to 8 bytes per pixel) files. This broad range of supported image types will enable creators to include everything from detailed illustrations to web-optimized, highly-compressed images in their projects. The format includes:

- **AI, EPS:** For Adobe Illustrator vector files with excellent qualities of scalable graphics.
- **TIFF:** It is a high-quality format supported both in the publishing and photography industries.

- **BMP, DIB, RLE:** Default Bitmap files for general purpose.
- **TGA, ICB, VDA, VST:** This format offers textures of high quality and other options of transparency.
- **PNG:** Lossless compression format for graphics where much detail and transparency are needed.
- **DPX**: Cineon/DPX for professional-grade color depth and fidelity.
- **GIF:** Good for simple animations and web graphics.
- **PTL, PRTL**: These are the title formats for Adobe Premiere. This file format gives easy access to the title assets.
- **ICO:** Icon files, with the majority of use under Windows.
- **PSD:** Adobe Photoshop files supporting layers for advanced editing.
- **JPEG (JPE, JPG, JFIF):** Very common photographic format with high compression.

Closed Captioning and Subtitle File Formats

Premiere Pro supports a variety of captioning and subtitle file formats for a wide range of accessibility options. Those include but are not limited to:

- **DFXP:** Distribution Format Exchange Profile for adaptive, timed-text options.
- **XML:** SMPTE/EBU timed-text options for flexible, standards-compliant captioning.
- **MCC**: MacCaption VANC for broadcast closed captions.
- **STL:** EBU N19, standardized for European broadcast.
- **SRT:** Subrip Subtitle format, widely used for online streaming platforms.
- **SCC**: Scenarist format for DVD authoring and broadcast use.

Video Project File Formats

Premiere Pro supports a range of project file formats to allow for easy collaboration with other Adobe and third-party video-editing applications. The supported project formats are as follows:

- **AAF:** Advanced Authoring Format for media interchange between different platforms.
- **AEP, AEPX:** After Effects project files give seamless integration with Adobe applications.
- **CSV, PBL, TXT, TAB:** Batch lists that go a long way in organizing complex projects.
- **CHPROJ:** Character Animator projects for animation workflows.
- **EDL**: CMX3600 EDLs for the exchange of timelines.
- **XML:** FCP XML caters to the exchange of data with Final Cut Pro.
- **PREL**: Adobe Premiere Elements project files (Windows-specific).
- **PRPROJ:** Premiere Pro opens these project files natively.

Support for Growing Files

Premiere Pro has deep support for growing files, which are files still being written to disk but that can be edited as they grow in real-time. Supported growing file codecs within an MXF wrapper include the following:

- **AVC-Intra Class 50/100**
- **XDCAM HD 50/35/25/18 RDD9**
- **IMX 30/40/50**

Through Premiere Pro, these files are refreshed dynamically; editors can see updated durations directly in the Project panel, Source Monitor, and Timeline.

Variable Frame Rate File Support in Adobe Premiere Pro

Variable Frame Rate (VFR) is a form of video compression wherein the frame rate changes during playback. The more data it needs, it uses more frames. In those places where the image doesn't contain much information, it uses fewer frames.

VFR formats are being used virtually everywhere in video creation from mobile devices such as iOS and Android and also in creating content which normally is made to be posted on e-learning platforms and popular streams like ScreenFlow and Twitch.

Adobe Premiere Pro features versatile tools to detect, synchronize, and edit VFR footage, thereby making workflows easier and ensuring broad compatibility with these commonly used formats.

Detection of VFR Footage in Premiere Pro

Premiere Pro detects VFR footage in several different ways, which empowers editors to seamlessly identify VFR properties:

- **By using the File Menu:** Once the footage is selected, navigate to the **File menu**. After that, click on **Get Properties** for and the **Selection tab.** In the resultant window, Premiere Pro will indicate if it has a variable frame rate.

- **Timeline Properties Panel:** Right-clicking the clip in the Timeline and opening **Properties** will bring up VFR status and related metadata.

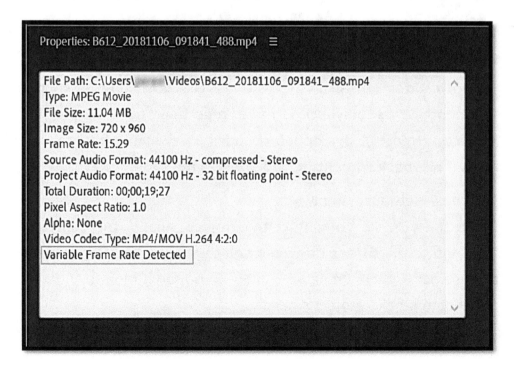

Properties: B612_20181106_091841_488.mp4 ≡

File Path: C:\Users\ \Videos\B612_20181106_091841_488.mp4
Type: MPEG Movie
File Size: 11.04 MB
Image Size: 720 x 960
Frame Rate: 15.29
Source Audio Format: 44100 Hz - compressed - Stereo
Project Audio Format: 44100 Hz - 32 bit floating point - Stereo
Total Duration: 00;00;19;27
Pixel Aspect Ratio: 1.0
Alpha: None
Video Codec Type: MP4/MOV H.264 4:2:0
Variable Frame Rate Detected

Audio-Video Synchronization Options for VFR Footage

In Premiere Pro, advanced options to manage audio sync and smooth video motion for VFR clips let the editors make an optimal choice between smooth video and audio-video sync.

- **Preserve Audio Sync:** On VFR clips containing audio, it uses an additive / DROP frame approach to keep the audio and video in sync. This may lead to slightly choppy video playback, but the sound will be in sync.

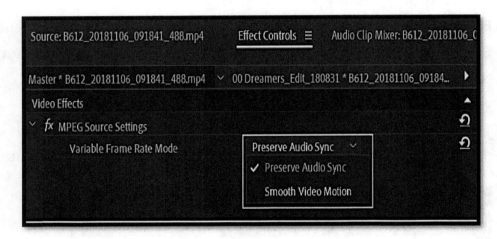

- **Smooth Video Motion:** When the VFR clip either doesn't contain audio or smooth visual playback is more important (for example, in motion graphics projects), this option decodes all available frames for smooth motion playback without forcing audio sync.

To apply these settings, simply;
- Select the VFR clip from either the Project panel or the Source Monitor.
- Then, go to the **Effect Controls tab** to access the **Master Clip Effect** and select either Preserve Audio Sync or Smooth Video Motion, depending on the project's needs.

Considerations and Limitations for VFR Files

Although Premiere Pro supports VFR footage, some considerations can help with certain workflows:

- **Proxy, Consolidate, and Transcode Workflows**: Transcoding VFR clips to a constant frame rate before editing can improve stability and compatibility, especially when working with proxies or consolidating media.

- **Projects Migrated from Previous Versions**: In projects where VFR clips have been manually synced in earlier versions of Premiere Pro, it is advisable to re-sync the clips in the most recent Premiere Pro version for accuracy's sake.

Support for Blackmagic RAW

Blackmagic RAW is a premium, flexible raw video format created by Blackmagic Design. It carries an extended reputation for strong support across professional video production workflows. Native support of this format is included in many Blackmagic Design products, from leading cameras to recorders, and therefore finds favor with videographers and filmmakers who are looking to capture the greatest amount of image fidelity and control in post.

Blackmagic Design provides a specialized plugin that integrates Blackmagic RAW support from within Adobe's suite of video applications, ranging from Premiere Pro and After Effects to Adobe Media Encoder. Once installed, users can import Blackmagic RAW natively into Adobe for effortless editing, leveraging the unique capabilities of the format directly from within their existing workflow.

Access to the Blackmagic RAW Plugin is done via the following:

- First and foremost, go to blackmagicdesign.com/blackmagicrawinstaller

- After that, download the Blackmagic RAW installer for your operating system.
- Follow the prompts to install.

With the plugin installed, direct access to Blackmagic RAW files is integrated right inside the Adobe suite, affording flexibility in color grading, resolution management, and image processing.

How to work with timecode

Timecode is a very precise tracking system used in video production for locating, synchronizing, and organizing visual and audio elements. Represented in seconds, minutes, hours, and frames HH:MM:SS, it provides an organized, accurate reference throughout the timeline of a project.

Importance of Timecode

The importance of timecode can be viewed for several reasons:

- **Organization and Retrieval:** Timecode, through the use of exact points in a recording, can be easily logged, cataloged, and retrieved at any scene, shot, or segment. This facilitates and simplifies the editing process and makes post-production more efficient.
- **Precise Synchronization**: Timecode allows editors to precisely align multiple video and audio tracks, which is very important in synchronizing the sound, effects, and video footage. The precision afforded by timecode allows effortless editing, even with the most complex multi-track projects.
- **Team Collaboration:** Timecode acts like a standard reference in collaboration environments; that is, multiple teams or editors can work together in unison. Because there is one timebase, all of them would exactly know where changes, adjustments, or edits are required.
- **Continuous Timecode:** Timecode should never be interrupted during the whole recording session for maximum quality. Timecode should run

without breaks to ensure smooth editing and playback; restarting may pose problems later on.

Best Practices for Continuous Timecode

Continuity of timecode gives effortless and continuous timecode. To do so:

- **Use Professional Equipment**: Professional cameras and audio recorders often have timecode generators in their make-up and hence can provide continuous timecode between takes.

- **Monitor the Timecode:** Always double-check the time code display for any breaks in its movement.

- **Record Extra Footage:** Always shoot a few extra seconds at the beginning and end of every shot as this helps the editor maintain continuity and for sync purposes.

Timecode Display in Premiere Pro: How to Customize

Premiere Pro offers some flexibility with timecode display, which can be tweaked for various editing requirements.

- **Choose Source Timecode or Custom Start**: By default, Premiere Pro will always display the source timecode of that original footage, even when the source timecode is different from the timebase of the project sequence. You can set it to start with 00:00:00:00 for each clip if that is what works best for your workflow.

- **Frames or Feet and Frames:** In the Frames or Feet and Frames display format, it is possible in Premiere Pro to edit the beginning frame number. You can create a beginning of frame count either from 0 or 1 or convert them from source time code.

To customize timecode and frame count preferences:

1. **Launch Preferences:**
   - On your Windows: Go to the **Edit tab.** After that, click on **Preferences** before selecting **Media.**

- On your macOs access the **Premiere Pro**. After that, click on **Preferences** before selecting **Media.**

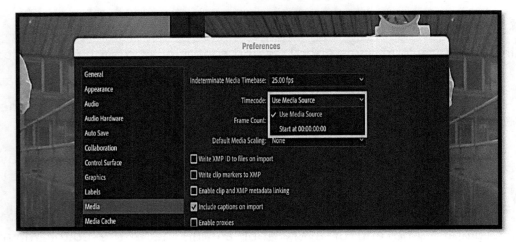

2. **Select Timecode Options:**
   - Use Media Source: This shows the timecode of the original media that the clip was sourced from.
   - Start At 00:00:00:00: This sets the start timecode for all clips to 00:00:00:00

3. **Set Frame Count Options:**
   - Frame Start At 0: Frames are numbered contiguously starting at 0
   - Frame Start At 1: Frames are numbered starting at 1
   - Timecode Conversion: Timecode numbers are translated to their number of frames equivalent.

4. **Save Preference:**
   - Click **OK** to save these settings.

Timecode Display Format Changes in Premiere Pro

Premiere Pro provides flexible options to adapt the time code display formats as editors prefer to make views and workflows very effective within panels and sequences. This overview will show the different settings available for displaying, editing, and navigating timecodes across different panels and workflows.

Timecode Display in Audio Units

You can display timecode in audio units for audio-heavy projects either in samples or milliseconds:

- **Timeline Panel:** To change the time display to an audio-based one, open the menu on the Timeline panel and select the option **Show Audio Time Units**.

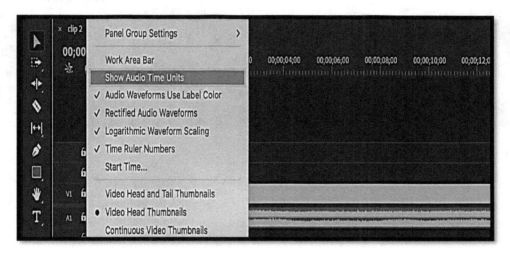

- **Project Settings:** For a more permanent setting across your project, navigate to the **File menu** before clicking on **Project Settings**. After accessing the Project settings, click on **Audio** before selecting the **Display Format** to select your preferred audio unit.

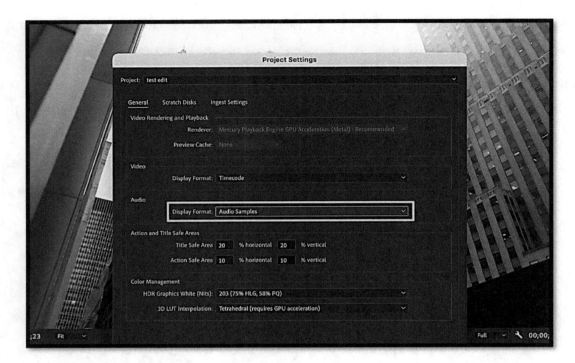

Changing Timecode Formats

Premiere Pro provides a few different ways to display timecode within the interface. The following time code types can be changed using these steps:

- Drop-Frame
- Frames
- Non-Drop-Frame
- Feet + Frames 16mm or 35mm

To cycle through the available timecode formats in any panel that contains hot text timecode, **Ctrl-click (Windows) or Command-click (macOS)** the timecode display. The format selected will be applied to both the **Program Monitor** and **Timeline panels**, so the two will match each other.

Editing Clip Timecode

You can edit the timecode for any clip by:

- Selecting the clip you want to edit, in the Project panel.

- Change Timecode by clicking on **Clip** to access the **Modify tab**, which also enables you to access the **Timecode.** When you access the Timecode, simply make your edit and click **OK.**

Note: Don't use proxies if your workflow involves manually adjusting source clip timecode.

Timecode Entry for Precise edits

Timecode entry is fundamental for setting **In and Out points** or for relocating the playhead to a specific frame:

- **Basic Entry**: Type timecodes without punctuation to allow Premiere Pro interpret your input as hours, minutes, seconds, and frames.
- **Relative Frame Offset:** To shift a number of frames from the current timecode, type the plus or minus sign followed by the number of frames.
- **Shorthand Entries:** Premiere Pro accepts shorthand such as 1 for 00:00:01:00 or .24 for 00:00:01:00 in a 23.976 fps sequence.

Using Burn-In Timecode

To have frame-accurate previews, include a burn-in timecode:

- **Metadata & Timecode Burn-in Effect**: This effect places onscreen timecode on any clip you apply it to during preview. It's ideal for use in a rough cut or while doing review. You can also add the effect to a transparent clip for burnt-in timecode over an entire sequence.

Source Timecode While Editing

Allow for source timecode to be visible in the Program Monitor to provide greater control over edits:

- **Trims and Adjustments**: If clips have been trimmed, the source timecode will appear and automatically update when performing slip and slide edits.

- **Overlay Option:** Once the Program Monitor menu option has been activated, you can activate Timecode Overlay during Edit, so the timecode will appear while editing.

Timecode Panel: Sophisticated Timecode Display Options

The Timecode panel offers a dedicated, customizable display of sequence and clip time code with many display options:

- **Timecode Display Options:** Choose from Current Time, Absolute (starting from zero), Duration, In/Out, Remaining, and Top Clip Name.

- **Source Track selection:** Choose which video or audio source track timecode to show.

- **Compact and Full-Size View:** Click this button to switch to compact or full-size view. Options include label color and/or display tags.

- **Customization Tools:** Add or delete lines, store your layouts in presets, and assign any desired shortcuts; this is how you might manage timecodes efficiently.

The Timecode panel can be resized by dragging the lower-right corner, allowing flexibility in UI arrangement to suit various editing needs.

CHAPTER FIVE

WORKSPACES AND WORKFLOWS

Workspaces and header bar

Adobe has a complete, consistent workspace system throughout its video and audio applications to ensure that user experiences are enriched in a customized way. Although every application has its special panels, such as Metadata, Project, and Timeline panels, all applications share that users can customize and group these consistently across products, making the workspace environment easy for users to navigate and personalize.

The application window is the central interface for any application, and it hosts panels organized within a layout called the workspace. The default workspace organizes panels in both grouped and standalone configurations. Users can work within this setup or customize it by moving and resizing panels to create an environment that best suits their workflow. While it moves some panels, others automatically adjust for space, and you can save multiple custom workspaces for different tasks such as editing and previewing.

Premiere Pro Home Screen

On the Home screen of Premiere Pro, you can create a new project and open an existing one, or cross through tutorials and documentation. When you are experienced with the use of the application, the content of the Home screen will be modified: it will show recent projects and change the tutorial offers according to the level of your experience.

The Premiere Pro header bar provides easy access to and navigation within the application. It contains the Home screen and the Edit, Import, and Export modes of the application, among other options relating to the workspace.

Key features include:

A.   Home – Open the Home screen

B.   Import, Edit, Export Tabs – Use to toggle between states of a project

C.   Project Name – Lists the name of the project

D.   Workspaces – Options to select and toggle workspaces

E.   Quick Export – Quickly export your video

F.   Maximize Video Output - View content in full screen

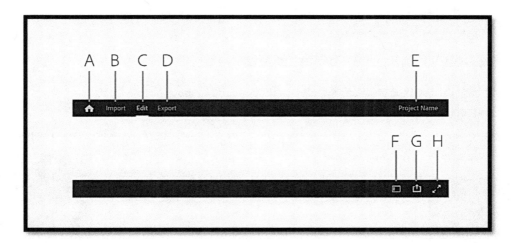

By default, Premiere defaults into **Import mode** with the opening of a new project. In other words, if a project is opened or created, by default it changes to **Edit mode**. In the case of exporting a project, the user can change it to **Export mode.**

Workspaces

By default, Premiere Pro allows 15 different default workspaces with customized selections for various post-production tasks ranging from color correction to audio and graphics. The general workspaces among them include the following;

•   **Essentials:** Organized, accessible layout designed for single-monitor editing. Starter: Simplified layout for beginners to easily get into using Premiere Pro.

- **Vertical:** Optimized for vertical video workflows, including the ability to toggle between Source and Program Monitor.
- **Learn:** Offers in-app tutorials to get started in Premiere while you edit.
- **Assembly:** Large Project panel for quick rough cuts, with hover scrubbing and In/Out point setting.
- **Captions and Graphics**: Dedicated layout optimized for captioning and graphic work.
- **Text-Based Editing:** Enabling transcription-based editing, helps create rough cuts effortlessly.
- **Review**: For Frame. io-based reviews.
- **Production:** Intended for collaborative projects within a Production. Switching and Managing Workspaces

These are available either from the drop-down menu or through Window > Workspace. Keyboard hotkeys for opening them quickly are Alt + Shift + 1 through 9. The user can also create keyboard shortcuts to open favorite or custom workspaces directly.

Managing Workspaces in Premiere Pro

Premiere Pro offers a number of advanced features to customize and manage workspaces according to your workflow. You can import workspaces, rearrange them and delete them, create and save custom layouts, reset panels to their default arrangement, and so on. This will allow you to customize the interface for every unique project, optimize the screen space, and keep your layouts clean and tidy.

a. **Opening a Project in a Custom Workspace**

By default, Premiere Pro opens any new project in the current workspace, but you can change this behavior to open each project in the workspace last used with the project.

To import a workspace for a project:
- Enable the option by heading over to **Window.**
- Then, access the **Workspaces.**
- Also, select **Import Workspace From Projects.**

Note: If a workspace is blank after import, then close the project and uncheck the box **Import Workspace From Projects**. Afterward, re-import and check on an existing workspace layout.

b. **Creating and Managing Workspaces**

To let you work as effortlessly as possible, Premiere Pro allows you to modify, organize, and even delete workspaces.

To access the workspace preferences:
- Enable the option by heading over to **Window.**
- Then, access the **Workspaces.**
- Also, click on **Edit Workspaces** or access the Workspaces menu and select **Edit Workspaces.**

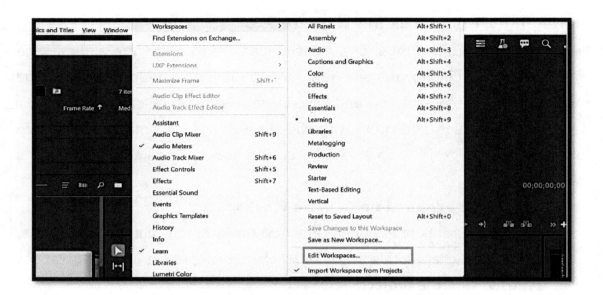

Options include:

- **Reorder:** Change the order of workspace listings in the Workspaces menu.

- **Hide:** Keep your menu from becoming too cluttered by hiding a workspace you no longer use.

- **Delete:** Remove a custom workspace you don't need.

- **Cancel changes**: This button reverses the changes.

c. **Saving Custom Workspaces**

You can save a workspace layout that you have modified and then easily switch between custom workspace configurations as needed.

Saving a custom workspace includes the following steps;

- Arrange panels and groups to display your preferred layout.

- Click the Workspaces dropdown and select **Save as New Workspace** or go to Window to access the **Workspace.** After accessing the Workspace, simply click on **Save as New Workspace.**

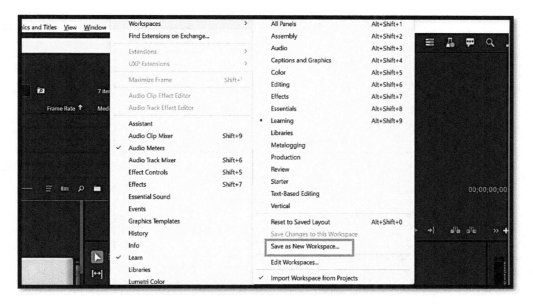

Note: You cannot use the **Undo command** to undo the changes to a default workspace. You would have to manually delete the configuration file of the workspace from your Layouts folder.

d. **Reset a Workspace**

Quickly restore a workspace to its original, saved layout.

To reset the layout:

- Click the Workspaces dropdown and choose **Reset to Saved Layout** or select **Window** to access the **Workspace.** After accessing the Workspace, simply click on **Reset to Saved Layout.**

Work with Panels by Docking, Grouping, and Undocking

Premiere Pro offers a variety of ways to work with panels either by docking, undocking, or grouping.

1. **Docking Panels**: Using the highlighted areas along any edge of panel or group of panels, which are called the docking zones, you can drop the panel into place alongside other panels. All groups will automatically adjust to fit.

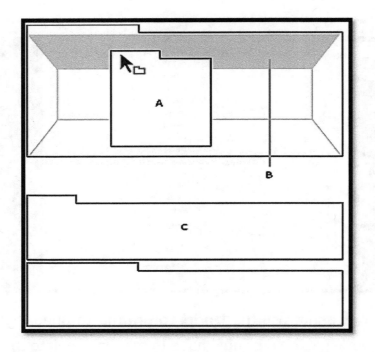

2. **Grouping Panels:** Grouping zones (center and tab areas within panels or groups) tab a new panel on top of already opened panels or stack them.

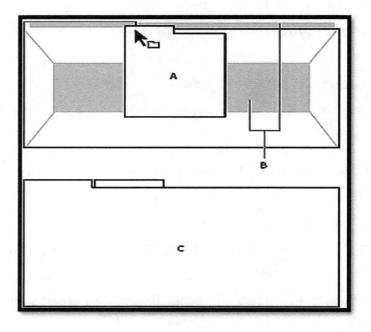

3. **Floating Panels:** To float a panel and create a floating window:
   - Click the **Undock Panel/Undock Panel Group** from the panel menu.
   - Or, hold Ctrl (Windows) / Command (Mac OS) while dragging the panel/group to the new location outside of the main application window.
4. **Panel Group Display Options**: Have panel groups personalized to either be in a stacked, expandable/collapsible view or even a tabbed interface for better accessibility and ease of organization in your workspace.

Panel Groups and Interface Settings: The Definitive Guide to Resizing Resizing Panel Groups in a workspace, resizing panels is instinctive-click and drag on dividers between panel groups. By hovering over these dividers, resize icons appear that let you drag and resize the panels:

- **Single Divider Resize**: When the divider is dragged between two groups of panels, their sizes will relatively change to each other, without affecting any other groups. In other words, assume that you have three-panel groups positioned vertically; now you move the divider between the two bottom groups. Only those two will be resized, and the top group will remain unchanged.
- **Maximize a Panel Quickly:** To instantly expand a panel beneath the pointer, press the accent key (without Shift). Press the accent key again to revert to the original size.

For other general resize options follow these:

- **Horizontal or Vertical Resize**: Move the cursor to one of the dividers between two sets of panels. Cursor changes to a double arrow that can be then pulled for a horizontal or vertical resize.

- **Multi-Directional Resize**: To resize in all directions simultaneously, click the pointer on a point where three or more panel groups meet. The pointer then transforms into a four-way arrow and by pressing down your mouse button and dragging, you can resize groups in several directions.

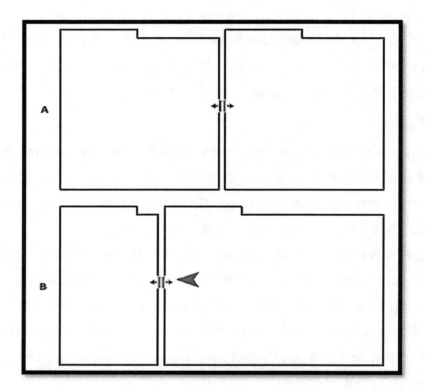

Setting Panel Visibility and Organization

To efficiently work within your workspace you'll need to open and close panel groups and organize them:

- **Opening and Closing Panels:** Open panels from the Window menu. To close a panel or floating window, press Control-W (Windows) or Command-W (macOS) or click the **Close button.** When panels are closed within the application window, the other groups automatically expand into the freed space.

- **Scroll and Arrange Panels**: If the panel group is narrow, use the horizontal scroll bar to see all the tabs. To bring a panel forward, click its tab or hover anywhere over the tab area and use your mouse wheel to roll through panels. You can also reorder the tabs by dragging them left or right.

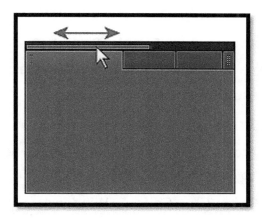

Extend Your Workspace:

It describes how to work with multiple monitors. For increased available screen space, you can have your computer run multiple monitors. You can have your main application window on one screen, place the floating panels on a secondary monitor. Your multi-monitor setup is saved as part of your workspace configuration, providing you with a customized, extended workspace.

Interface Brightness:

Adjusting the brightness of the interface can go a long way in comfort and clear vision when working in specific environments, such as dark editing suites. You can choose to switch to a lighter or darker theme that includes panels, windows, and dialog except for a few elements like scroll bars and title bars on Windows:

1. **Open the Preferences:**
   - On your Windows, simply head over to the **Edit Preferences** before clicking on **Appearance**.
   - On your macOS, simply head over to the **Premiere Pro.** After that, access the **Settings tab** before clicking on **Appearance.**
2. **Choose Theme and Toggle Contrast:** Pick the color theme of your choice and whether you want Accessible color contrast to meet accessibility guidelines.

How to work with Panels

For easy navigation through panels, the following keyboard hotkeys will allow you to cycle through opened panels either way:

- **Cycle Panels Right**: Ctrl+Shift+. (Windows), Control+Shift+. (Mac).
- **Cycle Panels Left**: Ctrl+Shift+, (Windows), Control+Shift+, (Mac).

These keyboard hotkeys provide a graceful way around your workspace without having to reach for your mouse.

Full-Screen Panels

To see any panel in full-screen view and then toggle back to normal view:

- Hover the mouse over the panel you want to expand.
- Strike the **Accent Key (`)** to go to full screen. The Accent Key is usually found to the immediate left of the numeral one (1) key on most keyboards.
- Strike the **Accent Key** again to return the panel to normal size.
  To set the selected frame to maximize, go to **Window** and click on **Maximize Frame** or use the quick shortcut of **Shift+Accent** and it will immediately set this. To bring it back, select **Window** and click on **Restore Frame Size.**

Note: For non-U.S. keyboards, this maximize shortcut might be different. You can look and adjust this in Keyboard Shortcuts by searching for **Maximize** or **Restore Frame Under Cursor**.

Opening Panel Options and Menus

- **Panel Options:** Once a panel is minimized, click its panel menu icon, located in the upper-right, to access options specific to that panel.
- **Context Menus:** Right-click on any panel to pop the context menu, showing options relevant either to the active tool or active selection.

Tools Panel and Options Panel Navigation

When tools are activated, the Options panel proliferates beneath the menu bar for easy access to its preferred settings and customizations. You could undock and move the **Tools panel** or dock it in the Options panel.

- **Open the Options Panel**: To open the options panel go to **Window** and select **Options.**
- **Docking Tools Panel**: Once you have opened any of the tools panel, simply click on the panel menu and select **Dock** in the Options Panel.
- **Undocking Tools Panel:** Click the dotted area next to the **Selection Tool** in the Options panel to undock and return the **Tools panel** to its default location.

Premiere Pro's Toolbox Overview

The Toolbox is a rather extensive set of tools for editing and arranging your clips. Each tool in the Tools panel has a special purpose and can be adapted with keyboard shortcuts for faster work. Here is a short overview:

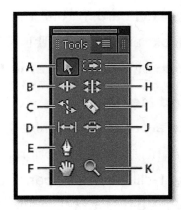

A. **Selection Tool:** This is the default tool used to select clips and items generally on the interface. It will allow the editor to perform most of the basic edits in the timeline.

B. **Track Selection Tool:** This tool will select all clips to the right-hand side of the cursor position in a sequence. Shift-click to turn this on for multi-track selections.

C. **Ripple Edit Tool**: This trims the **In or Out point** of a clip and instantly closes the gap.

D. **Rolling Edit Tool**: This adjusts the edit point between two clips but does not change the overall duration of both combined.

E. **Rate Stretch Tool:** Changes clip speed but doesn't change its start and end points.

F. **Razor Tool:** Splits the clip at an accurate position. Shift-click will make it cut across all tracks.

G. **Slip Tool:** Changes the **In and Out points** but maintains a fixed duration in the sequence.

H. **Slide Tool**: Moves the clip in the timeline, which automatically changes the neighboring clips.

I. **Pen Tool:** This is used for adding and editing keyframes and connector lines.

J. **Hand Tool**: This tool pans the view left or right in the Timeline.

K. **Zoom Tool**: This tool is used to zoom in and out in discrete steps.

Tip: If you hover over any tool in the Photoshop interface's Tools panel, the tool's name and its keyboard shortcut appear.

Info Panel: Your Real-Time Information Source

The Info panel provides you with useful information about the item that you have selected as a clip or in the timeline. Depending on the type of media and the active panel, the info panel will pop up with the following information:

A. **Video:** Frame rate, frame size, and pixel aspect ratio.

B. **Audio:** Sample rate, bit depth, and channels.

C. **Tape:** Displays the name of the tape source if applicable.

D. **In and Out Points:** Timecode for selected clip-in and out points.

Below the current selection information, the **Info panel** displays timecode for each track in a sequence, matching the stacking order of the Timeline.

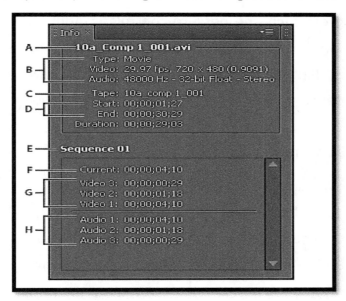

A. Name of selected clip

B. Data for selected clip

C.   Tape name

D.   Sequence timecode locations of clip (Start and End points)

E.   Name of active sequence

F.   Source timecode location in selected clip of current-time indicator

G.   Source timecode location in clips on video tracks of current-time indicator

H.   Source timecode location in clips on audio tracks of current-time indicator

Note: The **Info panel** dynamically updates itself with added or removed tracks as sequences are updated.

Mastering these panels, tools, and shortcuts will help you work more smoothly in your video editing workflow, thus saving time and increasing your productivity in Premiere Pro.

Windows touch and gesture controls

With the addition of touch and gesture controls in Adobe Premiere Pro 2025, editors working with touch-enabled devices like the Microsoft Surface Pro experience fluid and intuitive, tactile editing. The release which was years back builds on multi-touch to further improve the editing workflow by including features that give users an easy way to intuitively mix gestures with traditional keyboard and mouse interactions.

Swiping, tapping, pinching, and dragging all introduce a new palette of touch gestures aimed at making faster scrubbing of the media, cuts, and dropping clips into the timeline. The touch interface is designed to help an editor intuitively build and refine rough cuts early in the edit with greater efficiency. Many of these gestures are also available in mouse-driven workflows, ensuring flexibility across a variety of different devices and user preferences.

Key Touch Gestures and Features

- **Single-Finger Tap and Drag:**

  Tap and select clips using one finger in the Project panel; access thumbnail controls such as play and scrub. Dragging clips from the Project panel or Program Monitor into the Timeline is now well and painless, ensuring that users can quickly assemble clips sans keyboard intervention.

- **Two-Finger Pinch to Zoom:**

  This 'normal' gesture zooms in and out of clips and sequences in the Project panel, Monitor panels, and Timeline. The pinch inward zooms out, and by spreading the fingers, it zooms in, giving complete control over the level of visual detail in the workspace.

- **Two-Finger Scroll:**

  Scrolling through panels with two fingers is a piece of cake. If you need to see different parts of the sequence, or the contents of a panel, scroll horizontally and/or vertically inside the Project and Timeline panels.

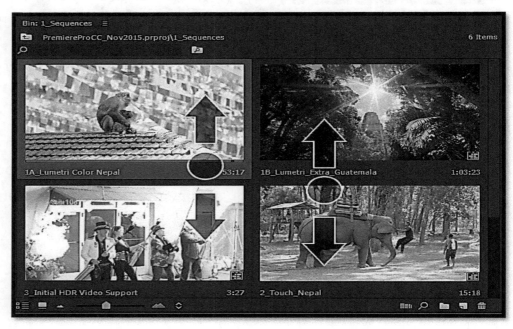

- **Two-Finger Scrub:**

  Similar to scrolling, two fingers can scrub through media, moving the playhead backward or forward on a 1:1 scale relative to the clip length. This is ideal when you want to meander through video content without having to jump around in time frames.

Improved Project Panel Thumbnail Controls:

When working with clips in the **Icon View** of the Project panel, touch gestures open up additional controls on thumbnails. Every clip provides play and scrubbing, as well as setting in and out points. Just tap to start either playback or scrubbing and drag your finger for fine adjustments.

00002.mxf   12:21

Additional Controls with Touch Gestures:

- **Frame Step Button:** Tapping or dragging on this button plays a clip one frame at a time.

- **Shuttle Button:** This button plays a clip at an increasingly faster rate, incrementing to 32x speed.

- **In-point and Out-point Buttons**: These allow establishing exact points where users want to enter or leave during playback or scrubbing a clip.

Drag-and-Drop Editing in the Program Monitor:

The touch interface extends basic drag-and-drop editing with multiple "drop zones" in the Program Monitor, each targeting a specific type of edit:

- **Insert:** Inserts clips at the playhead position, or between in/out points, and ripple all other clips later in the sequence.

- **Overwrite**: Overwriting content right in the timeline at the position of the playhead.

- **Insert Before/After:** Inserts a new clip before/after the active clip in the sequence.

- **Replace:** Replace content at the playhead, using existing selections.
- **Overlay:** Overlays a clip on to the first empty track without displacing other content.

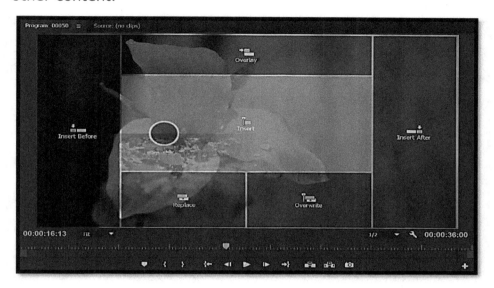

Notes on Drop-Zone Behavior:

Sometimes, depending on the playhead's placement within the timeline and its contents, more than one drop zone will yield the same result. For instance, adding clips to the end of a sequence might mean that dropping an item onto "Insert After," "Insert," or "Overwrite" does the same thing.

In short, the touch functionality of Premiere Pro unfolds a very intuitive, yet powerful option for editors who would like to integrate touch gestures into their workflow. These improvements target the core of faster and more immersive editing experiences that the users will get whether they use a touch device or any traditional peripheral.

How to use Premiere Pro in a dual-monitor setup

Setting up Adobe Premiere Pro with a dual-monitor setup is a very straightforward method of improving your editing workflow through workspace expansion, viewing video outputs separately, or splitting different sections of the interface across screens. Here's how you can set up and customize Premiere Pro for an optimized dual-monitor experience.

Getting Started

- **Connect Your Monitors:** Attach your second monitor to the computer. Most desktops and laptops have a port that supports HDMI, DVI, or even Thunderbolt connections with adapters if supported. For example, if both your computer and monitor support HDMI, connect them using an HDMI cable.
- **Check Display Functionality**: Check that your computer detects the second monitor in your system display settings. Adjust display settings as needed to confirm both monitors are active.

Setting Up Premiere Pro for Second-Monitor Video Playback

This is nice to use when color grading or if you want to play back video full-screen. Using Premiere Pro, you can have it play only the Program Monitor's video to the second monitor while your primary screen stays open to the editing controls.

1. **Adjust Playback Preferences**
   - To access this on a Mac: Go to **Premiere Pro** to access **Preferences**. After accessing Preferences, simply click on **Playback.**
   - On Windows, go to the Edit tab to access **Preferences**. After accessing Preferences, simply click on **Playback.**

2. **Enable Mercury Transmit:** Select this check box to enable playback on an extended desktop monitor.

3. **Choose Your Output Monitor:**
   - **Adobe DV:** For FireWire connections.
   - **Adobe Monitor x**: A listing of computer monitors connected to your computer for video preview.
   - **Third-Party Video Hardware**: This will include AJA Kona, Blackmagic Playback, Matrox, among others depending upon your configuration.

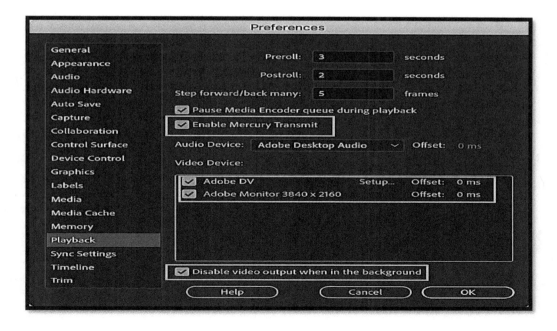

4. **Optional:** Check the box for "Disable video output when in the background" if you want it to revert to a standard display when you switch away from Premiere Pro.

   Now, as you play back your project, that monitor will display full-screen video output, immersing you in the editing experience.

Displaying the Premiere Pro Interface on a Second Monitor

You can set up a dual-monitor workspace so that your interface can be extended, moving tools, panels, or specific parts of the interface to the second monitor for an extended workspace.

1. **Move Panels to the Second Monitor:**
   - Hover over the panel that you intend to move.
   - Drag it onto your second monitor and release.

2. **Organize Your Workspace:** Put panels on your second screen for quick access to tools or timeline views. You can expand the Program Monitor, Effects, or any panel to maximize visibility.

3. **Save Custom Workspace Configurations:**
   - Once the panels are set up, save the configuration as a custom workspace by going to **Window** to access the **Workspaces tab**. After accessing Workspaces, click on **Save as New Workspace.**
   - You can make different configurations - one for editing and one for color grading, for example - and easily flip back and forth between them.

Tips and Tricks to Improve Workflow

- **Multiple Configurations**: Set up separate workspaces for specific tasks, such as an edit layout and a color grading layout, for a more effective workflow.
- **Quick Panel Adjustments**: Undock, resize, and reorganize panels in Premiere Pro to quickly and efficiently switch between different editing needs.

Troubleshooting Common Issues

If you have any problems moving panels or playing video on the second monitor, here are a few simple troubleshooting steps to try:

- **Panel Dragging:** The panel must be undocked to drag it to the other screen.
- **Display Overhang Problem:** Sometimes, Premiere Pro overlaps the secondary display a little, which can make it not too useful. Try adjusting monitor alignment in your OS display settings.
- **GPU Compatibility:** An outdated GPU driver version may also contribute to the malfunction of dual-monitor functionality in Premiere Pro. Update your drivers and check compatibility by going to the **File menu.** Afterward, access the **Project Settings** before clicking on **General.** Finally, click on **Renderer.**

By setting up a dual-monitor workspace in Premiere Pro, you create a wide, flexible editing environment that you can modify to meet your specific needs for any given project. This goes a long way in organizing your workflow and allowing you to improve on your overall editing speed.

CHAPTER SIX

FRAME.IO

How to install and activate Frame.io

Frame.io centers all of your communication, feedback, and media management on the most important thing in video production. No endless email threads, scattered spreadsheets, or app switching. With Frame.io coming right inside of Adobe Premiere Pro and After Effects starting with the latest version, it eases your entire workflow so that you can create.

Unified Integration for Adobe Creative Cloud Users

Open Frame.io by downloading the latest version of Premiere Pro. To access Frame.io at no additional cost, you must subscribe to Creative Cloud All Apps (as an individual or a member of Creative Cloud Team), or be a Single App subscriber for Premiere Pro. To access the Frame.io panel in your app:

- Head over to **Window.**
- Then, access the **Workspaces tab**.
- Also, click on the **Review with Frame.io.**
- To begin using Frame.io, sign in with your existing Adobe ID. If you have any trouble finding it, check out Adobe Account for assistance.
- When you log in, you will be taken through a series of steps to activate and launch Frame.io. To have the best experience and to access all the extensive functionality, check out the web application at app.frame.io, where you will find everything you need to manage and collaborate with ease on your projects.

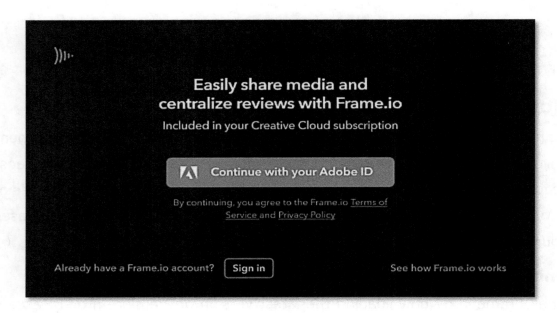

Getting Started with Frame.io

Sign in with your Adobe ID. To easily access your Adobe ID, go to Adobe Account. Take the cues to activate Frame.io and start collaborative creative work within your app or on the web at app.frame.io.

Activate Frame.io for Creative Cloud

To activate Frame.io, follow these steps:

- Open the Frame.io panel in-app (That is, select **Window** to access **Extensions.** After accessing Extensions, simply select **Frame.io** and click **Continue** or **Sign In)**.

- You will be directed to the Frame.io authentication portal. Make sure to use your Creative Cloud email and click **Let's Go.**

- Click **Continue with Adobe** before logging into your Adobe account. After which, you head back to the app.

How to use Frame.io with Premiere Pro and After Effects

Frame.io makes collaboration on videos smooth, allows you to share projects with anyone who needs access to it or wants to give feedback on it. Frame.io was designed to keep all project notes, feedback, and comments connected to your Adobe Premiere Pro or After Effects files, making it easy to track reviews and approvals in one organized space.

Getting Started

Before you begin working in Frame.io, ensure that the latest versions of Premiere Pro and After Effects are installed, then install and activate the Frame.io extension.

Frame.io Key Features

- **Integrated Panel:** A dedicated panel for Frame.io is available in Premiere Pro and After Effects. You can use the Frame.io panel for seamless work right from within your Adobe applications while adding collaborators, uploading media, sharing timelines, and importing comments.

- **Full Access Web App:** For the full capability, visit app.frame.io. The web application provides a more significant scale when it comes to versioning and permission settings.

- **Collaborative Workflow:** Start working in Premiere Pro/After Effects Frame.io panel, then into the web app for advanced functions.

Overview of the Frame.io Panel

The tools you'll find inside the Frame.io panel allow you to:

A. **Select Projects**: Click to select or create new projects.

B. **Upload and Download Media:** Transfer files directly from your editing timeline.

C. **Manage Versions:** Keep track of multiple versions of your projects.

D. **Add Collaborators**: Invite team members for review and feedback.

E. **Share Projects:** Send for review or present projects with just a few clicks.

Media Uploads

With Frame.io, you have a vast amount of file types supported, including but not limited to video, images, audio, and PDFs. Upload media directly from your editing timeline to review:

- **In Premiere Pro:** Drag files or folders into the Frame.io project, or use **Upload > Active Sequence** to upload an open sequence.

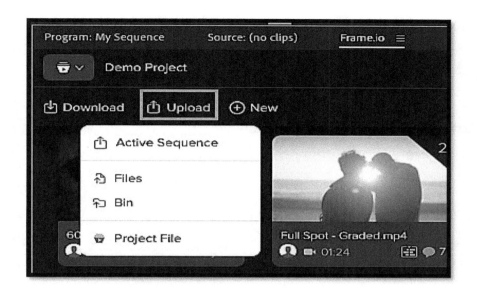

- **In After Effects:** You can directly upload using Active Comp, or Queued Comps for comps that are waiting to render in the Render Queue.

File Upload Tips

- **Organize Folders:** When uploading folders, folder structures automatically persist. There is no need to reorganize after uploading your content.

- **High Quality Playback:** Frame.io's accelerated uploader will let you upload big uncompressed files with no lag, encoding them into H.264 for smooth web playback. However, you can still have access to the original files for download.

- **Smarter Review:** Once uploaded, Frame.io generates hover scrubs for video files and thumbnails for stills to easily review media at a glance. Non-media files are denoted with file icons.

Upload and Render Timelines

To share projects without ever having to leave the app:

- **Enable Active Sequence options in Premiere Pro and Active Comp options in After Effects**: Enable either of the two for direct uploading onto the timeline. Now, set your export options such as the disk location, render preset, file name, export range, and whether you want to convert timeline markers to comments or retain rendered files on your local storage.

- **Auto-Versioning:** Automatically version-stack new versions so that it's easy to refer and compare.

Sharing and Collaborating on Frame.io Projects: A Quick Overview

Frame.io allows you to streamline sharing and collaboration on media projects by providing you with a variety of in-app and web-based tools. Here is an extended view of core features to review, comment, and collaborate with your team.

140

Sharing Projects for Review

1. **Share for Review from In-App Panel:**

   - **Quick Share:** Sharing from the Frame.io panel is instant. Simply open up your project by clicking on "Share For Review," and in an instant, a shareable link is created. Copy this link to share for immediate offline access.

   - **Advanced Sharing**: For more sharing options and permission management, head to Frame.io on the web.

Commenting and Feedback Tools

2. **Adding Comments and Annotations:**

   - **Frame-Specific Feedback**: Comments can be left by reviewers on specific frames within the video, directly below the composition window.

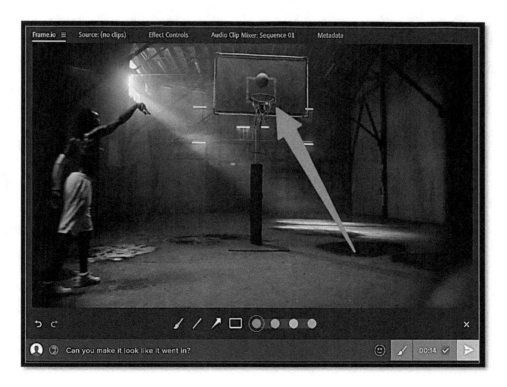

- **Annotation Customization:** Use font color and other annotation features to emphasize comments for clarity. Comments with their timestamp show up on the left in the **Comment List,** which you can reply to, delete, or mark as resolved.

3. **Timeline Navigation with Comments**:
   - Click any comment in this list, and immediately go to that video frame to make navigation easy and contextual review.

Integrating Feedback in Premiere Pro

4. **Importing Comments as Markers:**
   - **Link your Sequences:** Connect your Premiere Pro sequence to the Frame.io video to enable an easy comment integration. If the video was uploaded via the Frame.io extension, this happens automatically, but sequences can also be linked manually.

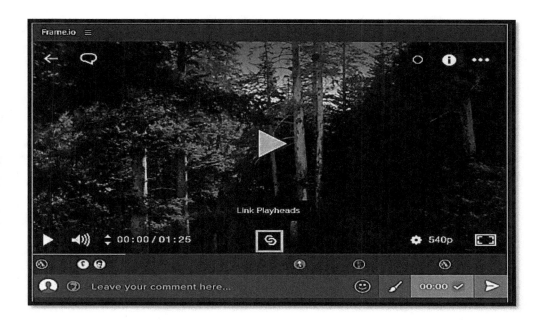

- **Import Comments:** Import comments are viewed as markers on your timeline, with each one displaying the comment, collaborator, and timestamp for ease in identifying feedback directly on your project.

Managing Collaborators

5. **Adding Collaborators:**

- **Options In-App and Web**: Open the project in the Frame.io web app or through the in-app panel, click the "+" icon, and add collaborators. You will be able to search for users by name or email, and if they are not under your account, you can send them a direct email invite.

- **Project Invite Link:** For quick access to projects, generate a URL from within the "project invite" link, share it, and collaborators can add themselves.

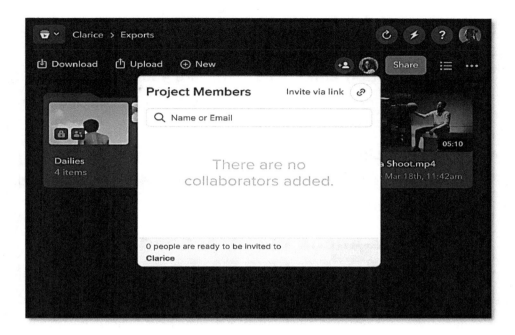

6. Deleting of Collaborators:

- To delete collaborators, select the project and go to the Collaborator icon to click the "-" icon that is next to the username. Confirm to complete the removal.

Sharing Edits Externally

7. **External Sharing Options:**

   - **Presentation Links:** You can share your clips for viewing and download only, with the possibility to add brand logos on them for delivering final previews.

   - **Review Links:** You can also let links be used for interactive external reviews by allowing your reviewers to comment directly on the content using annotations.

How to integrate Adobe Workfront and Frame.io

Video production is a multi-faceted process dependent on unified coordination between project management, reviews, revisions, and approvals of content. Successful integrations, such as Adobe Workfront and Frame.io, allow for the harmonious unification of such workflows, hence enabling the production teams to easily manage their operations right from creative development to tracking the same.

With Frame.io, creative teams can easily share video sequences from within Adobe Premiere Pro, capture feedback and approvals right within the production flow. Meanwhile, marketing and project management teams benefit a lot from robust tracking and oversight provided by Adobe Workfront, which keeps production progress visible and organized.

Integrating Adobe Workfront and Frame.io bridges project management, creative reviews, and content approvals to enhance the efficiency and alignment of video production teams. The following step-by-step guide gets you started with this integration.

1. **Set up Adobe Workfront and Frame.io Accounts**

   - First, make sure the Adobe Workfront and Frame.io accounts are properly set up and permissions are granted to your team.

- For larger teams, it may be worth creating Workfront templates that mirror how videos are typically produced.

2. **Configure Adobe Premiere Pro for Integration with Frame.io**

   - The Frame.io extension should be installed inside Adobe Premiere Pro so editors can upload sequences directly from it into Frame.io for review.

   - Connect your Frame.io account to enable team members to comment, review, and approve video files from within the editing software of their choice.

3. **Integrate Workfront with Frame.io using API or Third-Party Tools**

   - Workfront can be integrated with Frame.io using APIs or integration tools such as Zapier or Make (formerly Integromat). This could be helpful in further automating processes concerning video file uploads. For example, it automatically uploads the final approved files coming from Frame.io into a Workfront project.

   - Developers can then customize API settings for the option to further configure the workflows between Workfront and Frame.io.

4. **Streamline Feedback and Approvals in Frame.io**
   - Set up your Frame.io projects to map with your Workfront project structure. This way, all comments and feedback from within Frame.io are accessible to team members in Workfront.
   - Leverage Frame.io commenting and markup to capture exact feedback on video frames to help hasten revision and approval cycles.

5. **Enable Workfront to Track and Assign Work**

   - Use Adobe Workfront to show when a task needs to be executed at every stage of the video production, and a due date required for it.

- Connect review tasks within Frame.io with Workfront to indicate what's waiting for feedback, revision, or approval to help keep projects on schedule.

6. **Automate Notifications and Workflow Updates**

- Setup automated notifications in Workfront to let team members know exactly when an update happens in Frame.io, such as new feedback or when approvals are completed.
- This will allow teams to stay on the same page and be current with project activity without having to log on and check multiple platforms manually.

7. **Document Processes and Best Practices**

- Create documentation that guides on the most effective usage of each platform in conjunction so consistency is maintained across all video production projects.
- Provide training, when necessary, in order for all users to become familiar with the use of Adobe Workfront and Frame.io in their day-to-day work.

Workfront and Frame.io Integration Benefits

- This integration will guarantee smoother collaboration between project management and creative production and reduce overtime, thus keeping all team members on one wavelength.
- The integration will support activity alignment, speed up workflows, and improve the quality and efficiency of video production in general.

How to share for review with Frame.io

Adobe Premiere Pro 2025 has made sharing sequences in review smooth, group-oriented, and easy through integration with Frame.io. The "Share for Review" feature will enable editors to send sequences more effectively to receive feedback in real-time. Reviewers instantly obtain access via shared links where they will interact with the latest edits and have the opportunity to leverage commenting and annotating from Frame.io directly on the exact frames of the timeline to enhance the precision and effectiveness of feedback.

Also, included with all Adobe Premiere Pro and Creative Cloud subscriptions, Frame.io provides a robust collaboration environment with tools such as two users, five concurrent projects, 100GB of Frame.io storage, and Camera to Cloud.

1. **Getting Started**

- First, create and edit a sequence in your Premiere Pro project.
- Click the **Share button** from the header bar to open options for sharing.

- From here, you have two options: you can share the active sequence for review or turn the project into a Team Project. In the **Share for Review** section, select where your sequence will be saved using the option labeled **Select Frame.io Location.** This is how you organize and eventually will find your work in Frame.io's folder structure to make it easy for you and your reviewers to find it.

You need to be logged in to Frame.io for this destination to be chosen. The location picker allows you to browse through Frame.io folders and choose where the sequence will live for shared review.

2. Customizing Resolution

Click the **Preset Settings** dropdown to determine what resolution the video will export at. Options include:

- **Web 1080:** This will export Full HD, 1920x1080 pixels, good for higher resolution for more detail.

- **Web 720:** This exports HD at 1280x720 pixels. It is good quality, though the files are smaller, and is ideal when bandwidth is lower.

- **ProRes 4444:** A high-end, above-UHD quality codec that offers clarity for professional review.

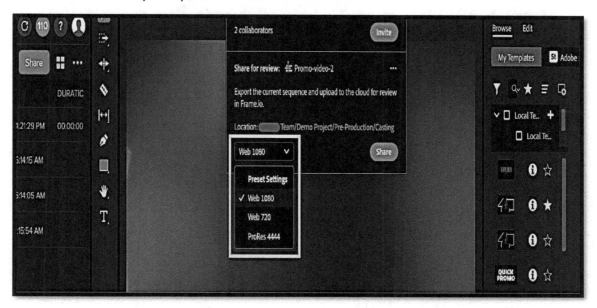

3. **Export and Upload**

- Once the resolution setting is set, click **Share** to launch **Adobe Media Encoder** and export and upload your sequence to Frame.io in the background while you continue editing.

- After the upload is completed, a review link will be created for sharing. Just copy this link to share it with reviewers.

4. Updating and Revising

- As you make changes to the shared sequence, Premiere Pro logs the changes and allows you to push updated versions to Frame.io. To refresh the shared sequence, just simply click **Share**, after which, you click on **Update shared content** to make sure that the reviewers get the latest version.

- You can also, to add flexibility, generate a review link for a new version of the sequence. To do that, select the options icon next to the sequence name and then select **Create a new link** for a fresh, independent review session.

This step refines the workflow by providing easy, fluid feedback loops for video projects, and thus efficient and potent collaboration in Premiere Pro.

How to invite collaborators to co-edit a project

Learn how to easily invite other editors into your Premiere Pro project and allow them to edit the video in real time in the cloud. You will activate the feature called **Team Projects**, through which any individual project can be transformed into a collaborative workplace, enabling multiple editors to work and make changes instantaneously.

1. **Getting Started with Team Projects**
   - **Open Your Project:** Open the Premiere Pro project you want to share for collaboration in editing.
   - **Convert to Team Project:** Click **Share**, then click **Invite** to convert your project to a Team Project, enabling you to invite and add collaborators while controlling their level of access.

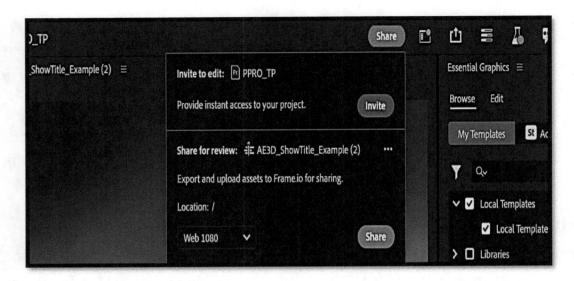

2. **Sending Invitations**

   In the **Convert to Team Projects** and **Invite dialog**, do as follows:

   - Under the General tab, give a name and description to your Team Project.

   - Click Invite and enter email addresses of collaborators. They will be sent an invite to the document, where they can edit along with others in real time.

3. **Configure Project Settings Before You Invite**

   Configure the project settings to best suit their purpose and ensure high performance and quality:

   - **Options**: Define the settings related to video rendering and playback, as well as audio and capture display format: video, audio, capture display format.

   - **Color Settings:** Modify advanced color settings, including the Viewer Gamma, 3D LUT Interpolation, HDR Graphics White, and Auto Detect Log Video Color Space.

- **Scratch Disks:** Establish storage locations for captured video/audio, Creative Cloud Libraries, preview files, and Motion Graphics templates.

- **Ingest Settings:** Allow the **Ingest Settings** to select your import actions, presets, and storage locations for primary and proxy media files.

4. **Manage Collaborators**

Once you have invited collaborators, additional management can be done by:

- In the **Edit Collaborators dialog box**, you will see a list with the invited collaborators, the status of the invitations already sent and the option to remove the ones that are not needed anymore.

- Click **OK** once you have these set to your liking, and the invites will be sent. A progress pop-up dialog box appears showing the status of each invitation.

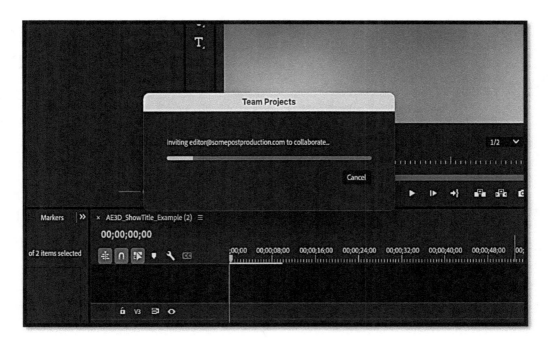

A backup copy of your project is auto-saved in the cloud, letting you invite others to collaborate freely and safely. Notifications of new invitations will be available within both the Creative Cloud desktop app and the Premiere Pro app, so it keeps everyone in sync.

CHAPTER SEVEN

ANIMATION AND KEYFRAMING

How to add, navigate, and set keyframes

Animation of a property in Adobe Premiere Pro means to introduce dynamic changes regarding time, developing visual or audio augmentations by changing some of its attributes, such as position, opacity, or volume. This is accomplished through keyframes-set specific moments in time along a timeline where you define values for these properties. By setting at least two keyframes, (an initial and one final-one) Premiere Pro will automatically calculate and interpolate the transition that occurs between them.

Key frames can be added, edited, and deleted from both the **Timeline panel** and from within the **Effect Controls panel**. For the best use of keyframes in Premiere Pro, here is a general look at how to use them effectively within the program:

Using Keyframes

1. **Adding Keyframes**

    - To animate any property, select the clip first in the Timeline panel.

    - If the Timeline is not displaying keyframes, then turn them on by clicking on the **Wrench icon** and select **Show Video Keyframes**.

    - In the **Effect Controls panel**, any effect is 'opened' by clicking the triangle, then keyframing is turned on by clicking the **Toggle Animation button**.

    - Click the **Add/Remove Keyframe icon** after you have moved the playhead to the point of your desired time and changed the property value. Or from within an **Effect Controls panel**, simply changing any effect property will by default create a keyframe at the current playhead position.

2. **Keyframe Selection**

Selecting keyframes allows you to modify or duplicate them.

- To select a single keyframe in the Timeline, click with the **Selection tool or the Pen tool or Shiftclick** to select multiple keyframes.

- In the **Effect Controls panel**, drag a marquee selection to select multiple keyframes or click a property name to select all keyframes for that property.

3. **Deleting Keyframes**

- To delete keyframes, either highlight the keyframes you want to delete and press the **Delete key,** or click the **Add/Remove Keyframe button** while the playhead is at that keyframe.

- To delete all keyframes for property in the **Effect Controls panel**, click the **Animation button** to toggle it off—this deletes all keyframes for that effect.

4. **Additional Controls**

- **Fine tuning:** The Keyframe Navigator, through the Effect Controls panel, permits you to jump from keyframe to keyframe for fine-tuning. In adjustments in segments, any selected segment between keyframes automatically realigns when doing keyframe adjustments to accommodate ease management of smooth transitions.

Introduction to Keyframe and Graph in Effect Controls and Timeline Panels

The Effect Controls and Timeline panels in most editing software each offer ways to control keyframes and other properties for effects. Each has unique ways of controlling timing and values. The Effect Controls panel offers a comprehensive view into all of the effect properties with keyframes and interpolation methods applied. You will have full control over your keyframe adjustments here, including properties that use x and y coordinates like Position.

By comparison, Timeline panels can show only one effect property per clip at a time, and you have minimal control over keyframe values. However, Timeline panels allow you to make quick adjustments without needing to toggle to the Effect Controls panel.

Displaying Keyframes and Interpolation as a Graph: Both the Timeline and Effect Controls panels represent each keyframe's value graphically and interpolate transitions between them. A flat graph indicates no change between two keyframes, whereas an ascending or descending graph line reflects increased or decreased values. Transitions speed is controlled by adjusting the interpolation methods and by editing Bezier curves.

Keyframes in the Effect Controls Panel

You see and edit the keyframes for a clip you have effected in the Effect Controls panel. Collapsed effects in it will show you a **Summary Keyframe icon**, which is a shortcut to refer to your keyframed properties within an effect. The summary keyframes themselves are static and cannot be edited directly; however, they give you an overview of active keyframes for each effect.

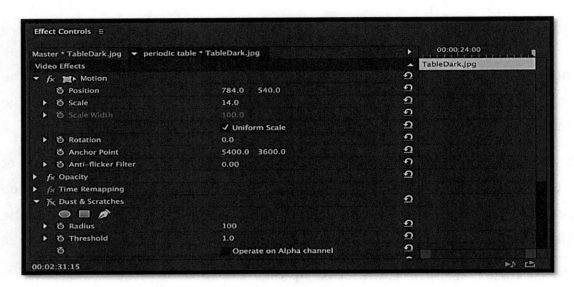

Steps to View and Adjust Keyframes;

- Select an effect applied clip in the Timeline panel and then open its **Effect Controls panel**.

- If the effects timeline is not visible, click the **Show/Hide Timeline View button.**

- To display keyframes for an effect, click the triangle next to the effect's name to expand it in the Effect Controls timeline.

- For more detailed work with the keyframes, click the triangle next to the **Toggle Animation icon** to open the Value and Velocity graphs.

Previewing Keyframes in a Timeline Panel

In the Timeline panel, you can view both video and audio effect keyframes of every clip. You can only view one effect property's keyframes at a time per track. All-track keyframes can also be viewed for Audio tracks. Both clip-specific as well as track-wide adjustments can be made.

Steps for Viewing and Managing Keyframes:

- If necessary, click the triangle next to the name of a track to expand it.

- Click the **Show Keyframes icon** on a video or audio track and do one of the following:

160

a. **Show Keyframes**: This option activates the display of any applied effect graphs and keyframes to clips in the track.

b. **Show Opacity Handles (video) or Show Clip Volume (audio):** This option shows you only those keyframes that have been created for either the Opacity (video) or Volume (audio) effects.

c. **Show Track Keyframes (audio):** This option displays keyframes representing audio effects applied to the entire track.

d. **Hide Keyframes**: This option hides all graphs and keyframes for the track.

For more detail, use the **Zoom In control** to magnify the track or adjust track height by dragging track boundaries. You can also resize all expanded tracks by holding **Shift** while dragging.

Keyframe Navigator and Precise Adjustments

Both the Effect Controls and Timeline panels have keyframe navigators, which contain arrows for moving the current-time indicator from one keyframe to another. You can Shift-drag the current-time indicator in the Effect Controls panel to snap it to the nearest keyframe.

To Move Between Keyframes:
- Click the left and right arrows of the keyframe navigator.
- In the Effect Controls panel, Shift-drag to snap.

Editing Keyframe Values in the Effect Controls Panel

After having an effect property set to keyframe, the Effect Controls panel presents an advanced editing using **Value and Velocity graph**. In general, Value graphs show time-based variations of non-spatial properties such as Scale and Velocity graphs illustrate how a value changes over time. A Velocity graph reveals the velocity of change between keyframes.

How to Edit Keyframes in the Effect Controls Panel:

- Select any clip and make sure its effect is opened into the **Effect Control panel.**

- Open the **Value and Velocity graphs** by clicking the triangle next to the property's name.

- With the **Selection or Pen tool**, drag keyframes up or down in the Value graph to change values.

- Drag the **Bezier curves** in the Velocity graph to fine tune the transitions of the values.

Modifying Keyframe Graphs in the Timeline Panel:

- Have the Timeline panel open to the clip that includes the keyframes.

- In the clip or track, select from the effect menu the property to be affected.

- Drag the keyframes with the **Selection or Pen tool;** value changed by dragging up or down, time location changed by dragging left or right. Changes made in the Timeline panel are dynamically reflected in the Value and Velocity graphs of the Effect Controls panel for dynamic feedback and unified integration of these panels.

Animating effects

In Premiere Pro, "animation" is more than just making something move around the screen. In other words, it means changing things dynamically over time. That can include anything from a property that changes over time, like moving a clip from one corner of the screen to another, a sharpness changing over time from focused to blurry, or color changing from one hue to another. Here, animation means any kind of change that occurs over time, and all or almost all effects in Premiere Pro can be animated, though some have limitations.

Keyframe in Premiere Pro

The basis through which animations of changes in motion, effects, audio, and other properties are created is through keyframes. Every keyframe represents a point in time for which some property value of an object is known. For instance, its position, its opacity, or its volume. To animate using keyframes, Premiere Pro interpolates values between the keyframes to make the movement continuous and smooth. You will commonly create at least two keyframes that define the beginning and end of what you want to change.

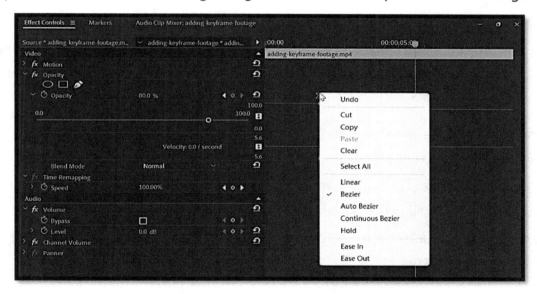

Working with Keyframes

Keyframes can be set, viewed, and manipulated in the Effect Controls and Timeline panels, but each serves a different purpose:

- **Timeline Panel:** Good to have a quick look and to modify simple one-dimensional properties, such as opacity or audio volume. Changes in the value of keyframes are visual; hence, it is easy to see how the values evolve. By default, the interpolation is linear, but some adjustments can produce subtle transitions, such as easing motion to a smooth halt. You can have even more control over the speed and smoothness of the animation with Bezier handles.

- **Effect Controls Panel**: Used to adjust those properties that are a bit more complicated, such as position, rotation, or scale. This panel also displays a lot of keyframes, but it will show only keyframes for a particular selected clip. The Value and Velocity graphs allow the visualization of the exact change of an effect's value, which allows for modifying its editing speed and smoothness with precision.

Editing Keyframes for Audio

You can adjust audio keyframes either in the Timeline panel or Audio Mixer. Similar to video clip keyframes, audio clip keyframes also provide the option of editing both in the Timeline and the Effect Controls panels.

Customizing the Workspace

Premiere Pro allows a lot of flexibility in managing panels. You are allowed to set up the panels according to your preference to work with and then save that setup as a new workspace by heading to **Window.** After which, you access the **Workspace** and select **New Workspace**. Just name your workspace to easily access it in the future.

Premiere Pro's very versatile keyframing system is great, and powerful, and allows for precise control over animated properties, which is an indispensable development tool for video projects with dynamic visual and auditory effects.

How to use Motion effects to edit and animate clips

Motion effect in Premiere Pro gives you precise positioning, scaling, and rotation of clips in the video frame with a powerful base for visual customization. Automatically applied as a fixed effect to any clip in the Timeline panel, the settings for the Motion effect are accessed in the Effect Controls panel, where, to refine your settings, you can expand the Motion section.

With Motion properties, you can achieve creative motion by setting keyframes to animate clips. By doing so, you unlock new creative potential. Premiere Pro also provides many of the standard effects that can be used to manipulate clips directly inside of the Program Monitor, including but not limited to Corner Pin, Generate effects, Lighting Effects, Crop, Mirror, Transform, and Twirl.

a. **Moving Clip Position**

To move the position of a clip in the Program Monitor:

1. Select the clip in the Timeline and place the current-time indicator over a frame in the clip.

2. Deselect the "Uniform Scale" check box for the Motion effect to get non-proportional scaling.

3. Choose one of the following methods:

    - **Lighting Effects:** To add a Lighting Effects lens flare or other lighting effects, select **Lighting Effects** from the Effects panel. In the Effect Controls panel, drag the light to change the position.

Before adding lighting effects

After adding lighting effects

- **Motion Effect**: Click the clip in the Program Monitor to see handles and the anchor point, and drag the clip to change the position.

b. Scaling a Clip

To scale, do one of the following:

- **Move the clip**: Double-click the clip and then drag the anchor point or handles to move without scaling.
- **Scale freely:** Drag a corner handle to scale freely.
- **Scale one dimension**: Drag a side handle to scale horizontally or vertically.
- **Scale proportional:** Hold Shift while you drag a corner handle to scale proportionally.

Scale assets manually

Scaled frame

If scaling over 100%, notice that this will lower the image quality.

c. **Scaling Assets in a Sequence**

By default, Premiere Pro maintains the original frame size and centers assets within the sequence frame. To adjust scaling options:

- **Manual Scaling:** Highlight the asset to be scaled inside the timeline, open the Effect Controls panel and adjust the Scale slider under **Motion controls.**

- **Auto Scaling to Frame Size**: Right-click (or Control-click on macOS) the asset in the Timeline then select "Scale to Frame Size" to scale it to the sequence frame size.

Note: "Scale to Frame Size" resamples the asset to match sequence dimensions, while "Set to Frame Size" fits the asset without resampling.

d. **Rotating Clips**

To rotate a clip:

- Hover just outside any handle until the **Rotate icon** appears, then drag to adjust.

- Or in the Effect Controls panel, twirl open **Motion controls** and specify a Rotation value.

- To flip a clip, enter a negative number in the Rotation field.

Select frame

Rotated clip

Note: If you want one of these transformations to change over time, just set keyframes and the Program Monitor will transition smoothly between values for smoother animation.

Key Points

By default, clips are centered in the Program Monitor and appear at their original size. All transforms such as Position, Scale and Rotation happen around the anchor point, which by default is the center of a clip. It becomes very intuitive to perform spatial transformations directly by manipulating these properties in the Program Monitor.

Animating Motion in the Program Monitor

The Program Monitor provides an interactive means to animate and compose dynamically, and through which you can create motion paths, keyframe properties, as well as adjust anchor points in real time. By adjusting a clip's Motion effect in the Program Monitor you will be able to do some very cool things such as creating animated insets, split screens, and transitions that bring your layers to life in complex and visually interesting ways.

Clip displaying motion path

Clip displaying disparity of speed in motion path

a. **Creating Motion with Keyframes**

Motion over a clip is achieved through the Motion effect that is available within the Effect Controls panel. You can directly adjust **Position** and **Scale values** in the Program Monitor to control what you see of the clips in lower tracks to create layered visuals.

To achieve that, you would need to set keyframes that determine the clip's starting and ending points so that there are smooth transitions or user-designed animations.

- **Motion Paths:** A motion path, at the head of a clip, appears in the **Program Monitor**, small blue squares at the head represent keyframes. Dotted lines between the keyframes represent interpolated frames. The spacing of these dots defines the speed of the motion. Closely spaced dots indicate slow motion whereas wide spacing indicates faster motion.

- **Keyframe Manipulation:** Keyframe value adjustment for things like **Position and Scale** is directly done within the Program Monitor. By clicking and dragging the clip's eight corner handles, you are able to set specific values of those properties to refine the movements to be linear or curved, depending on the design needs.

b. **How to Animate Clips**

- **Select and Prepare the Clip:** Make sure your clip is selected in the **Timeline panel**. Then, go to the **Motion effect** within the **Effect Controls panel.**

- **Define Start and End**: The points of the start and end are determined by the movement of the current-time indicator where the animation begins. Click on the **Toggle Animation button** next to **Position** and establish your first keyframe. Drag the current-time indicator further along the timeline, move the clip to its ending position, and a motion path will join these points in the **Program Monitor.**

- **Edit Motion Path Curvature:** In Effect Controls, twirl down the **Position property** to reveal its Bezier handles. Use these controls to sculpt the motion path, smoothing out corners or creating sharp angles, respectively.

- **Adjust Speed and Timing:** Right-click (Control-click on macOS) on a keyframe to open **Temporal or Spatial Interpolation settings** to adjust acceleration for finer control over the animation.

c. **Advanced Motion with Anchor Points**

By default, the anchor point of a clip is always the center of a clip. This means that any rotation or scaling takes place around this anchor point. The anchor point is able to be changed so that the clip moves in relation to its frame or a motion path. This is useful for creating pan effects or if you want to change where the action is within a frame.

- **Setting the Anchor Point**: The anchor point can be set in **Effects Controls** that is opened by clicking an arrow next to the anchor point opens. Drag the horizontal or vertical controls to set the anchor point at any point off center, toward any edges, or to any corner of the clip for a variety of creative motion effects.

- **Keyframe the Anchor Point for Dynamic Movement**: Setting keyframes to the position of the anchor point is able to move independently with time as well. This can be used to simulate camera panning or to introduce shifting points of focus in the clip, adding storytelling value to your animation.

d. Refining Precision with Program Monitor Controls

For fine-tuning with a high degree of accuracy, there are several advantages in using the Program Monitor's Direct Manipulation Tool:

- **Pan Behind Tool:** Make detailed adjustments to an anchor point by selecting the **Pan Behind Tool** using Alt for Windows or Option for macOS. This will adjust the anchor point but won't change the clip's Position.

- **Snap to Guides:** Snap on by pressing **Ctrl** while dragging the anchor point to guide it to snap on frame edges and centers.

- **Anchor Point Display Adjustments:** Size the Program Monitor larger if you need to see beyond the frame for more extended movements, or reduce the size for display for a wider view.

e. Advanced Keyframe Adjustments

Refine the shape of motion speed across curves in the motion path using the **Bezier handles**. You will, as a result, be in a position to control acceleration and deceleration past both smooth natural motion and Sharp, abrupt changes that draw emphasis.

How to optimize keyframe automation

Automating audio adjustments in the Audio Mixer can sometimes lead to an excess of keyframes in the audio track, impacting performance. Keeping fewer but more sufficient keyframes will keep the audio quality higher and the efficiency of the system, especially when working on big projects. By optimizing the density of keyframes, you provide minimal loss of performance, as well as ease and precision in keyframe editing.

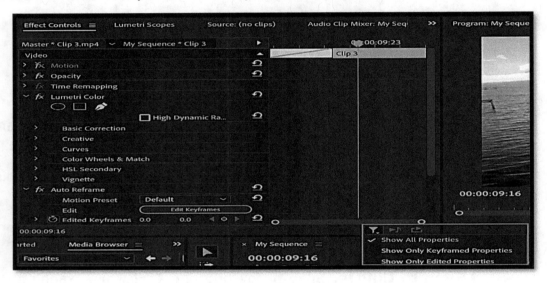

To set these preferences, follow these steps:

a. On your Windows, choose the **Edit tab**. After that, access the **Preferences tab** and click on **Audio.**

b. On your Mac OS, access the Premiere pro. After that, access the **Preferences tab** and click on **Audio.**

c. In the Automation Keyframe Optimization area, select one or both of the following options:

   • **Linear Keyframe Thinning**: It will only set keyframes at points that don't lie on a direct line between the start and end key frames. For instance, if you are automating a fade from 0 dB to -

12 dB, Premiere Pro will only place keyframes at points that reflect the progression of the fade from 0 dB to -12 dB. This setting eliminates unnecessary keyframes when you're dealing with gradual changes. Therefore, it's selected by default.

- **Minimum Time Interval Thinning:** It sets the key frames at key interval values more than what is set here. You can enter values from 1 to 2000 milliseconds and space would be set. The feature controls the frequency of setting the keyframes, pretty important in high-speed settings. It maintains equidistant key frames while optimizing the playback performance.

d.   Hit **OK** and save changes to simplify key frame management.

How to move and copy keyframes

The first and last keyframes of any sequence have special functions: the first keyframe is identified with the **Start Keyframe icon,** the last with the **End Keyframe icon**. These icons make quick identification of the starting and ending points for animated adjustments easy to see.

Adjusting Keyframe Timing

You can move keyframes to fine tune the timing of your animations. To do this, using the **Selection Tool or the Pen Too**l, simply select and drag one or multiple keyframes in either the **Timeline panel** or the **Effect Controls panel**:

- **Timeline Panel:** Select one or more keyframes and drag them to your preferred point in time.
- **Effect Controls Panel**: With the keyframe markers selected, drag them to their new positions.

In the **Effect Controls panel**, when a keyframe is selected, there is an overlaid black vertical line extending above and below the keyframe. It will help you visually as a guide to align the keyframe against any of the markings on the time ruler or against other objects. If the keyframe snapping is enabled, that line would turn white to indicate that it has snapped with the selected objects.

How to Set Up Keyframe Snapping

When you drag and drop your keyframes, keyframe snapping aligns your keyframes with proximal objects. You can toggle this feature on and off in the **Effect Controls panel** as well as determine what type of objects keyframes snap to as follows.

- Click the menu button at the upper-right corner of the **Effect Controls panel** to open the panel menu.
- Choose "Snap To" and select the objects, such as Video Keyframes, for snapping alignment.

Copying and Pasting Keyframes

Duplicating keyframes means you can quickly reuse an animation at different times, or in different clips. You can copy keyframes and then paste them into a new time in the same clip or into another clip or into another track. Here's how:

In the Effect Controls Panel:

- Click the triangle to expand the effect that includes the keyframes.
- Select one or more keyframes, then choose the **Edit tab** before clicking on **Copy.**
- Move the current-time indicator to the new time position, select the appropriate clip or property, and choose the **Edit tab** and click **Paste.**

If the target clip is shorter than the source clip, keyframes that extend beyond the Out point of the target clip are not shown unless you deselect the **Pin To Clip option.**

Timeline Panel:

- Open the clip's or track's effect menu to show the property you want to paste.

- Select the keyframes you want to copy and choose the **Edit tab** before clicking on **Copy.** Place the current-time indicator in the target clip or track where you want to paste the keyframes.

- Choose the **Edit tab** and click **Paste to** make sure that the target clip or track has the same property visible that you copied the keyframes from.

When it executes a paste, it does so with the earliest keyframe aligning with the current-time indicator, but subsequent keyframes keep their relative order. If a target track or clip is missing an appropriate property to take the Paste, the Paste command will gray out.

When you paste audio, Premiere Pro places the copied keyframes into the first matching property track, in order, first checking for an audio track, then for a submix track and finally the master track.

How to view and adjust effects and keyframes

The **Effects Control panel** provides a detailed interface for operating and editing all the effects applied to a selected clip. You can modify fixed effects and those that you can customize according to your needs so that you have fine-tuned control over every visual and audio property for every clip. Fixed effects include Time Remapping, Opacity, Motion, and Volume, and these are always a part of a clip. All but **Volume** are under the heading, Video Effects and Volume is under **Audio** Effects and is only available for clips that have audio or that have audio linked to them.

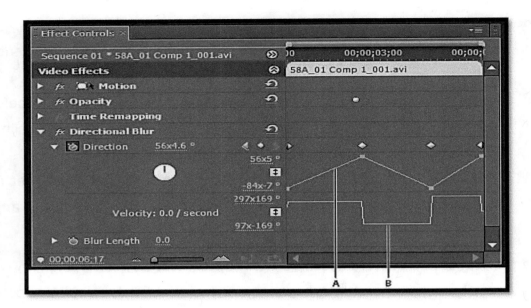

To facilitate your work, simply;

- Open the Effects workspace by choosing **Window.**
- After that, select the **Workspace** and click on **Effects**. This arrangement of the interface is designed to streamline working with effects.

An **Effect Controls panel** layout includes the name of the sequence, the name of the clip, the effects applied, and other controls, such as the **Show/Hide Timeline View button**, used to toggle on/off the timeline display to make more detailed edits.

Normally, this timeline view is turned off by default. To enable it, click this button; if necessary, expand the width of the panel. In this extended view, the properties of the applied effects, such as **Value graph** and **Velocity graph** will be made available for finer tuning.

When you click on a clip in the Timeline, the **Effect Controls panel** automatically centers the **Timeline view** on the clip's **In and Out points**. If you turn off "Pin To Clip" from the menu of the Effect Controls, you are able to reveal areas beyond those two points. Below the time ruler is the keyframe area where you can specify values at particular frames for the properties of an effect.

Viewing and Adjusting Effects

- To view the effects that have been applied to a clip, select it in the Timeline. There's no need to position the current-time indicator over the clip to turn on Effect Controls.

- Click the **Show/Hide arrows** beside each heading to open and close effect categories (many effects will be hidden by default). When the arrow points up, all the effects in that category are showing; when pointing down, the category heading is closed.

- Click an **effect heading** to expand it and expose its associated properties and controls. For example, in the ThreeWay Color Corrector effect, Tonal Range Definition is a property group, while Shadow Threshold is a property. Most properties include graphical controls such as sliders and dials with which you adjust the property interactively. Drag any effects by their headings to reorder them. Note that fixed effects are always pinned in place.

  You can also choose to display a timeline outside of the clip boundaries by deselecting "Pin To Clip." What lies outside of the clip boundaries now appears grey. If you have clips with audio, the **Play Audio button** will play the audio within the panel.

Access keyframes for an effect property in the Timeline panel

To view and manage keyframes and effect properties, including the ability to see keyframes in the Timeline and Effect Controls panels, simply do the following:

a. **Viewing Keyframes in the Timeline Panel**

- **Using the Show Keyframes Button:** Click the **Show Keyframes button** in a video or audio track's track header, and choose a keyframe option from the Show Keyframes menu. Now you can see keyframe data for a range of effect properties.

- **Playing Clip Keyframes via Right-Click:** Right-click (Windows) or Control-click (Mac OS) on the clip that contains keyframe properties you wish to view. Click on **Show Clip Keyframes** and then select the specific effect that contains the keyframes you want to view.

b. **Filtering Properties in the Effect Controls Panel**

As you're working in the Effect Controls panel you can streamline your display by filtering the properties to reduce your display to only those properties most relevant to your work.

- **Open the Filter Menu:** At the bottom of the Effect Controls panel, click the **Filter icon** to open options to filter properties in the panel:

  1. **Show All Properties:** All of the effect properties appear.

  2. **Show Only Keyframed Properties:** Only the properties that were keyed (when the blue stopwatch icon next to it was clicked) show up.

  3. **Show Only Edited Properties**: Only the properties with values different from its default appear.

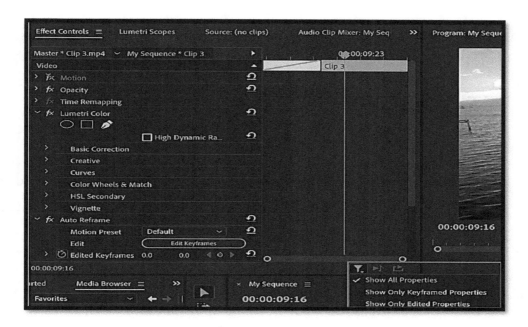

- **Assign Keyboard Shortcuts for Filtering:** You can create shortcuts to toggle between them more rapidly. Go to the **Premiere Pro menu**, then access the **Keyboard Shortcuts** and search by the name of the filter. You can also create a shortcut to cycle through all filters using the **Select Next Effect Controls Properties Filter.**

c. **Changing and Resetting Properties in the Effect Control Panel**

- **How to Change Property Values:**

    1. Hold your cursor over an underlined value of a property and left click drag to the left or right.

    2. Click the property value and edit the value in the text field; press **Enter** (Windows) or **Return** (Mac OS).

    3. Click the triangle to the left of a property if an arrowhead is displayed to open the property's slider controls; drag or scrub the sliders, or type directly into a text value area.

4. To input an angle, drag in the angle value area, scrub the underlined text value, or enter a value directly in the text area.

- **Editing Colors:**
  1. The Eyedropper Tool samples any color on your screen. To sample a 5x5 pixel area to get a more accurate color reading, Ctrl-click (Windows) or Command-click (Mac OS).
  2. Click the **color swatch**, select a color in the Adobe Color Picker, and click **OK.**

- **Resets Effect Properties:**
  1. Click the **Reset button** alongside an effect to restore default settings. Settings that have no keyframes are fully reset, and those with keyframes are only reset at the current time, inserting new keyframes as necessary.
  2. Mistakenly reset? Immediately use the **Edit tab** and then click on **Undo** to retrieve changes.

CHAPTER EIGHT

COMPOSITING

Compositing, alpha channels, and adjusting clip opacity

The powerful set of tools available in **Adobe After Effects and Premiere Pro** allows for the combining and layering of images and clips together to make visually dynamic composites. After Effects is specialized in advanced compositing; hence, it's an ideal application for creating detailed compositions which can be imported flawlessly into Premiere Pro for further editing.

In Premiere Pro, multiple techniques allow you to control transparency in images and video clips, which is key to effective compositing. For example, you can use mattes and effects to create transparent areas in an image or clip to reveal the content from other layers. You can also adjust clip opacity uniformly over a selected duration or animate the clip's opacity to fade it in or out during playback. This is done through the **Effect Controls** or **Timeline panel**, where you control each element with great detail. In cases where a simple fade to black is needed, one can apply a transition effect, like Dip to Black, to facilitate this with no manual keyframe animation required.

Alpha information, or transparency for clips, is stored in an alpha channel, which is a special channel dedicated to transparency information only so that the color channels are not affected. An alpha channel has the ability to composite in detail: it provides both opacity and transparency regions for each clip. When the alpha channels are on, Premiere Pro composites footage by layering clips from the lowest track up, showing black for any empty or completely transparent regions.

In addition to directly setting clip transparency, you can combine clips using blending modes or channel effects. Blending modes are creative choices that let you merge image data from several sources to create complex, multilayered compositions. To change the way opacity might interact with other effects, Premiere Pro provides for a specific rendering order when it applies effects. To alter this sequence, add the **Alpha Adjust effect** to allow more control over where and when in the production opacity is rendered compared to other visual effects.

Premiere Pro also provides options for interpreting and changing the alpha channel such as invert or to ignore it completely in the **Interpret Footage dialogue box**. If you are not sure what part of a clip is transparent, then playing the clip's alpha channel in the **Programme Monitor** will help you identify the transparency level using black for transparency, white for opacity, and gray for partial transparency.

Images can have alpha channels in various formats, like Photoshop, ElectricImage, TIFF, and QuickTime-if the image has been saved with a proper codec. An alpha channel can also be a matte. And, there are more robust methods for describing transparency. A matte is one method of specifying transparency by using black, white, and grey to give a far more subtle approach to composite fine-tuning than you can obtain with a basic alpha channel.

Whether you're compositing clips through the addition of an effect, layering videos through adding an alpha channel or even creating complex motion animations, Premiere Pro and After Effects have the robust detailed compositing features to achieve professional visuals.

Overview of Straight and Premultiplied Alpha Channels

Alpha channels come in two main forms: **straight and premultiplied**. Both do similar functions in that they can both store information on the transparency of an image, but different methods are used in handling color information; hence, they have different compositing and editing implications across different pieces of software.

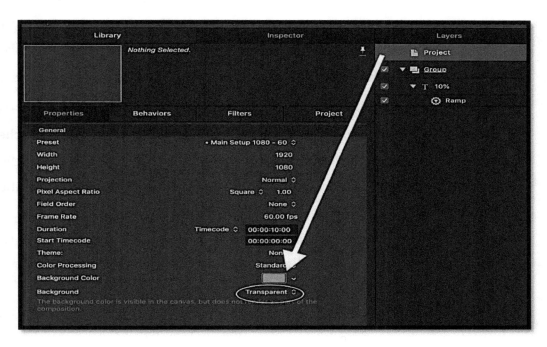

- **Straight Channels**

    In straight, or unmatted alpha channels, transparency information is contained solely within the alpha channel, while the color channels remain untouched. This method ensures that actual colors of the image remain intact even in areas with partial transparency. For instance, feathered edges or gradients within semi-transparent areas maintain their original color details without blending to some background color.

    This could be an advantage where high fidelity in color accuracy is required. However, straight channels require supporting applications to interpret transparency correctly. Until then, any transparency effects remain invisible, as the alpha information is applied only at the point of rendering or compositing.

- **Premultiplied Channels**

  Premultiplied, or matted alpha channels, differ in that they store transparency not only in the alpha channel but also in the visible RGB channels, blending these with a designated background color. In such a configuration, colors of semi-transparent regions are pre-shifted toward the background color according to the quantity of transparency.

  This may also facilitate a rendering process in programs that do not support straight alpha channels, thus making those premultiplied channels more compatible with a greater range of software, including **QuickTime Player**. The background color used for the premultiplication usually defaults to black or white by most applications; although some programs may have a custom color option for that. Still, this compromise is practical for a video and animation workflow because it does not affect the slight color accuracy in favor of compatibility.

Software Compatibility and Workflow Considerations

The choice between straight and premultiplied channels often depends upon requirements pertaining to software compatibility. For example, Adobe Premiere Pro and After Effects are flexible in supporting both types of alpha channels but will only process the first alpha channel in files containing more than one.

While Adobe Flash supports only premultiplied alpha channels. These differences in software support mean that, often, the type of alpha channel to be used has already been determined by the time you receive the assets, and knowing how to work with both types can facilitate easier compositing.

Keying Techniques

Keying is perhaps the most important technique to know to achieve transparency in a shot. It involves selecting a color or brightness range and is one of the basic tasks in replacing backgrounds for video productions.

This process may be performed by **chroma key**, which relies on color, or luminance key, relying on brightness. In chroma keying, the selected color—frequently blue or green—is removed to composite another background behind the subject.

Difference keying is yet another approach in which transparency is defined relative to a baseline background, which allows for the removal of more complex and non-uniform backgrounds. Keying tools in applications like Premiere Pro ease this process by offering various effects that tend to suit the deletion of selected colors or levels of brightness. These include the **Garbage Matte effect** and the **Track Matte Key effect** that enable detailed and intricate compositing between layers.

Adjusting Opacity in the Timeline

Opacity adjustments within the Timeline panel involve direct manipulation for creating transparency. By expanding the track views and by using an opacity control rubber band, one can specify opacity levels at various points in time to achieve dynamic changes in the level of opacity.

Since animations allow to set keyframes that adjust the values of opacity at any particular point, thus it is quite easy to make clips fade in or out or to create gradual transparency. It involves using either the **Selection or Pen tool** to set and adjust keyframes and fine tuning between smoothness and style by switching interpolation modes from linear to Bezier curves.

Compositing Best Practices

While performing compositing, some strategic practices will make things easier and of better quality:

- In case the entire clip needs to have uniform transparency, adjust the opacity in the **Effect Controls panel.**

- Where possible, use source files that contain an alpha channel. This maintains integrity of the transparency across sequences for both continuity and consistency.

- When there is no alpha channel in the source, transparency effects should be added or clip opacity adjusted by hand to achieve what's required.

- Save files containing an alpha channel in a format compatible with After Effects, Photoshop, or Illustrator to retain transparency settings between applications.

This option for transparency, either by means of an alpha channel or through keying technique, is supposed to simplify the process of compositing while allowing for flexibility across a wide range of video and imaging applications.

How to mask and track

Masks are a feature in video clip editing, enabling the editing in relatively small areas and thus making covering, blurring out, color correcting, highlighting, and other visual effects precise. Masks can be created in an ellipsoidal, rectangular, or freehand shape using **Bezier curves** with the **Pen tool**. These shapes provide the means for flexibly defining areas where selective adjustments will be made.

Shape-Based Mask Creation

Choose your mask from basic shapes: The **Ellipse tool** creates a mask in the shape of a circle or oval, while the **Rectangle tool** will create a mask as a four-sided polygon. Alternatively, select the **Pen tool** to create a free-form mask that traces more intricate outlines of objects.

Steps on Adding Effects with Masks;

- **Select the Clip:** In the Timeline, highlight the clip you want to add masking.

- **Apply an Effect**: Select an effect such as Mosaic from Video Effects > Stylize in the Effects panel. Drag the effect onto the selected clip or double-click the effect to apply it instantly.

- **Open Effect Controls:** Inside the **Effect Controls panel**, open any mask properties. The controls here are variable based on your mask for size, shape, and placement.

- **Shape Selection:** The **Ellipse and Rectangle tools** are used to create simple shapes, while the Pen allows creation of complex, freeform masks.

Editing Masks Using Shape Tools

The selected mask shape will be visible in the Program Monitor and is constrained within the bounds of the applied effect. To further define your mask shape, its size or shape can be adjusted within the **Effect Controls panel.**

- **Multiple Applications**: You can apply the same effect multiple times with different settings for each mask. Note that some effects, like the

Warp Stabilizer, do not support masking, and masks are not saved as an effect preset.

Drawing Freeform Shapes with the Pen Tool

The pen tool allows detailed control and is good for drawing around an irregularly shaped object. To draw a mask using straight or curved paths, follow these steps:

1. **Linear Mask (Straight Lines)**
   - Click to set vertex points for a straight line path. Each click adds a new vertex to create a polygonal shape.
   - Pressing the **Shift button** will constrain the angle to 0°, 45° or 90°. Alt + click (Windows) or Option + click (macOS) the first vertex to complete the path.

2. **Curved Bezier Paths:**
   - To create smooth curves, drag with the **Pen tool** to build Bezier handles at each vertex. These allow for precise manipulation of the angle and length of the curve, making it C-shaped or S-shaped depending on the direction of the drag.

Mask Adjustments and Moves

Masks can flexibly be adjusted in shape, size, rotation, and position. Because modification of vertex points is possible, it will be easy to change the dimension, orientation, and even the form of a mask.

a. **Shape, Size, and Rotation Adjustment of Masks**
   - **Shape Adjustment:** Any handles of the mask can be dragged to change its shape. This makes reshaping of the mask fast and easy.

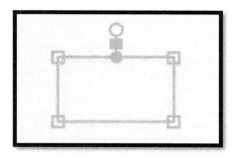

- **Converting an Ellipse to a Polygon**: To convert an elliptical mask to a polygon, press and hold **Alt,** then click on one of the vertices. You can now break the circular shape into multiple sides.

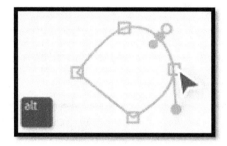

- **Resizing a Mask**: To resize a mask hover just outside a vertex, press Shift (the cursor will change to a double-sided arrow) and drag to scale the mask.

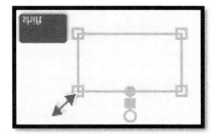

- **Rotating a Mask:** To rotate, click your cursor just outside a vertex (cursor will change to a curved double-sided arrow), and drag to rotate the mask.

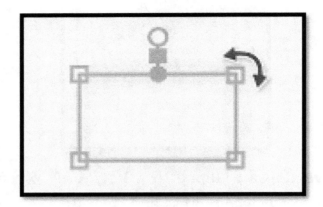

b. Move, Add, or Remove a Vertex

- **Move a Vertex:** To move a vertex, simply drag it using the **Selection tool**. Note that when an elliptical-shaped mask is being dragged the ellipse may morph into more of a polygonal shape.

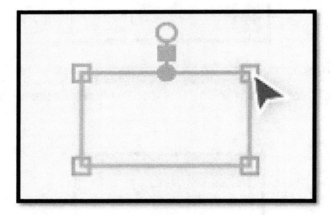

- **Add a Vertex**: To add a vertex, you need to be hovering over the mask edge with the Ctrl key-press. At that point, the cursor will switch to a pen icon with a "+" in it, which you can click to add a vertex at that location.

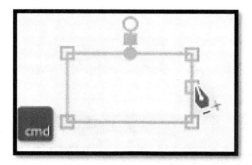

- **Remove a Vertex:** To remove a vertex, hover over the point to be removed while holding **Ctrl** for Windows or **Cmd** for macOS. The cursor will transform into a pen shape with a minus inside it. Left-click with your mouse to remove the vertex.

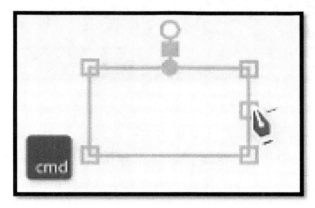

Other Handy Commands and Shortcuts

- Arrow keys nudge selected control points one unit.
- Shift + arrow keys nudge control points by five units.
- Deselect all control points by clicking outside of the active mask.
- To disable direct manipulation of a mask, click outside of the mask or deselect the clip in the sequence.
- To delete a mask, select it in the **Effect Controls panel** and press **Delete** on your keyboard.

Adjusting Mask Settings

Masks can be further refined through the Effect Controls panel by adjusting properties such as feathering, opacity, expansion, and inversion to further improve visual effects of your video.

- **Feathering a Mask:** The Feather slider of the Mask controls can soften the edges of the mask. You'll want to adjust the amount over which the mask feathering gradually blends the masked and unmasked areas together. The feathering guide shown as a dashed line is used as a visual reference for the effect.

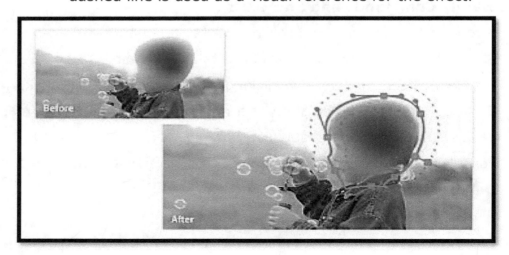

- **Adjusting Mask Opacity:** The opacity control dictates how much the masked area is see through. At 100% the mask is totally opaque and blacks out all underlying footage totally. As the opacity is lowered, the underlying footage increasingly shows thru the mask.

- **Expand a Mask:** Refine the Mask Expansion amount to expand the mask's edges outward (positive values) or contract them inward (negative values). The expansion handle allows you to drag to fine tune the mask reach.

- **Inverting a Mask:** The Invert Mask check box is an on/off toggle that switches which parts of the mask are selected and which aren't, so you can either protect certain areas or affect everything else.

Copying and Pasting Masks

Premiere Pro 2025 offers quick ways of duplicating masks between clips and effects to expedite your workflow:

1. **Copy and Paste Masks across Clips**
   - Select the clip that contains the mask effect that you want to use in the Timeline panel.
   - In the Effect Controls panel, select the effect that you want to copy.
   - Select **Edit** and click **Copy** or Ctrl+C (Cmd+C on macOS). After that, select the destination clip and paste using the Edit tab before selecting **Paste** or Ctrl+V (Cmd+V on macOS).

2. **Copy and Paste Masks between Effects**

- In the Effect Controls panel, expand the effect to show applied masks.

- Copy the mask and then paste onto another effect by selecting the destination effect in the panel.

Mask Tracking in Premiere Pro

With moving objects, Premiere Pro can auto-track a mask movement across frames, morphing the mask to follow a face, object, or any subject in your video. This is particularly effective for tasks like blurring moving faces.

1. **Tracking Options**

- Click the **wrench icon** in the Effect Controls panel to access the tracking settings available. Following are some of the tracking options available:

  a. **Position:** This option tracks the mask's movement from frame to frame.

  b. **Position and Rotation:** It monitors the position as well as a rotation of the mask.

  c. **Position, Scale, and Rotation:** This option follows the position of the mask and accordingly scales it and corrects its rotation as per the scene requirements

2. **Improving Mask Tracking Speed**

Mask tracking performance is improved if **Live Preview** is off.

- Head over to the Timeline panel to choose the specific clip that contains the effect with masks.

- To preview the adjustments in the track, select the **mask wrench icon** before heading to the drop-down list to choose **preview.**

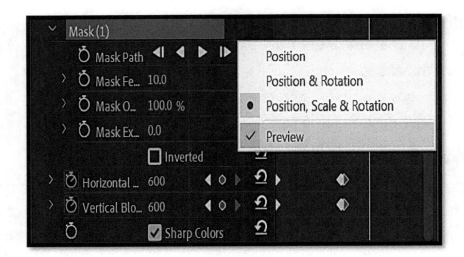

- To turn this off, click the **mask wrench icon**.
- After that, de-select **Preview** from the drop-down list.

Premiere Pro will improve tracking for clips taller than 1080p through auto scaling the frame pre-tracking and using low-quality renders to enhance processing.

For advanced tracking options, Premiere Pro uses **Dynamic Link** with After Effects to unlock additional tracking capabilities.

How to blend modes

In Premiere Pro, you can control how a clip overlays, or superimposes on other underlying clips in the **Timeline** to accomplish particular special effects by changing the opacity and blending mode of a clip.

- To start, place a clip on an upper track in the Timeline over any other clip on a lower track. By doing that, the clip on the upper track overlays or superimposes itself onto the clip on a lower track.

- Select the clip on the upper track and open the **Effect Controls panel** to turn that on. Inside the panel you will notice a triangle beside the word Opacity; click it to open it out.

- Adjust the opacity by dragging the value to the left, reducing it from the default 100%. This will make the top clip partially transparent, allowing the clip below to show through.

- Below the Opacity option is the **Blend Mode selection pull-down menu**. It's accompanied by a small triangle; clicking that triangle opens options on what kind of blend mode to use.

There are several different blend modes, which are designed to facilitate everything from subtle interactions between layers to extreme ones, and they're grouped into six different categories based on how they uniquely affect the final result of the blend. These categories include;

1. **Normal:** This includes modes like **Normal** and **Dissolve**. The normal essentially overrides the one underneath, except when the opacity is lowered. In Dissolve, random transparency is added in, where a few of the top clip's pixels disappear.

2. **Subtractive:** These will include things like Darken, Multiply, Color Burn, and other similar modes that darken the image by blending colors of the two layers based on darker values.

3. **Additive:** Modes such as Screen, Lighten, Color Dodge, and Linear Dodge (Add) lighten the image by blending according to lighter-colored values to create a bright, washed-out effect.

4. **Complex**: This includes Soft Light, Overlay, Hard Light, among others. These are dynamic in nature once more, since they change contrast and lighting effects per the content of the layer, producing results like spotlighting, playing with the shadows, and much more.

5. **Difference**: The modes such as Subtract, Exclusion, Difference, and Divide show the difference of the top from the bottom clip. Most of these modes can change color inside out or show jarring contrasts depending upon the differences which are used in special effects.

The HSL mode includes Saturation, Color, Hue, and Luminosity. This acts on the specific parts of the color model, namely hue, saturation, or brightness, whereby the result might be sophisticated color manipulations like tinting, saturation adjustment, or changing luminosity while preserving other properties of the underlying clip.

These blend modes allow for amazing diversities of visual expressions by changing ways in which the pixels of the topmost layer interact with the pixels of underlying layers. They make everything possible from subtle lighting effects to dramatic color shifts.

Now to explain each one in a bit more detail:

- **Normal** is the default and displays the top clip independent of the underlying layer.
- **Multiply** darkens by blending the color of the two clips together, like mixing pigments.
- **Screen** lightens by combining the inverse of the colors.
- **Overlay** uses a mix of multiply and screen modes depending on the brightness of the underlying clip.

- **Difference** modes, such as the Exclusion mode, let you contrast and give focus to the difference between the two clips. This could also be useful if it is required to align elements or get some other special visual effect.

When playing with the blending mode, pay attention to visible effects that will happen in your project. Some modes work best for certain specific effects: **Multiply** does well with shadows, and **Screen** does wonders for highlights or lightening up dark imagery.

CHAPTER NINE

EDIT VIDEOS

How to prepare Your Video Clips Ready for Editing

In editing your video in Adobe Premiere Pro 2025, prepare all video clips you are going to use. Whether the files are in your computer's internal hard drive or in external storage, preparing them will be a good starting point. Here is a step-by-step guide to get you started.

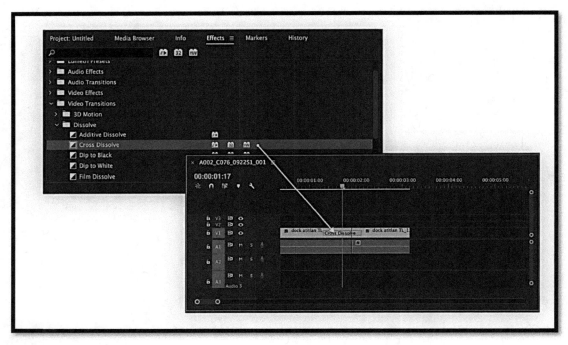

Step 1: Locate and Organize Your Video Files

First, you'll want to gather all of your video files from the sources. Typically, these are exported into a general format such as .MP4 or .MOV. Such file formats are usually well-supported by Adobe Premiere Pro and make for a good way of keeping the quality of the video during editing. Make certain that all the files are named and stored in a folder which will be easy to identify later. Organize your raw footage by storing them in well-organized, clearly labeled folders: by date, location, or theme. It will save a lot of time during the editing process.

Step 2: Select a Storage Solution

Determine whether you store those files directly onto your computer's hard drive or use an external hard drive. For projects containing larger video files, using an external drive may be quite handy because it keeps your internal storage from getting bogged down with that. External drives even make sharing projects across many devices easy, especially when collaborative work is involved.

Step 3: Import your footage into Premiere Pro

Now that your files are organized and you have made your storage decisions, it is time to bring all these into Adobe Premiere Pro. Open Adobe, go down onto the Project panel because that is where you want all your project assets to appear. Now, there are several ways by which you can import:

- **Drag and Drop:** Highlight your video files from their storage location and drag them directly into the Project panel. This is the fastest and easiest way to go about it, especially if the files are already organized.

- **Import:** Import the file via the "Import" command via File-Import, or press the general shortcut key for **Ctrl + I** on Windows and **Command + I** on Mac. The option opens a browser window through which you will locate your files and select them for import.

Step 4: Review and Organize Your Clips in Premiere Pro

Once imported, Premiere Pro displays your files in the Project panel. Here, you can further organize them into folders called "bins." You could do a separate bin for each day of shooting, or separate bins for different types of shots, or different locations - any way you need. This just adds an extra level of organization so you can find specific clips in a flash without an editing mess on your hands.

Step 5: Verify File Properties and Settings

Keep in mind that before you begin editing, confirm the properties of your clips. You can easily view in Premiere Pro the resolution, frame rate, and other key information about each file by right-clicking on a clip and selecting "Properties." This is a real-time-saver if your project requires consistent video settings, as it will enable you to make sure that your files all meet the requirements called for by your final output.

Understanding Your Video File Formats

When working with Adobe Premiere Pro 2025, a deeper understanding of file format and video settings can make a significant difference in the quality and flexibility of your video projects. The most important decisions are those that involve how your shooting setup will tie into both the editing process and the final output. The proper shooting format and picture style will afford you great creative control and give you ease with a DSLR, mirrorless camera, or professional camera.

a. Shooting in C-LOG for More Creative Control

Shooting your footage in Canon's C-LOG (Canon Log) format can be a game-changer in terms of color grading and creative control during post-production. C-LOG footage is captured within a "flat" picture profile; it looks desaturated and low in contrast straight out of the camera. While this might look unimpressive on the surface, it becomes a powerful tool for editors and colorists; all this is because good latitude is available when color correction and adjustments are made.

This desaturated flat look captures more dynamic range, meaning that more detail in both highlights and shadows can be maintained. It's like shooting RAW in photography: the format retains more data, which therefore allows finer adjustments without losing quality.

With C-LOG, you are free to enrich colors, adjust exposure, and create a mood or style specific to your project. For instance, you may want to improve the warmth in a sunset, bring out the lush greens in a forest, or stylize a night scene cool. The flip side of this is that a lot of time will have to be spent in post-production. Color grading C-LOG footage can be very labor-intensive and time-consuming, especially if you are trying to achieve a cinematic or professional-looking quality.

b. Choosing a Different Picture Style for Streamlined Editing

If you're the type that wants to spend minimal time in the editing phase, shoot in a pre-set picture style like Landscape, Portrait, or Monochrome. These styles do basic adjustments to your footage right in the camera, offering full or more saturated colors, higher contrast, and ready-to-use right out of the camera. This technique requires fewer adjustments during post-production, which can be great for quick turnarounds or projects where heavy color grading isn't a priority.

For example, if you're shooting some travel vlog and need saturated colors with minimal tweaking, then the Landscape setting will give that pop, high-saturation look to your footage. Portrait mode is designed to emphasize skin tones, which makes it perfect for interviews or any piece of work that centers on people. The Monochrome option captures in black-and-white and could be great for stylized projects or if you try to reach for that never-aging look.

c. **Shooting in 4K for Higher Quality and Flexibility**

Shooting in 4K has, over time, become the gold standard for quality video production. Shooting in 4K (a horizontal resolution of about 4,000 pixels wide) offers several key advantages. It produces sharper detail with greater clarity, and more flexibility while editing. You may reframe or crop shots without losing much quality if you are shooting in 4K resolution. This is particularly helpful for adding motion to static shots, simulating zooms, or readjusting the composition to enhance framing for a content creator or editor. In addition, 4K footage tends to be more "future-proof" in many ways, since viewers currently are using either 4K screens or other ultra-high-definition-enabled devices.

On the other hand, 4K format files are far larger compared to standard HDs. If you are shooting in 4K, that will require more storage space both on the memory cards of your camera and the editing workstation. Editing in 4K will also demand more from your computer, so make sure the hardware can process these larger files fluidly in Adobe Premiere Pro 2025. A good practice is to invest in fast SSDs, external drives, and a good, powerful computer with enough RAM and GPU power. This will make all the difference in workflow efficiency and avoid frustrations of lag or stuttering during playback.

d. File Management and Storage Considerations

This becomes even more important with the increase in file sizes when shooting in high-resolution formats, such as 4K, or log formats, like C-LOG. You might consider project-by-project file organization and then backing up data to circumvent data loss on external hard drives or through cloud storage.

There are also several utilities for file management inside of Adobe Premiere Pro 2025; one such utility is **proxy workflows**. A proxy file is a low-resolution version of your 4K footage so that editing can be smoother without constant access to the high-resolution originals. You can toggle between proxies and full-resolution files easily in Premiere Pro, which makes it versatile for handling large projects.

How to Sequence and Trim Your Video Clips

With your footage inside Adobe Premiere Pro, now you're finally ready to put it into your timeline. Sequencing is the term for the ordering of your clips to establish the overall desired narrative and flow of your video. Sequencing is the kind of art that could make all the difference in how your story unfolds. Take time to consider which shots should come first, how each of the scenes will merge with the next, and at what pace to fit the mood you want to portray. Start by dragging and dropping your clips from the **Project panel** directly onto the timeline. Move them around in the order that best suits your vision, so that the order is supportive of the story you want to tell.

When a number of your clips are placed, you might want to trim them to get the right length to maintain an even tempo, or to cut out superfluous parts. This is where the 'Cut' tool also called **Razor** in Premiere Pro becomes handy. With the 'Cut' tool, you can shorten each clip by trimming footage from the beginning or the end. This flexibility helps in narrowing down the exact moments that highlight your video, be it expression, action, or detail. Cut out parts that distract from your message or invite unwanted pauses, making sure only the most engaging and relevant portions of each clip remain.

The trimming will keep the story tighter and help to achieve a better viewing feeling due to the highlights of the scenes. This is the time for refining footage so that it represents your creative intention and allows you to make different cuts and placements of shots. By sequencing and trimming, you will be able to build a cohesive, visually engaging story that flows from beginning to end.

How to Edit the Look and Feel of Your Video Clips

Improving the aesthetic quality of your clips is important in making your final clip interesting and professional in Adobe Premiere Pro 2025. When you first import your footage into the application, you might notice it looks a bit flat or washed out especially if you've shot in a log profile such as **C-LOG**, which is designed to capture a broad dynamic range but requires additional adjustments for an appealing look. This is where powerful effects and basic correction settings in Adobe Premiere Pro can make a difference in molding the look and feel of your project to better communicate your story and vision.

Refine your footage in the **Lumetri Color panel** with basic edits, including exposure, white balance, temperature, saturation, and contrast. These controls enable you to emerge with a bright and more visually stimulating result by taking care of any dullness or unwanted color casts in the original footage.

Start with **exposure adjustment**, as this sets the brightness of your image. It's the temptation to make things pop, but exposure should be used very little. Too much exposure can blow out the highlights without even trying, making your shadows muddy, or vice versa, and this degrades any detail and quality that may exist in the footage. You want balanced exposure, that holds highlight and shadow details for depth and clarity without losing key visual information.

One important thing to remember is that, unlike photography, exposure adjustments in video editing are not that forgiving. In most cases, while shooting photography, you have ample room for maneuvers during post-processing. Video files, though, can easily degrade if exposure changes are too extreme. Because of this, nailing the exposure as best you can in-camera pays off considerably, especially when working with high dynamic range or log footage.

Further refinements in white balance and temperature will further establish the mood for your video and refine the accuracy of your colors. White balance can be used to get rid of color shifts caused by lighting conditions. Moving the temperature slider adds warmth or coolness to the image, enhancing the atmosphere. For instance, a gloomy scenario or wintry scene should be better defined with cool shades, while sunset shots look quite appealing with warm ones.

Saturation and contrast adjustments can also help to set the look of your footage. For example, desaturating or increasing saturation can help bring out the colors and make them more vivid or even popping out, while adjusting contrast can help make the image pop by highlighting the difference between the darkest and lightest parts of the frame. Again, subtlety is key. Colors that are too saturated, or levels of contrast that are too high, can lend an unnatural look to your production, maybe detracting from the immersive experience one might want.

You might notice, finally, that if you've shot in C-LOG, the footage might need a bit of sharpness boost to be more defined. A higher sharpness may result in more detail in your shots, but sometimes over-sharpening gives your footage an unnatural grainy feel that takes away from the quality. Use your **sharpening**, just like your exposure and contrast, balanced- neither too little nor too much.

In other words, Lumetri Color in Adobe Premiere Pro 2025 offers all the tools that will make your footage pop. Being careful with settings, including exposure, white balance, temperature, saturation, contrast, and sharpness, you'll get a visually brilliant piece that shows your style while giving life to your story. Remember that the best possible exposure and color balance at the time of shooting will make post-production smoother and get you closer to your required result with fewer adjustments.

How to Copy and Paste Your Video Settings

If you have completed color correction for your first video clip in Adobe Premiere Pro 2025, you can then apply those very settings to other clips on your timeline with ease. Not only does this technique accelerate your editing process, but it also allows you to maintain a consistent look throughout your entire project. This is how you copy and paste color correction settings across multiple clips in Premiere Pro.

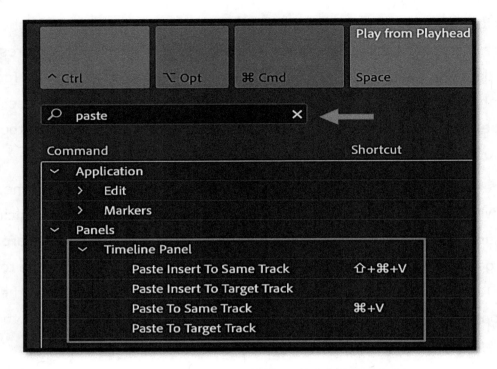

1. **Complete Color Correction on the First Clip**

   Adjust color, exposure, contrast, and anything else on the first clip until it looks just right. If this clip looks good to you, then you're ready to take these settings to the rest.

2. **Copy Color Settings**

   Still having the first clip selected, go to the **Effects Control panel** where your color corrections are, and right-click the adjustments easily with either the **Ctrl + C** (Windows) or **Command + C** (Mac) to copy them.

3. **Select the Other Clips**

   Then, in your timeline, select all the other clips you'd like to paste the color into. To select multiple clips hold the **Shift key** and click each clip, or drag across them.

4. **Paste the Settings**

   With the additional clips selected, use **Ctrl + V** for Windows or **Command + V** for Mac to paste the color settings. The copied settings will apply in just about the same color and lighting profile to each of the selected clips.

5. **Fine-Tune if Necessary**

   This method will eventually have the same color correction settings applied to each clip, but there can still be slight variations in exposure, lighting, or color balance across your footage due to different conditions when shooting. Go through each clip and make minor adjustments to ensure the look remains consistent but also works for that particular scene.

   The steps described above will save you a lot of time on color correction, improving at the same time visual continuity of your project. When you get accustomed to this technique, it will be an integral part of your editing workflow, hence you will be able to create professional-looking videos without too much hassle.

How to Add Dynamic Transitions to Make Your Video Flow

Transitions can indeed be such a great tool in video editing. If applied effectively, they truly improve the look and feel, adding to the continuity of your project. By adding a unique style to the way each clip flows into the next, transitions create this fluid viewing experience that will have your audience engaged and immersed in your video. Adobe Premiere Pro 2025 has a great variety of transitions you can use to make your video edits both interesting and smooth. In this presentation, we take a look at how these transitions will make your project even better and some handy tips on how to use them.

Transitions are meant to link different scenes or moments and to set the mood and emotions by which the recipient will have to view your video. The **Cross Dissolve transition** for instance creates a soft, natural effect of one clip dissolving into another. Such transitions work perfectly in instances where that soft, unobtrusive shift is to be made, like in documentaries or even narrative scenes where the focus relies on continuity and natural flow.

Or the **Wipe transition,** which offers even more formal and structured effects; the next clip is introduced through directional movement to the right, top to bottom, and even diagonally. This sort of transition can add energy to fast-action scenes or introduce new settings and characters with flair. For example, wipes can be very effective in action sequences, highlight reels, and stylistic videos, as the mood requires dynamic movements.

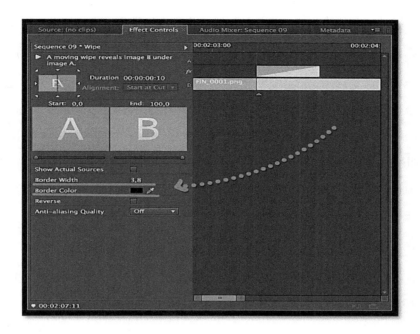

Other than the regular **Cross Dissolve** and **Wipe effects**, Adobe Premiere Pro 2025 has **Zoom Transitions** and **Whip Pan Transitions** to notch it up a level and make the video cinematic. The transition can have a zoom for the effect of depth and travel, pulling the viewer into the next shot or scene. This would work great for dramatic reveals, action sequences, and even in travel videos because each new scene offers new visuals.

Other transitions might involve the **Fade to Black or White**, which is generally used to indicate a shift in time, location, or mood. Transitions such as this allow for a brief pause to reset before the next clip. They work well with any indication of the end of a scene, a dramatic change in pace, or a reflective moment within the story.

- To apply all of these transitions, open the **Effects Panel** in Premiere Pro, where you will find several preset transitions located under the **Video Transitions folder**.

- You drag and drop any of these desired transitions between two clips on your timeline. You will be able to adjust each transition's duration,

215

direction, and style in **the Effect Controls Panel** to best fit the mood and pacing of your project.

Adding transitions dynamically within Adobe Premiere Pro 2025 is less about transitioning from one clip to another and more about adding greater depth to the story you're trying to tell. Each different transition type will be able to express a different feeling and visual cue, which lets your video make many fascinating turns. Whatever you want, be it subtlety or excitement, your piece deserves the right transition.

How to Export Your Video at the Highest Quality

Exporting your video at the highest quality in Adobe Premiere Pro 2025 preserves the detail, color accuracy, and professionalism of your final product. Once you have a video project cut to perfection, sequenced, timed, and color corrected, it's time to get ready to export. Here are steps you can use to ensure that the video output meets the best quality for the intended platform.

Step 1: Open the Export Menu

Go to top menu in your screen and click 'File'. After that, click 'Export', then 'Media'. This brings up an export settings menu where you can tweak your video to get better playback and sharing.

Step 2: Opt for the Right Export Options

Within the export settings menu, Adobe Premiere Pro will allow you an option to preset different platforms such as Facebook, YouTube, Vimeo, and Twitter, and all these presets will have different sizes and settings according to requirements for a single platform. To achieve the highest quality, try to set it to 1080p HD which is high definition or 4K. The 4K is much sharper, especially on the platforms where it is supported; however, 1080p still makes for an excellent choice if you want faster uploads and smaller file sizes.

- **1080p (Full HD)** resolution is the standard for high-definition and finds its application in almost all online platforms. It offers a good balance between quality and file size.
- **4K Ultra HD** provides the viewer with a resolution four times that of 1080p. It is great for content to be viewed on large screens or high-resolution displays.

With your resolution selected, you can then further customize other settings to satisfy your needs-specifically frame rate, aspect ratio, and codec.

Step 3: Tuning Bitrate Encoding for Better Quality

Bitrate controls the data rate of your video file and directly influences both its quality and file size. Social media platforms like Facebook, Instagram, and Twitter often compress uploaded videos into smaller files to save memory, which affects their quality. You can minimize this by exporting them at a high quality, adjusting the settings for bitrate encoding.

- **VBR, 1 pass:** This uses a single pass of encoding and balances quality and faster export time, although it would slightly lower the quality in output.
- **VBR, 2 pass:** With this option, the file is analyzed on the first pass for optimal quality and then does the encoding on the second pass. VBR, 2 pass encodes the file and ensures that the quality is very much improved, which is quite important if you're going to upload your video to social media or any other platform which applies compression of their own.

For maximum quality, you'll also need to allow the **Use Maximum Render Quality option** under the **Video tab.** This will further improve render quality of complex scenes so that no artifacts arise and the output is clear.

Step 4: Output Location and File Name

Then, fill in the destination where you want the exported file to be saved. In the **Output Name field,** select a file name and destination folder. If you are working on a big project and don't want to hog your local storage, export your file to an external hard drive for more free space.

Step 5: Additional Settings

Under **Basic Video Settings,** you can make any final adjustments, such as ensuring that the aspect ratio matches your project. For ease of upload, Premiere Pro also allows you to save a Preview File, should you revisit the project at any later date. It just creates a lighter version of your video, perfect for previews or selecting a thumbnail image if needed.

Step 6: Export Your Video

Once all settings are established, ensure that everything is set correctly and then click the **Export button.** Premiere Pro will start rendering and exporting your video with selected settings.

These next steps will ensure your video is exported with the highest quality possible, ready for viewing or sharing on the platform of your choice.

CHAPTER TEN

EXPORTING MEDIA

How to export video

You can modify your export in Adobe Premiere Pro to zero in on whatever platforms or destinations you need for that job fast, efficiently, and professionally. From the Export workspace, speedier presets are available for popular social media platforms such as YouTube, TikTok, Facebook, and X, formerly known as Twitter, and some advanced and customizable settings allow you to have full control over your output.

Opening the **Export window** will present three key areas highlighted:

a) **Choose Export Destinations:** Choose between several available destinations in the left-hand column, like TikTok, YouTube, Vimeo, or a local drive (Media File).

b) **Access Output Settings**: In this section, you will specify your destination platform's most crucial output settings.

c) **Customize Export Preset:** Choose from a range of optimized preset options for quick setup, or create and save custom presets for your particular needs.

To get started:

1. **Choose Sequence to Export:**

   Select which sequence you want to export. If the Project panel is forward, Premiere Pro will export the currently selected sequence or clip. If the Project panel is active, Premiere Pro uses the currently selected sequence or clip; multiple selections are supported but with limitations:

   • Export preview is disabled.

   • Export settings apply to all selected items.

2. **Access Export Mode:**

   • Open the Export workspace

   • After that, click the **Export** in the header bar. Alternatively, you can choose to head over to the **File menu,** then click on **Export** and **Media**, or use the Cmd/Ctrl + M shortcut.

3. **Set Up Export Settings:**

   The export workflow is designed to work from left to right and starts with your export destination. After that, Premiere Pro will automatically offer you some optimized export settings for the platform you've selected.

- You can either select the default preset H. 264 or click the **Preset menu** to choose among several choices. Advanced settings let you tweak almost every export setting imaginable and save your own presets, which can be accessed in the **Preset Manager** via the More Presets option.

The **Match Source prese**t is adaptive; it takes the original frame size, frame rate, and other attributes of your source sequence, so this is an excellent choice if quality has to be maintained. The **High Bitrate preset** is best if quality output is needed.

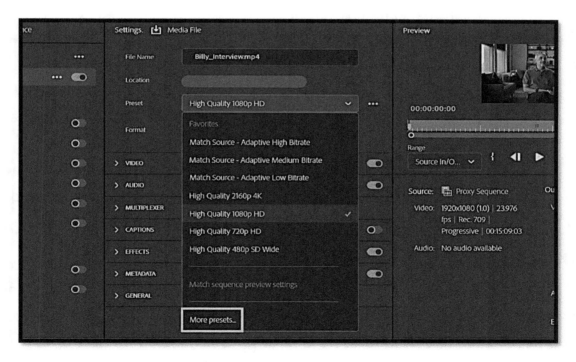

4. **Preview and Adjust:**

Use the **Preview window** to review and adjust your media before exporting. You can scrub, play back, and see how your video will appear with various export settings. The **Export Range** can customize an export to define what amount of your sequence is exported:

- **Entire Source:** exports full sequence.
- **Source In/Out:** uses In/Out points set within your sequence.
- **Work Area:** exports Work Area Bar - sequences only.
- **Custom:** uses a custom In/Out set in Export mode.

Adjust **Scaling** to control how your video fits within the output frame when exporting into a different frame size:

- **Scale to Fit:** Resizes to fit the frame but will never crop. There may also be black bars that show up.
- **Scale to Fill:** The frame gets completely filled, although there might be some pixel cropping.
- **Stretch to Fill:** It stretches to fill the entire frame, which might distort the video.

5. **Final Export:**
   - After making the settings, click the **Export option** to process your video.
   - Click the **Send to Media Encoder button** to open up the **Adobe Media Encoder** with all the export destinations queued up, ready for batch processing or exporting in the background.

How to Export Preset Manager

The Preset Manager allows for an easy, versatile, and effective way of managing all your export settings. This is because it can allow you to select one out of several system presets that are pre-configured, import or export presets for sharing between devices or workflows, and even create custom presets that match particular requirements. Whether you want to have a quick export with default settings or you need some specific configuration for projects, Preset Manager gives you a unified point to ease your workflow of export.

a. **Access the Preset Manager**

- Click the **Quick Export option** on the header bar to open the Preset Manager.

- You can export your project using a default preset by choosing **Export** from there, or you can choose **More Presets** to get into the full Preset Manager.

- Also, you can enter this interface through the **Export Mode** in Premiere Pro because it opens the list of all available presets and allows you to modify, save, and use them later.

b. **System Presets Installed by Default**

A series of system presets are installed in Preset Manager that correspond to several general export requirements. These default favorites are intended to ease the effort of export configuration by matching popular formats and quality standards. Key system presets include:

- **Match Source H.264 Presets:** A set of presets that automatically match your source video parameters at varying quality levels.

- **H.264 Presets**: This includes standard presets for common frame sizes such as 4K, HD 1080, HD 720 and SD 480 widescreen for easy exports in popular resolutions.

c. **Navigating the Preset Manager Screen**

The Preset Manager dialog box provides one central place you can access, create, and manage all your presets. Important elements of the interface include:

a) **Full Preset List:** Shows all the presets available in Premiere Pro- system and custom.

b) **System Presets:** Presets that are installed with Premiere Pro.

c) **Custom Preset**: Presets you have created and saved.

d) **Favorites:** Quick access to your favorite presets.

e) **Preset Info:** Details listing of any given selected preset.

f) **Preset Actions:** Delete, Import, or Export options for presets.

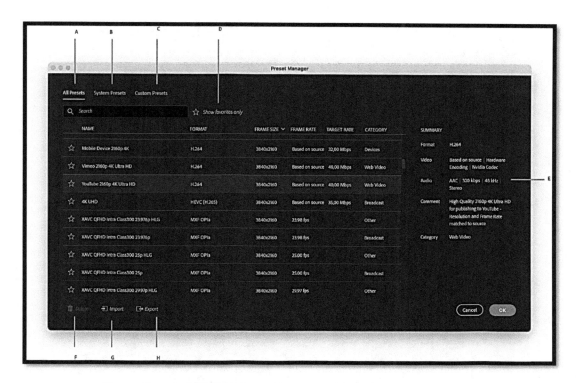

d. Creating and Saving Custom Presets

If you have specific export needs, then creating custom presets is quite easily done as you shall see in this part of the section:

- Open the **Export Dialogue** before choosing any preset that is closest to what you want the settings to be like.
- Adjust the pre-set settings so it will conform to the specifics of your export details.
- Click **Save Custom Preset** and it will be added into the **Custom Presets folder** in the Preset Manager dialog box.

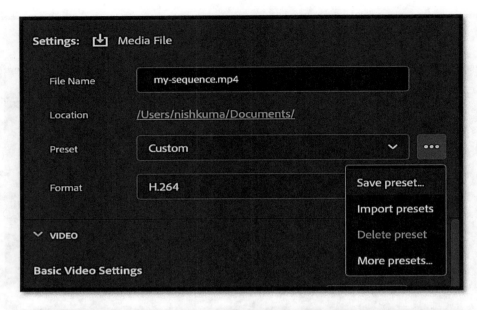

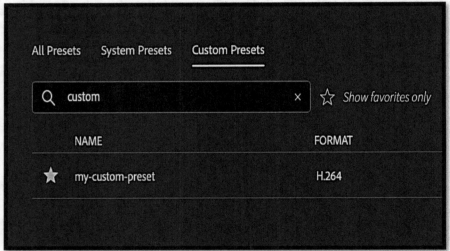

e. **Arranging Presets for Efficiency**

To take your workflow to an even smoother level, you can also sort, favorite, filter, and arrange your presets by several attributes:

- **Arrange Presets:** You can sort your presets up or down by format, frame size or category, etc. by clicking on each column header.

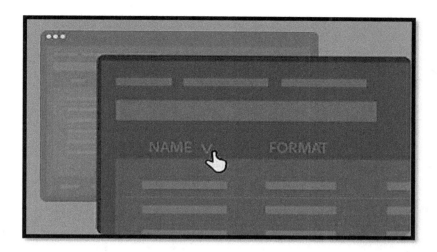

- **Mark Favorites:** Star your most-used presets to give you easy access via the Preset Menu for Quick Export and Export Mode.

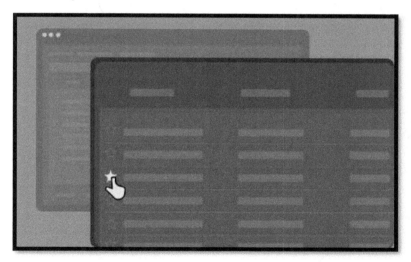

- **Search:** The search bar will filter the presets by name, format, etc. For example, you can just type in "ProRes" to show only ProRes presets.

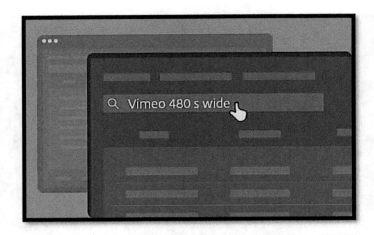

f. **Deleting and Organizing Custom Presets**

To delete any custom preset, select it in the **Preset Manager** and click **Delete.** Note that you cannot delete system presets, you can only choose to hide them.

Import and Export Presets for Portability

The Preset Manager makes it easy to import and export presets between different computers, perhaps in order to collaborate or work in an offline environment.

- **Exporting Presets:** To export presets, with the source computer open the **Preset Manager** and select which presets you want to migrate. From there you're able to export them into a transportable folder.

- **Importing Presets:** Open the **Preset Manager** in the destination computer and select **Import Presets**, you will import the files. The presets you import from Adobe Media Encoder will get added automatically; however, you need to mark those as Favorite to show them in the Preset menu.

Workflow and overview for exporting

Adobe Premiere Pro facilitates the export of videos to famous social platforms like YouTube, Vimeo, Facebook, and Twitter with much ease and speed. At the same time, in the Export mode, render settings are optimized by default for high-quality content so as to meet every specification of a certain platform. You can export completed projects in an easy manner without compromising on the perfection required.

You can also use a free-standing encoding application called **Adobe Media Encoder** for added flexibility by exporting projects in the background. All presets and settings transferred from **Export mode** in Premiere Pro when export jobs are sent to Media Encoder will allow batch processing and continuous work on other projects within Premiere Pro while rendering. Here are ways you send export jobs to Adobe Media Encoder:

- From Export mode, click the **Send to Media Encoder button.**
- Alternatively, export directly from the timeline or Project panel by heading to the **File menu**. After that, click on the **Export tab** to select the **Send to Adobe Media Encoder tab.** You can also opt for pressing **Opt + Shift + M** (macOS) / **Alt + Shift + M** (Windows).

The default preset for exporting from Media Encoder is H.264 Match Source (Adaptive High Bitrate), but you can switch to any previously used setting or a custom preset. This setting allows you to fine-tune your export options in the Export Settings dialogue of Media Encoder before you start queuing.

In this respect, different formats are available in Premiere Pro for export, suitable for various workflows that range from options to continue editing, creating still images from the project, to optimizing the said projects for different devices, platforms, and systems.

Exporting for Further Editing

You can export editable video and audio files, allowing you to view your work with all the effects and transitions fully rendered or to continue editing in other applications. Other than video and audio export, Premiere Pro also allows you to export still-image sequences or single-frame stills that could be used in titles, graphics, or other design elements.

Premiere Pro supports two major export workflows: direct export and Adobe Media Encoder export. In direct export, new files are created directly from within Premiere Pro. Conversely, an Adobe Media Encoder export sends the files to this program for extended rendering options to render the assets immediately or add to a render queue for batch processing.

Exporting Project Files for Other Editing Systems

In addition to exporting clips, Premiere Pro allows you to export full project files as AAF files compatible with a variety of third-party editing systems for further finishing work. You can also prepare Premiere Pro projects for archiving by condensing them to only what's necessary, including or not including source media.

Formats for Devices and Online Platforms

With Media Encoder, you will be able to export the video in a format most compatible with specific devices and web platforms. This will also include a number of web destination presets for the most popular websites: YouTube, Twitter, Facebook, Vimeo. It makes exporting media to a platform very easy.

General Workflow for Exporting Video and Audio

To export from Premiere Pro:

- In the Timeline, Project panel, or Source Monitor, select the sequence, clip or source you want to export.

- Click the **Export** in the header bar, or navigate to the **File menu** to access the **Export tab.** Then, click on **Media** to enter Export mode.

- Some optional steps for when you are in Export mode include setting a **Source Range** of either the sequence or clip by being able to adjust in and out points, or set crop options in the Source panel if cropping needs to occur.

- Choose your file export format. Premiere Pro has presets based on where you want to play or distribute the video, and even for social media platforms.

With the customized export settings, clicking on particular headings such as Video or Audio can adjust the parameters according to your need. Click the **Match Sequence Settings** for seamless export of the files with settings exactly matching with the original sequence settings.

Customization and Efficiency in Export Mode

With Premiere Pro's Export mode, you will be able to configure and maintain one set of export destinations, which is customizable and shareable across projects and sequences. Once set, export by choosing one of the following options:

- **Send to Media Encoder:** This option queues the job for further processing in Adobe Media Encoder.

- **Export**: Export immediately starts rendering and exporting within Premiere Pro.

By default, Adobe Media Encoder will save exported files in the source file's folder, adding the appropriate extension to the filename. Another way to further automate your workflow is to set up watched folders for different export types.

How to use Quick export

Conserve time and easily export your video with Quick Export, intuitively designed to accelerate the export of your video. You will be able to export your project in a high-quality H.264 format just in a couple of clicks.

Besides, use the **Match Source preset** that automatically sets things like resolution and frame rate to your sequence for easy exporting or choose from popular resolution presets and export fast and optimized.

- **Open Your Project**: Open the sequence or select a sequence or media file from the Project panel.
- **Access Quick Export**: Select the **Quick Export icon** to launch the dialog box.
- **Setup Export Details**: Set your exported file name and saving location.
- **Select a Preset:** Select a preset from the dropdown menu for your preferred settings.
- **Customize Your Presets**: To edit the preset list, click on "More presets..." and open the Preset Manager where you can favorite either system or custom presets for ease of access.

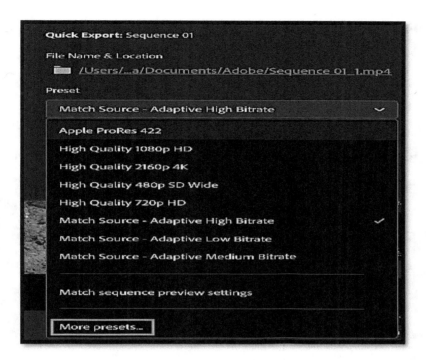

- **Export**: Click **Export** to finish.

  Your video will export effortlessly, with matched settings to the project, ready to instantly share or publish. Try it in-app and see how Quick Export saves you time and effort.

How to Export for the Web and mobile devices

Adobe Premiere Pro goes all out to provide extended tools that make creating and sharing video material easier; it allows users to export content directly into various platforms that are optimized for the Web and mobile viewing.

With integrated publishing options, videos can be posted instantly to popular social media sites like Facebook, TikTok, YouTube, and more, right from within the Premiere Pro interface.

Direct Social Media Integration and Export Options:

- **Behance:** Share work directly to your Behance portfolio.

- **Facebook:** Faultlessly post videos to public or business Facebook pages.

- **TikTok:** Publish directly or save as a draft for further editing on TikTok.

- **X (formerly Twitter)**: Share instantaneously to your feed.

- **Vimeo:** Upload directly to your Vimeo channel.

- **YouTube:** Publish videos directly to YouTube or YouTube Shorts.

The Export tab in Premiere Pro features a clear, user-friendly UI with icons for each platform, making it easy to export media to a specific social destination.

Using Built-in Tools to Optimize Content for Social Media: Premiere Pro provides project templates specially designed for social media. The project templates help the creator align with destination-specific requirements and the safe zones. Besides, users will be able to get recommended presets right out of the box. To open all the recommended presets, a user has to click **More Presets** in the Preset Manager. Each different platform has its preset settings.

How to Export Direct to Social Media:

1. Select the sequence you'd like to export and head up to the **File menu.** Afterwards, click on **Export** and subsequently click on **Media.**

2. Click the toggles of any of the social media platforms you'd like to export to at the top of the **Publish tab**, then click the login button to link the accounts.

3. Select your export options:

    •   **Note:** The H.264 format and Match Source which is an **Adaptive High Bitrate preset** are great defaults for exports to most social media. Feel free to modify these to speed up upload times or for better playback performance.

4. Add your hashtags, title, descriptions, etc.

5. Finally, click **Export**. Premiere Pro will take care of the exporting for you, and even publish the video directly to the desired platforms with settings native to those platforms. You can also delete the rendered file after it has been uploaded if you wish.

How to Make Engaging Social Videos

The process of making successful social videos is packed with technical and creative decisions. Here's an extended tutorial on how to create videos that will appear professional, load fast, and play perfectly across platforms and devices.

a. **Know Your Audience and Data Rate**

    •   **Optimize Data Rate:** You shall have to ensure that the data rate for your video file is correctly set so that quality and download speed are in perfect balance. Higher data rates ensure crisp visuals on fast connections but can lead to long load times for users with slower connections. Consider keeping clips short to help dial-up or mobile users.

- **Audience Insights:** Use data that would bring insight into the viewing habits of your desired audience. The devices and possible network speeds of the target audience will then drive the decision behind file size, resolution, and bitrate.

b. **Choose the Right Frame Rate**

- **Adjust for platform and content:** Frame rate (frames per second or fps) is a vital factor that can impact the playback quality or data usage! While it saves data by reducing the frame rate, it reduces smoothness, which might be noticeable during high-motion scenes.

- **High-Quality Output:** If the platform and connection allow for it, aim for higher frame rates to make playback smoother. Consult optimal settings from your hosting provider in web videos. For mobile devices, use device-specific presets in Adobe Media Encoder.

- **Divide the Frame Rate Wisely:** Where needed, reduce the frame rate by whole numbers. For example, 30 fps to 15 fps which gives the best possible look with less data.

c. **Choose the Correctly-Sized Frame and Aspect Ratio**

- **Balance Frame Size with Data Rate:** Frames of larger size for the same data rate would decrease the quality. Choose a frame size that best fits the intended platform and a frame aspect ratio that best fits the source footage to avoid black bars or "pillarboxing.".

- **Maintain Aspect Ratio:** Keep the frame size the same aspect ratio as the original footage during encoding. In other words, it is highly important when converting between formats like NTSC and PAL.

-

d. **Optimize Progressive Download Times**

- **Download and Play**: Calculate the download time so videos play without pausing. Display alternate content (such as an eye-catching thumbnail or animation) during download to maintain viewer engagement until playback starts. For short videos, use this formula for initial pause time: Pause = download time - playtime + 10% of playtime.

e. **Noise Removal and Interlacing**

- **Improve Video Quality:** Remove noise and interlacing artifacts from your footage for the best possible encoding. These can be especially visible on computer monitors, which tend to display colors and details with high fidelity.

- **Prioritize Original Quality:** High-quality source material produces superior encoded videos, so aim for the best original footage possible.

f. **Apply the Same Standards to Audio**

- **Clean Audio Source:** Clean audio is just as important as sharp video. Minimize analog-to-digital conversions that introduce noise; instead use a direct digital transfers from CDs or decent quality sound cards.

- **Quality Compression**: For the best compression, start with clean high-quality audio and use direct digital transfer tools that are provided for a range of platforms.

Creating Videos for Mobile Devices

When creating for mobile devices, there are specific considerations for smaller screens as well as lower bandwidths and color spaces.

- **Focus on Close-ups:** Close-ups that are well-lit and that have good contrast between the subject and background are more visible and, therefore, more interesting for people with small screens.

- **Watch the Lighting:** Poor lighting can make videos hard to see on mobile; better to have enough lighting to improve visibility.

- **Limit Movement:** Refrain from fast pans or too much movement, which will blur or result in compression artifacts on mobile screens.

- **Device-Specific Frame Rates**: Choose the frame rate of the devices on which the platform is targeted. For example, 15 fps may be sufficient for mobile, while commercial broadcast would have to be 29.97 fps.

- **Pre-encoding for Less File Size:** This involves a proper shooting technique to avoid empty frames or excess motion and applications of post-production instruments such as stabilization and noise reduction, allowing for efficient compression.

- **Color Management:** Mobile devices often show a restricted color gamut. Test your video by using device emulators or tools like **Adobe Device Central** to make sure colors look good on all your target devices.

Final Touches

- **Test across Multi-Platforms**: Always do a preview before publishing, using various devices and different platforms for consistent quality. Check color balance, clarity, and responsiveness across devices.

How to Export a still image

To export a frame from a clip or sequence in Premiere Pro, follow the directions below:

1. **Add the Export Frame Button:** By default, the Export Frame button is not active in the button bar. To activate it, open the button editor inside the monitor panel and drag the **Export Frame button** into place.

2. **Move the Playhead:** Move the playhead to the exact frame in the clip or in the sequence that you want to export.

3. **Exporting the Frame**: Click the **Export Frame button**. This opens the Export Frame dialog box, which has the frame name ready for editing. By default:

   - The name field is preselected, showing the name of the clip or sequence with an auto-incremented number appended, like Clip.mov.Still001.

   - If you rename the frame, Premiere Pro will continue the naming sequence next time.

4. **Define Export Settings:** By default, Premiere Pro exports frames using the format selected the last time it was chosen for frame export. You can do the following:

   - Enter a new name for the frame.

   - Select a file format from the Format menu.

   - Select a destination folder by clicking the **Choose button.**

   After defining the above options click **OK** to export the frame. Or press **Enter** to confirm the default settings and immediately export the frame.

5. **Frame Bit Depth:** The default color depth for exported frames is 8-bit. To export in a higher bit depth, such as 10-bit or 16-bit, use Export mode and choose format options like DPX, PNG, Targa, or TIFF. Make sure the "Export as Sequence" option is turned off so that you can save a single frame in a higher bit depth.

   By doing the following mentioned above, you will be able to export high-quality frames from your clips and sequences efficiently.

How to Export projects for other applications

Premiere Pro provides the advanced export options like the **Edit Decision List** in the CMX3600 format that help to round out a portable, comprehensive project file that can easily be transferred, shared, or recreated across platforms.

An EDL provides a list of every clip in a project, including its placement, transitions, and edits critical to continuity between editing systems. **EDL export** can be customized to show either the source clip name from the Project panel or the timeline clip name. This flexibility provides options to make name changes during export without touching and renaming original source files. Switch between them by selecting "Show Source Clip Name and Label" from the wrench menu.

Increasing Project Portability with EDLs

EDLs are best used for projects that keep the structure lightweight. This typically means no more than one video track and two stereo audio tracks. EDLs support most common transitions, frame holds, and speed changes, so they are fairly versatile for simple editing.

Prepare for EDL export by capturing source materials with correct timecodes. Each videotape should be assigned a unique reel number and should be preformatted with timecode to ensure consistency in the EDL is accurate.

When exporting:

- Open or save a project to export
- Have an active Timeline panel then go to the File menu. After which, you click on **Export** to access the **EDL.**
- In the EDL Export Settings (CMX 3600) dialog, select which video and audio tracks to export-one video track and up to four audio channels (or two stereo tracks).
- Choose a destination and filename and click **Save** and **OK.**

Note: Merged clips are exported as standardized EDLs. The merged audio and video clips are separate entries and source timecode for both the video and audio components is preserved.

Augmenting Clip Name Visibility in EDLs

EDL format often truncates clip names to eight characters for projects with longer names. If you require longer names, activate the option for 32-character names in the EDL Export Settings CMX 3600 dialog box. This extends support for tape and clip names up to 32-character length.

Exporting and Sharing Final Cut Pro and Premiere Pro Projects via XML

Working with video editing software, either in a collaborative environment or when working cross-platform, it is common to have to share files between FCP and Adobe Premiere Pro. One good method of doing this is exporting projects as XML files: these are file types which retain much important project data and can therefore be read by both applications.

Final Cut Pro XML Export

The following describes how to export XML from within Final Cut Pro.

- Go to the **File menu** before clicking on **Export.**

- Afterwards, click on **Final Cut Pro XML**. This opens up a workflow for exporting in XML.

- After doing so, a dialog box opens labeled **Save Converted Project As**. Choose where the XML is to be saved, title it accordingly and click **Save.**

Exporting Notes

- If there are any conversion issues or unsupported features in the export process, Premiere Pro will auto-create a log file. Often called **FCP Translation Results**, the file can be found in the same location as the XML. Opening this will show where some discrepancies.

- Note that merged clips created in Premiere Pro will be translated to nested sequences when the XML file is imported into Final Cut Pro. This may have implications for how project structure is organized.

Importing XML into Premiere Pro

After exporting, the XML file can be easily imported into Premiere Pro:

1. **Import the XML File**

   - Open Premiere Pro and go to the **File menu** to access the **Import tab.**

   - Then, find and select the XML file so Premiere Pro can import it into the project.

2. **Compatibility Issues**

   For files created in Final Cut Pro 7 and earlier, Premiere Pro's XML import is typically smooth. For Final Cut Pro X projects, you may need a third-party tool like Xto7 (XtoCC) to convert files. Xto7 is widely used for converting newer Final Cut Pro project files into XMLs that Premiere Pro can interpret.

Working across software versions

This isn't an uncommon occurrence, where editors work with different versions of Premiere Pro. If you have to open a project that's been opened in newer versions with an older version of Premiere Pro (let's say your trial has expired), the export option of an XML file is decent. This could also facilitate access to such a file without having to have the latest Premiere Pro version.

1. **Export Premiere Pro Project as XML**
   - To do that, go to the **File menu** to access the **Export tab**.
   - After that, click the **Final Cut Pro XML** to select where to export.
   - You can then import this XML into an older version of Premiere Pro as required.
   - The **Save Converted Project As window** will pop up now. Go inside a location of your choice for your XML file, type the filename, then click **Save**. Premiere Pro will now save your sequence into the selected location, converted into an XML file.

2. **Limitations to Note**

   XML exports may not export all metadata or settings. What this means is that not all complex transitions effects or metadata are completely translated with newer versions.

How to Export OMF Files for Pro Tools

Adobe Premiere Pro does have the ability to export all audio tracks of a sequence via **OMF** to continue editing in Pro Tools. This workflow allows for advanced editing of audio by creating a compatible format for Pro Tools, particularly when the DigiTranslator feature is licensed within it. Using **DigiTranslator**, Pro Tools will be able to import OMF files so that soundtracks created in Premiere Pro can be fine-tuned and improved.

Note: The OMF export in Premiere Pro is designed specifically to work well in Pro Tools, and the support of OMF can be poor in other systems. Import of an OMF file is not supported directly within Premiere Pro.

How to Export an OMF File for Pro Tools:

1. **Select the Sequence:** In the Timeline panel, select a sequence that you want to export.

2. **Open Export Settings**: Go to the **File menu** before clicking **Export** to access the **OMF.**

3. **Setting OMF:**

   - **OMF Title:** Fill in the title for your OMF.

   - **Sample Rate and Bit Depth**: In the **Sample Rate and Bits Per Sample pull-down menus**, choose the one that best suits your sequence.

4. **Choose File Format:**

   - **Encapsulate:** This option encases metadata and audio of the chosen sequence in one OMF file. Remember, the encapsulated file will be huge.

- **Separate Audio:** This option exports each audio track as separate mono AIF files in a folder named after the OMF file. This separates the audio into different files in AIF format, which is better compatible with some legacy systems.

5. **Rendering Options:**
   - **Copy Complete Audio Files:** This always exports the full audio of each clip used, regardless of how many segments or instances appear in the sequence.
   - **Trim Audio Files:** This exports only that portion of each clip that's used in the sequence. These are sometimes called "clip instances." Check this box to include handles that will extend each clip a bit at the head and tail.

6. **Specify Handle Length:** In the **Handle Frames field,** specify the length of the handles in frames. The default is one second, by default using the frame rate of the sequence. If the specified handle length is larger than the available clip length, Premiere Pro exports the entire clip.

7. **Import into Pro Tools:** Launch Pro Tools and import the OMF file to begin working with the audio tracks. For more information on how to import, refer to the Pro Tools Help.

OMF File Export Supported Features

Exporting to OMF files gives Premiere Pro a full-service enablement of options, flexible in managing audio data and maintaining compatibility with Pro Tools. The following is a general overview of the attributes and options available in the exporting of OMF in Premiere Pro.

a. **General Export Attributes**

   1. **Sample Accurate Exports:** Premiere Pro ensures that all transitions and keyframe points align precisely with audio sample

boundaries, providing the potential for very accurate audio timing unencumbered by video frame boundaries.

2. **Sample Rates (48kHz and 96kHz):** Exported audio is converted to one consistent sample rate to meet the requirements of Pro Tools; the desired sample rate can be chosen at the point of export.

3. **Bit Depths 16-bit and 24-bit:** Users are given a choice of 16-bit and 24-bit audio depths, depending on the project requirements.

4. **Encapsulate and Separate Audio Options:** The Encapsulate option bundles the audio and metadata in a single big OMF file. It is ideal for smaller projects. The Separate Audio option lets the audio files be divided from outside while keeping the OMF file of smaller size (less than 2 GB) so that big projects become easier to handle.

b. **Metadata and Track Handling**

1. **Track and Clip Naming Conventions:** Because OMF supports only mono tracks, Premiere Pro exports each channel of multichannel (stereo, 5.1 and 16-channel) as individual mono tracks, appending a unique identifier, such as _L, _R to each track's name.

2. **Clip Volume and Keyframe Volume**: Clip volume levels and keyframe volume levels are exported to the **Clip Gain effect**, but DigiTranslator provides an option to either accept or ignore keyframe volume settings.

3. **Audio Transitions**: Audio transitions between adjacent clips, centered or uncentered, based on user preference also featured in Premiere Pro.

4. **Audio Mixer Pan Settings**: A single pan setting is applied per clip, extracted from the track and included in the export data.

5. **Stereo Channel Handling:** Premiere Pro does not change hard panned stereo tracks. Left channels are panned left and Right channels are panned right.

6. **Stereo Balance:** Clip-based balance adjustments are done directly to the **Clip Gain effect**. Track-based Audio Mixer balance is not included as it does not translate to clip-based OMF files.

7. **Channel Gain for Multi-channel Tracks 5.1 and 16-channel**: Premiere Pro exports the first gain value per clip channel excluding keyframes.

8. **Fill Left, Fill Right, and Swap Channel Effects**: First values of these effects are applied to each clip without keyframes.

9. **Toggle Track Output Settings**: Only audio tracks that have the **Toggle Track Output** enabled are exported, except for tracks that are muted using the Audio Mixer's Mute Track or Solo Track buttons.

c. **Special Clip Types**

1. **Nested Sequences:** Premiere Pro regards nested sequences as one clip and exports the audio for each nested sequence in exactly the same way.

2. **Merged Clips:** Audio for merged clips is exported in much the same way as for master clips and subclips.

Pro Tools Import Tips

Importing OMF files into Pro Tools: Here are the best settings to ensure optimal compatibility.

1. **In DigiTranslator:**

   - Leave **Sample Rate Conversion** deselected unless specific conversions are required.

   - Deselect **Pan Odd Tracks Left/Even Tracks Right.**

   - Select **Convert Clip Based Gain To Automation** for smoother gain transitions.

2. **In the Missing Files dialog box:**

   - The default is set to **Manually Find And Relink**.

   - Deselect all the other options before pointing to the project name and external media files folder to select and re-link files.

CHAPTER ELEVEN

COLLABORATIVE EDITING

Get started with collaborative video editing

Team Projects brings powerful cloud-based video editing collaboration to your team. Work together in one shared project, effortlessly syncing changes to sequences and compositions wherever you are.

Simplified Cloud-Based Collaboration

With Team Projects, editors can collaborate in real-time, hosted in the cloud, eliminating additional hardware.

- **Invite Collaborators with Ease:** Flawlessly add people or groups to new or existing Team Projects, making it fast to share projects and collaborate as a team anywhere, at any time.

- **Team Presence and Status Monitoring:** See in one place all the collaborators and their statuses in real-time so you know who is online and ready to contribute.

- **Visual Cues for Easy Workflows**: Multiple visual indications keep everyone on the same page to help avoid missteps that get in the way of smooth, uninterrupted collaboration.

- **Conflict-Free Editing via Sequence Locking**: Lock edits so that no one else overlaps in work and the work of no single editor gets overwritten.

- **Instant Publishing and Updates:** Publish edits instantly and thereby make changes available for all collaborators in near-to-real time.

- **Uninterrupted Editing, Even Offline**: Continue working in offline mode while changes are saved locally until you go back online.

- Automatic Saves and Version Control: Every change auto-saves to your local system, and Team Projects creates a version history with each save. You can revert, if needed, to any prior version or create a new project from an auto-save.

Team Projects Workspace

By design, the Team Projects interface offers minimalistic view to the user:

- Version History and Auto-Saves
- Sequence Locking
- Invite to Edit
- Collaborator Presence and Status
- Publish and Update Options

Getting Started and System Requirements

- The following steps will help you get started with Team Projects. You first need to be online and signed in with the Creative Cloud Desktop app.
- Team Projects is available in Adobe Premiere Pro, After Effects, and Adobe Media Encoder, starting with the October 2018 versions to the most recent version. If you are an Enterprise customer, ensure that your administrator has activated the service for your account. Sign in with your Adobe ID, Apple ID, Google, or Facebook account.

How to Create Team Projects

Collaboration in an Adobe Premiere Pro project is slick and offers various ways to initiate, manage, and customize it among groups. Here's how to get started with Team Projects, a feature that allows users to create a shared project with multiple collaborators.

a. **Creating a Team Project**

- **Direct Access:** To initiate a collaborative project, choose New Team Project from the start screen of After Effects or Premiere Pro.

250

- **Within the Application:** To create a new project that allows multi-collaborator editing and sharing within an application, one goes to the File menu. After that, click on **New** to access the **Team Project tab.**

- **Convert an Already Existing Project into a Team Project**: If you already have a project you want to collaborate on, you might navigate to the **Edit tab.** After that, select the **Team Project tab** before clicking on **Convert Project to Team Project** to transition your enterprise to a team setup.

When you create a **Team Project,** you will be prompted with the option to provide a name for the project, which is required, and a description, optional. You can immediately add collaborators or at a later time during the development of the project.

b. **Adding Collaborators**

To invite collaborators, perform the following steps:

- **Open the Edit Collaborators Dialog**: Once your Team Project has been created, click Edit to open the Edit Collaborators dialog.

- **Add Users:** You must type the team members' names or email addresses. As you start typing, Adobe will pop suggestions matching your past collaborators or your organizational address book if your setup is synced to the Adobe Admin Console.

- **Invite Groups:** If your organization uses Active Directory, you can invite groups. Note that changes to the membership of a group will not be reflected in your project automatically; you need to send a new invitation to refresh the list.

When ready, click **Invite**. Collaborators will receive an invitation in their Creative Cloud Desktop app and directly within Premiere Pro or After Effects.

c. **Managing Collaboration**

- **Removing Collaborators**: To remove a collaborator, click the "X" next to the name.

- **Re-invite Users:** If you need to add new members or update an existing list, make the changes within the **Edit Collaborators dialog**.

- **For Enterprise Users:** Make sure your IT administrator has activated the Team Projects service for your account so that you can collaborate impeccably.

With Team Projects, this makes collaborative video editing both effortless and flexible, allowing teams to collaborate effortlessly from anywhere.

Converting a Premiere Pro Project to a Team Project

To convert an existing Premiere Pro project to a collaborate Team Project, follow these steps:

- **Open the Project:** Open the Premiere Pro project that you want to convert.

- **Navigate to the Team Project Option:** Go to the top menu bar, then select the **edit tab.** After that, select the **Team Project** before clicking on **Convert Project to Team Project**. This setting will flawlessly guide your project into the workflow of the Team Projects, allowing multiple users to collaborate on edits together.

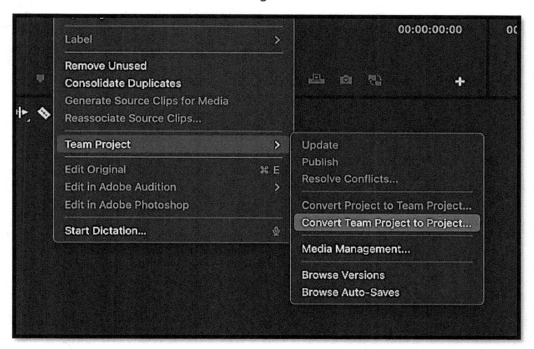

- **Create Your Team Project:** When prompted, name your Team Project, and optionally, add a description to it. This is your opportunity to define the project to your collaborators and put it into context.
- **Add Collaborators:** After naming the project, you can add collaborators to invite other people to the project. You will add their details for an invite to collaborate on the project.
- **Complete Setup**: In the details, add collaborators, then click **OK**. They will be notified through the Creative Cloud Desktop app, and the invitation will also appear in the **Manage Team Projects dialogu**e under the **Invites** tab, where they can accept it to join the project.

Opening Team Projects in After Effects

The following are the ways to work on an After Effects Team Project:

- **Open a Team Project:** Just launch **After Effects** and go to the **File menu** before selecting the tab titled **Open Team Project**. Immediately, it opens the **Manage Team Projects dialog** showing you all the Team Projects you have worked on.

- **View and Choose Projects:** In the dialog, the Team Projects are organized in three tabs.

  a. **Team Projects:** This shows all the active Team Projects that you can open.

  b. **Archive:** Lists the archived Team Projects that are no longer active but still can be accessed for reference or further use.

  c. **Invites:** Shows the Team Projects opened for you to collaborate on, but which you have not yet accepted.

- **Search for Certain Projects:** If your list of Team Projects is very long, you can locate a particular one simply by typing rapidly inside the search box.

- **Open Selected Project**: Once the project is found, choose it and click **Open.** After Effects will load project components in the background and display you that it's loading the project.

- **Work While Loading:** While other components of the project are loading, you can begin your work with those elements of the project that have loaded. With **After Effects**, you start working on the part of the project without waiting until everything is loaded.

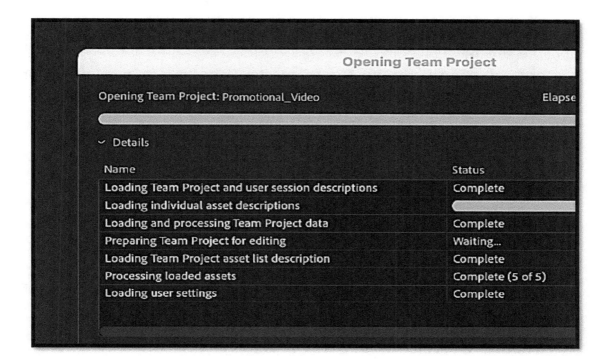

How to add and manage media in Team Projects

Starting October 1, 2024, the Creative Cloud Synced files for Business accounts will no longer be available within organizations created before December 11th, 2023. This will impact the workflow for Team Projects in Adobe Creative Cloud dependent on metadata and media references retained in an Adobe-owned database.

a. **Add and Manage Media in Team Projects**

Media files in Team Projects can be stored in one of the following locations:

- Cloud storage platforms with a syncing relationship to desktops including but not limited to Dropbox, LucidLink, Google Drive or OneDrive
- Network shared storage location or to local drives, shared amongst collaborators

Adding Media from Cloud Storage

You can add media files from cloud storage synced to your desktop such as OneDrive directly into Team Projects. This allows unified integration with existing assets.

Choosing Media-Sharing Locations

Adobe recommends shared storage options that are accessible to all team members. Options include:

- Public cloud-based file sharing
- NAS, VPN accessible (though VPNs can be slow to access for media)
- External drives (with copies of the media) distributed to each collaborator

Importing Media from Shared Storage

- To import media, either choose the **File menu**, then click on **Import**.
- Alternatively, open shared cloud storage or network drives to access the

Media Browser panel.

- Next, locate the media folder and highlight the files you want to import into your project.

Media Browser

The Media Browser panel supports the importing and access of your media files in an organized structure for efficiency, even within teams.

b.   **Manage and Relink Media in Team Projects**

If media were to become unlinked, the Link Media option within Premiere Pro provides the facility to reinstate a link in a non-destructive manner to the other collaborator's media paths. The relink is a local operation only and does not rewrite the original paths that other collaborators have written.

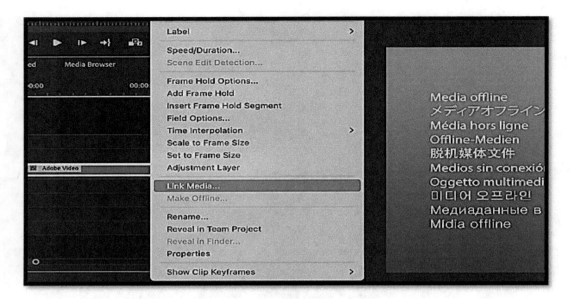

Mapping Media with Media Management

To do a large quantity of relinks, use the Media Management dialog:

- Select the **Edit tab.**
- After that, select the specific **Team Project.**
- Also, select the **Media Management.**
- Then, select **New Media Mapping** for the offline or missing files.
- In the popup window, select the folder where the correct media resides, highlight it, and click **OK.**
- Repeat the steps mentioned above for the remainder of the files.

This ability to relink locally prevents one member from impacting changes to another teammate's project but provides an agile method of keeping media for continuity between projects.

How to invite and manage collaborators

In this section, learn to use all the options to collaborate within Team Projects. In other words, how to invite individuals or groups, how to manage invites, view active collaborators of your team, and how to remove them. It will be covered step by step so that collaboration in shared projects is easy.

Overview

- Invite Collaborators to Team Projects
- Invite Groups to Collaborate
- Respond to Collaboration Invitations
- View Active Collaborators in Real-Time
- Remove Collaborators from Team Projects

a. **Invite Collaborators to Team Projects**

To bring others into a project, use the invite option (+) next to the collaborator icons. Collaboration settings can also be accessed via the **File menu.** After which, you select the **Team Project Settings** and click on **Edit.**

- **Add Collaborators:** Type the names or e-mail addresses of others you would like to invite. Previously invited collaborators will appear for you to select easily. A search feature allows you to locate specific names more quickly.
- **Send the Invite:** Once you've identified your collaborators, click **Invite**.

Note: For enterprise users, ensure that your IT administrator has activated the Team Projects service.

b. **Invite Groups to Collaborate**

Enterprise accounts can invite entire groups created through the Adobe Admin Console's Active Directory integration. You need only type the name of the group in the invitation field and all members of that group will be invited.

Note: Group invitations are static. If group membership changes after an invitation is issued, new members won't be automatically added, and removed members will remain unless they have been manually updated. Groups are limited to less than 150 members.

c. **Respond to Collaboration Invitations**

When invited into a Team Project, you will be notified both in the Creative Cloud desktop application and within Premiere Pro or After Effects themselves.

- **Join in Creative Cloud Desktop**: When you open the application, click on the **Accept option** to join.

- **Manage Invitation from Team Project Settings**: Select the **File menu.** After that, click on **Open Team Project** and select **Invites** to view the invitations and take action.

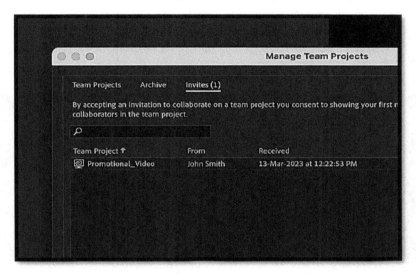

d. **View Active Collaborators in Real-Time**

Hover on the profile pictures of collaborators to see whose online working on the project. You also can show if they are online or offline.

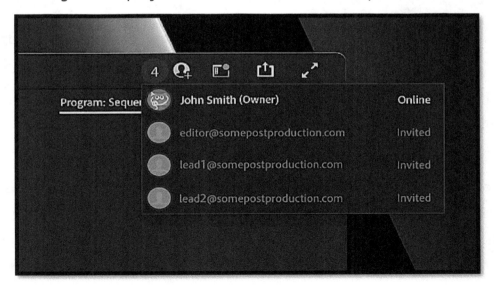

e. **Remove Collaborators from Team Projects**

- You can remove any collaborator by clicking on three dots next to the collaborator's name and click **Remove.**

- **You can also r**emove a collaborator by navigating to the **File menu**. Afterwards, click on the **Team Project Settings**, click **Edit,** and remove the collaborator from the list.

Hint: If you're removing yourself from a Team Project, be sure to close the project before doing so.

With these steps, collaboration in your Team Projects will go smoothly, and managing will become effective too.

How to share and manage changes with collaborators

Collaboration in video editing within Team Projects will entail several tools and workflows to effortlessly support collaborative teams, whether editors are working offline or not. Key features such as Sequence Locking, publish updates, visual cues, and offline editing allow multiple users to collaborate in 'conflict-free' environments and ensure everyone's edits correctly sync and appear in their right place.

Core Concepts and Tools

a.   Sequence Locking

If you enable this, you will exclusively work on a sequence, locking it in such a way that others can only view previous versions as you make changes. This allows you to avoid conflicts since the others will have only view rights until you publish your changed version. Visual indicators showing who is actively editing and if any changes have been published are shown in the Timeline, Project, and Program Monitor panels.

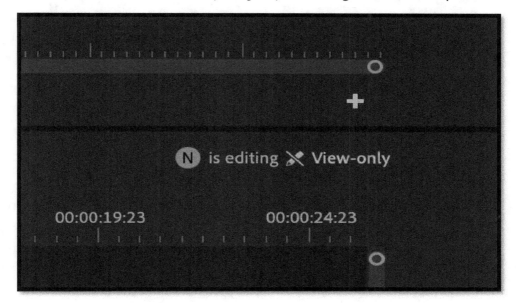

b.   Publish Changes

When you are done with your edits, click **Publish** to release the sequence. This ensures that collaborators have the latest version and are able to update their projects with these newly published changes. You may want to include a comment so collaborators know what you have updated.

c. Visual Cues in Collaboration

Visual cues in Team Projects make collaboration quick and easy. For example:

- **Active Collaborator Lock:** When you are editing, a lock is engaged and stops people from editing.
- **Publish Status:** When someone else is editing you will be offered a view of an older version of the sequence with the option to refresh once they publish.

- **Show Asset Status Icon**: Several icons such as a white pen or downward arrow will indicate if assets are edited or viewed only.

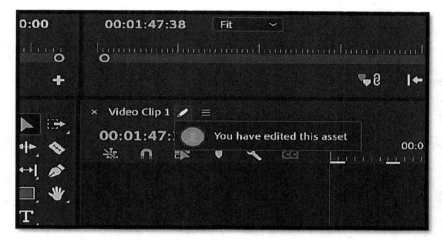

d. **Offline Editing and Sync Status**

Team Projects supports offline editing when you are temporarily disconnected. An icon indicates whether you are online or not, and whether the changes are synced or not. You see a **cloud icon**; if that cloud icon turns into a green checkmark, your changes are updated. If it is a yellow warning or grey cross, that means you have gone offline. Changes you make offline are saved locally and will automatically sync when you go online. However, working offline for longer periods is not advised as it can lead to conflicts when you merge data later.

e. **Sequence Locking in Offline Mode**

If you go offline during editing, Sequence Locking is disabled, and others can edit it. When you reconnect, as long as there isn't a conflict, you'll be able to publish your local changes. If there is a conflict, for example, two collaborators edit the same sequence offline but only the first to reconnect can publish. Other collaborators will be forced to save their work as a new sequence so as not to overwrite.

Conflict Management in Team Projects

- **No Conflict**: If no one else has edited anything when you reconnect, you can simply publish your edits made offline.

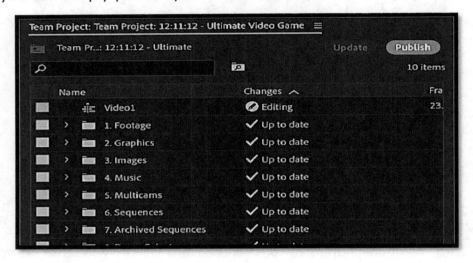

- **Conflict**: When this happens because another person edited the same sequence offline, you'll receive a conflict alert. You may use **Duplicate** to save your changes as a new sequence and avoid the conflict.

How to view autosaves and versions of Team Projects

In Team Projects, any edit you make instantly saves a new version, both to the cloud and to your local system. Every time a new update happens, a version is created, thus allowing you to keep a very clear and accessible history of what changed. You can easily view, and navigate or revert to any previous version to maintain a smooth workflow collaboratively, and robustly version-controlled.

Contents:

- Viewing Project Versions
- Setting Auto Save Cache Location
- Managing Auto Saves
- Creating New Team Projects from Versions or Auto Saves

   a. **Viewing Project Versions**

   Each time a collaborator publishes a change, a new version of the Team Project is saved. These versions allow for easy browsing and retrieval of any published version, keeping the entire project history. Access to and management of versions are simple and can be initiated in a couple of ways:

   1. **Header Menu Access:**
      - In the Premiere Pro header bar, select the Team Project name and select **Auto Save History**.

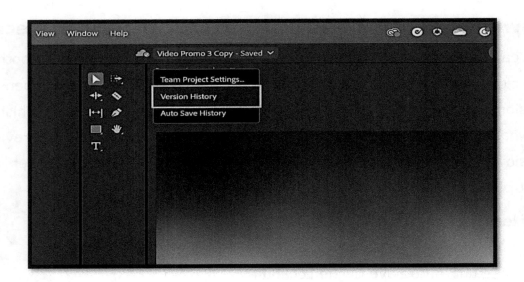

This opens a drop-down menu showing Version History, Team Project Settings, and Auto Save History.

2.   **Edit Menu:**

- Select the **Edit tab**.
- Afterward, click on **Team Project**, then select the **Browse Versions** to display all the available versions in the Media Browser panel.

3.   Media Browser Panel:

- Right-click the Team Project in the **Media Browser panel** and select **Team Project Versions.** This opens a dialog listing all versions, including shared comments and other information.

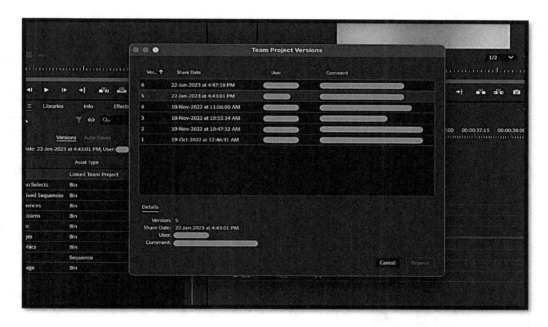

- Use the **Versions tab's vertical slider** to scroll through versions visually.

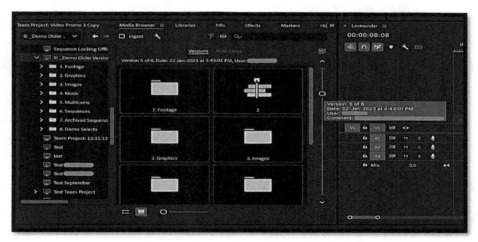

Creating a New Team Project from a Version

Easily create a new Team Project from a previous version:

- In the Media Browser panel, right-click the Team Project listed under **Creative Cloud** and select **New Team Project from Version**.

- A dialogue box opens. The current name of the Team Project is pre-populated with "Copy" added and the original list of collaborators. Click **OK** to confirm.

b.   **Setting Auto Save Cache Location**

Team Project offers autosave on every edit, both to the cloud and locally. You can choose a custom location for those AutoSave files so that they are easy to access. To do so:

- On your macOS, go to Premiere Pro, then click on **Settings** and **Auto Save**. On your Windows, click on **Preferences,** then click on **Auto Save.**

- In the Team Projects section click **Browse** to choose where you want your Auto Save cache to be.

Note: The format of auto-save files is .tpr and these files cannot be opened directly.

c.   Managing Auto Saves

The Auto Saves feature allows you to access your autosaves for reviewing, reverting, or even creating a new project from auto-saved edits.

1.   Browse Auto-Saves:

- To view the autosaves of the current project, navigate to the

Edit tab.

- After that, select **Team Project** before selecting **Browse   Auto-Saves.**

2.   Creating New Team Projects from Versions or Auto Saves

- Click the Team Project name in the Premiere Pro header bar, then click **Version History**.

3.   Media Browser Options:

Right-click in the Creative Cloud section of the Media Browser on the Team Project and select **Team Project**

Auto-Saves. Or use the **Auto-Saves vertical slider to** browse.

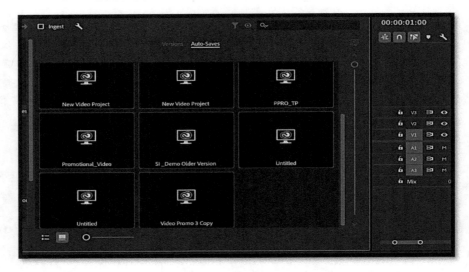

To revert to a previous edit, click **Make AutoSave the Latest.** To create an auto-save to a Team Project, right-click the **Team Project**, then select **New Team Project From Auto-Save** and confirm.

How to manage Team Projects

The following section describes how to effectively manage Team Projects by archiving completed projects, restoring those that have been archived when they are needed again and permanently deleting projects that are no longer needed.

Key Actions Covered:

- Searching and Filtering Team Projects
- Archiving Team Projects
- Restoring Archived Team Projects
- Deleting Archived Team Projects

   a.   **Searching and Filtering Team Projects**

If you manage multiple Team Projects, this can be time-consuming and cumbersome. If you want to find a project in a rush:

- To access the **Manage Team Project dialog**, go to the **File menu** before selecting the **Open Team Project.**
- Then, search for a project via the **search box** in the dialog.

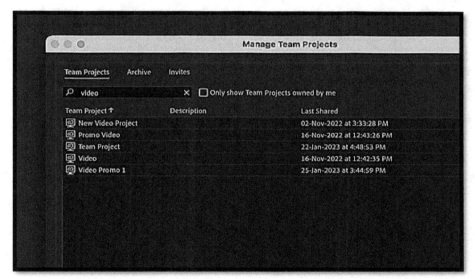

This method saves you from having to scroll through a long list, thus you find projects easier and in a more effective way.

b.   Archiving Team Projects

Once the work on a project is complete and the final output has been exported, archiving the Team Project removes it from active view and restricts access from collaborators.

- Choose the **File menu**
- Afterward, select the **Open Team Project** to access the **Archive tab.**
- Click **Archiv**e to confirm.

The project is no longer available in the active tab of the Team Projects. As the project owner, you will be able to access it in the Archive tab.

c.   Restoring Archived Team Projects

If you need to re-access a project, you can restore it from the archive.

- Choose the **File menu**
- Afterward, select the **Open Team Project** dialog.
- Then, go to the **Archive tab** to select Restore.

- Select the project and click **Restore.**

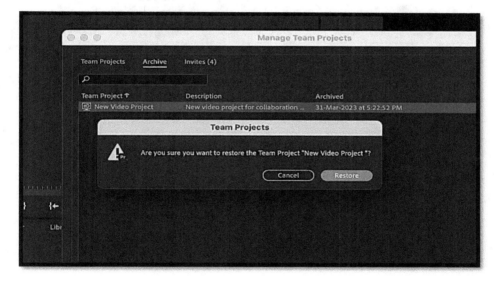

A confirmation dialog will pop up. Confirm your selection and the project will be moved back into the **Team Projects tab.**

d. **Deleting Archived Team Projects**

For projects that are no longer needed, you can permanently delete them from the archive.

- Move to the **Archive tab** of the **Manage Team Project panel.**

- Choose projects you want to be deleted and press **Delete**.

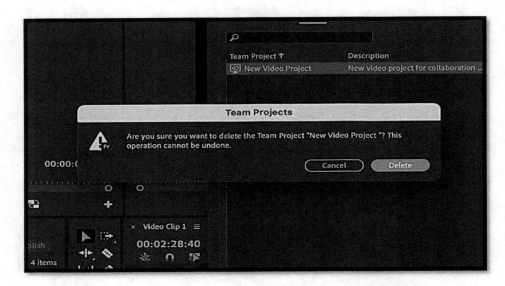

Note: Only the project owner has permission to archive, restore, or delete projects permanently.

CHAPTER TWELVE

WORKING WITH OTHER ADOBE APPLICATIONS

After Effects and Photoshop

Adobe Premiere Pro integrates smoothly into the Adobe ecosystem, offering a workflow that continues the editing, creation, and refining of video projects. Equipped with an expansive toolkit, users can make use of various specialized Adobe applications-including but not limited to After Effects and Photoshop refine, customize, or extend assets created within Premiere Pro projects. Premiere Pro also allows the importing and editing of content created in other applications, smoothing the multimedia production process within Adobe even further.

1. **Edit a Clip in its Original Application**

   In Premiere Pro, an option called "Edit Original" opens the media file in its associated application type for edits on the spot. If a clip is externally edited and saved, then Premiere Pro will automatically update the changes within a project, without needing any replacement of files. Similarly, sequences created in Premiere Pro and then imported into other Adobe applications, such as After Effects can also open in their native applications, and be edited and updated smoothly across applications using the "Edit Original" command.

   - Select a clip in either the Project or Timeline panel.
   - Choose the **Edit tab**, then select **Edit Original.**

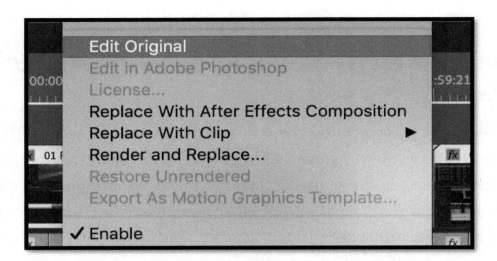

Note: You can incorporate information about the **Edit Original command** into the export settings. To do so, select **Project** from the **Embedding Options menu** in the Export Movie Settings dialog.

2. **Dynamic Copying Between After Effects and Premiere Pro**

    After Effects also demonstrates particularly dynamic integration with Premiere Pro, allowing you to copy and paste not just your media but also your timeline elements between applications. This means you can directly paste the layers of an After Effects Timeline into a Premiere Pro Timeline panel, complete with all their original settings, effects, and properties.

    -   **From After Effects:** Copy the audio, video, and solids layers, then paste them into the Premiere Pro Timeline.

    -   **From Premiere Pro:** Use the ability to copy assets within tracks and paste them directly into the After Effects Timeline.

    Besides, all of the footage items can be exchanged across each application's Project panel, but a few of the elements such as After Effects' unique shape and text layers are not transferable to Premiere Pro. If you want to work on full clips or sequences of Premiere Pro within

After Effects, then it is advisable to use an **Import command** to bring the Premiere Pro project into After Effects.

Tip: Use **Adobe Dynamic Link** to create live links between compositions across the two programs without rendering.

3. **Pasting After Effects Layers in Premiere Pro**

    After Effects compositions can be pasted into a Premiere Pro sequence, where layers become clips and effects with shared functionality between programs are preserved.

    Steps:

    - Open Premiere Pro and then copy the layers from After Effects.
    - In the After Effects Timeline, select and copy layers.
    - Open a sequence in the Premiere Pro Timeline panel.
    - Drag the current-time indicator to the desired location in the Premiere Pro Timeline, then select **Edit** and **Paste** or **Paste Insert.**

    Converted Properties in Premiere Pro;

    Some, but not all, keyframes, properties, and effects are translated when After Effects layers are pasted in Premiere Pro. Following is a list of some **After Effects** transfer the appropriate attributes including, but not limited to: Blending modes Audio effects, and Transformation.

    Everything else at this time stays offline, and expressions do not get transferred.

4. **Copying Premiere Pro Assets to After Effects**

    On the other hand, you can also copy assets such as audio/video clips and stills from the Premiere Pro timeline and then paste it into **After Effects**. The items that are copied are transferred as After Effects layers along with the retention of keyframes and effects as well as their settings if compatible.

- In Premiere Pro, highlight the assets to be copied.
- Open any composition in After Effects, paste them, and they will appear as the top-most layer in the timeline.

Note: Insert at current-time indicator point Ctrl+Alt+V (Windows) or Command+Option +V (Mac)

5. **Working with Photoshop and Premiere Pro**

    Photoshop is particularly good at detailed editing of still images, whether for PIPs or individual frames of any video in a Premiere Pro project. You can animate full-frame images or specific layers from Photoshop in Premiere Pro and use the robust select, mask, and draw tools in Photoshop to refine visual elements. Edits made in Photoshop can be saved as PSD files for use in Premiere Pro or rendered as QuickTime movies or image sequences.

Integration Tips with Photoshop and Premiere Pro

- **Create a New Photoshop File in Premiere Pro**: Use the **command File**, then select **New** and select the specific **Photoshop File** for creating a still image and that precisely fits the video frame size of your project.

- **Edit an Image in Photoshop:** Open any supported still image directly from Premiere Pro, make edits in Photoshop, and save. Changes will automatically be updated in Premiere Pro.

Benefits of Using Photoshop along with Premiere Pro: Although Premiere Pro is a very powerful video editing tool, it allows you to import layers from Photoshop for titles, graphics, or masks. On the other hand, selective and paint tools in Photoshop will allow for fine-tuning in a more precise manner.

By integrating your Adobe applications with Premiere Pro, you'll be able to extend creative opportunities with your project, taking advantage of application-specific tools and workflows to enhance and extend the video editing experience.

The Dynamic Link

Dynamic Link allows you to create solid, smooth integrations between **Adobe After Effects** and **Premiere Pro**, allowing you to share media assets impeccably between them. Consequently, this would allow users to share compositions and media back and forth in a very convenient manner with no need for any intermediate rendering. Dynamic linking of assets is quite easy, and this process happens much like the importation of other assets. In their display, unique icons and color labels will be used to differentiate these linked assets.

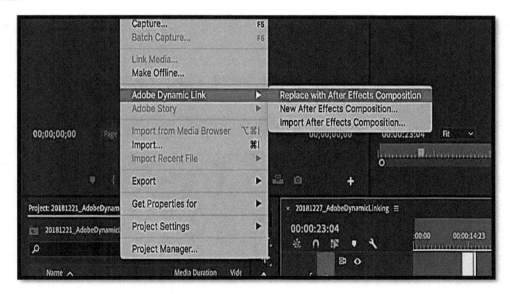

Preconditions of Using Dynamic Link

Make sure you are on the same version of After Effects and Premiere Pro. Dynamic Link is version-sensitive and will not work across major version mismatches. For Dynamic Link with **Character Animator** or **Adobe Media Encoder (AME)**, there is a minimum version requirement available, especially in the case of version 23.x of the Adobe applications. In case you are on

Character Animator 23.1, then for other applications, the versions should match between 23.0 to 23.4.

Optimizing Dynamic Link Performance

Linked to a complex composition, extra processing time in After Effects will be required before the final data will be available in Premiere Pro. Sometimes, these extra processes can lead to delays in preview or playback. To avoid delays, try the following:

- Temporarily taking linked compositions offline
- Deactivating the linked clips to stop referencing
- Rendering compositions and replacing linked compositions with rendered files

The **Render** and **Replace option** in Premiere Pro for heavy VFX projects helps users handle playback performance.

Dynamic Link Workflow Essentials

You will be able to create and link directly to After Effects compositions directly from Premiere Pro. Here's how:

- **Replace Premiere Clips with After Effects Composition:** In a Premiere Pro sequence, select clips that you want to use in After Effects. Right-click and select **Replace With After Effects Composition.**

- **Create New After Effects Composition:** To create a new linked composition, go to the File menu. After that, select **Adobe Dynamic Link** before clicking on **New After Effects Composition**. It will open up After Effects and create a project based on the Premiere Pro sequence settings.

- **Link to an Existing After Effects Composition**: To import an existing After Effects composition, choose the **File menu** and select the **Adobe Dynamic Link**. Also, select **Import After Effects Composition,** or drag a composition from the After Effects Project panel directly.

Note: The duration of a newly created linked composition is set by default to 30 seconds. To change the settings for a composition, edit the composition in After Effects.

Managing Linked Compositions

Dynamically linked compositions and clips can be deleted, modified, or re-linked.

- To open and make changes to a linked After Effects composition, select the **Edit tab.**
- After that, click **Edit Original** in Premiere Pro.
- To delete linked clips from the timeline or Project panel of Premiere Pro, highlight one or more and press **Delete.**

Handling Offline Linked Compositions

Compositions will go offline if their source After Effects project has been renamed, moved, or deleted.

- To take an attached composition offline in Premiere Pro go to the **Project** and select **Make Offline.** This may also be useful if playback is stuttering, as taking compositions offline can temporarily alleviate performance.

- Re-enable the composition by clicking on **Link Media** to re-link back to the source project.

Dynamic Link creates a powerful connection between After Effects and Premiere Pro, allowing for a great increase in workflow efficiency for real-time compositing and editing. Knowing these processes and how to optimize link performance are the keys to unleashing the full capability of Dynamic Link throughout Adobe's creative suite.

Working with Adobe Audition

Audio post-production with Adobe Audition opens incredibly powerful tools for the creation, refinement, and editing of audio with professional precision. If installed, an audio clip or the whole sequence can be transferred from Premiere Pro directly into Adobe Audition, allowing multi-layer detailed sound design.

When you send the audio clip to **Audition**, Premiere Pro renders the audio data so you can use the advanced **Wave Editor** in Audition to make fine-tuned adjustments in the audio. With this tight integration, any change done from within **Audition** automatically reflects instantly within Premiere Pro, thereby saving all the markers, effects, and other metadata that were applied to the original sequence.

Sending a sequence to Audition offers even broader editing possibilities. Premiere Pro transfers your composition with full fidelity, including all effects, keyframes, Essential Sound settings, and metadata intact. This opens the door to advanced mixing, layered sound editing, and comprehensive soundscape creation in Audition's Multitrack Editor.

How to Use Adobe Audition for Audio Editing in Premiere Pro
- In the Project panel, select an audio clip or sequence, or right-click on a clip or sequence in the Project panel or Timeline.
- Then, navigate to the **Edit tab.**

- Also, select **Edit in Adobe Audition** and click either **Clip** or **Sequence**.
- The audio opens in Adobe Audition for detailed editing.

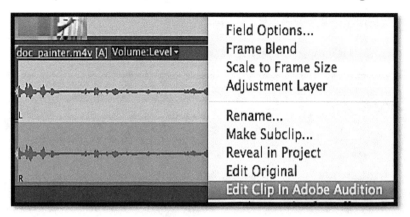

Editing Audio Clips in Adobe Audition

The **Edit** in Adobe Audition command allows Premiere Pro to open a new audio file in Audition for finer editing. If an In/Out range has been set in Premiere Pro, then those markers also transfer to Audition.

After being edited and saved, the edited clip refreshes in Premiere Pro. Premiere Pro allows multiple edits by creating a new render file for each edit, keeping the original clip intact, and updating only the rendered version.

Editing Sequences in Adobe Audition

When you wish to edit a sequence, Premiere Pro will send the whole audio arrangement as a Multitrack Session over to Audition where you can refine the composition. To export a project to Audition:

- Navigate to the **Edit tab.**
- Also, select **Edit in Adobe Audition** and click **Sequence**.
- Choose desired options in the **Edit in Adobe Audition dialog** and click **OK.**

This process exports your sequence with audio clips consolidated into a standalone project, allowing you to work on the audio independently of the source project. You are able to configure settings such as Audio Handles to include extra material beyond clip boundaries and Video Export options to include Dynamic Link streaming or exclude video.

Configuration Options in Adobe Audition

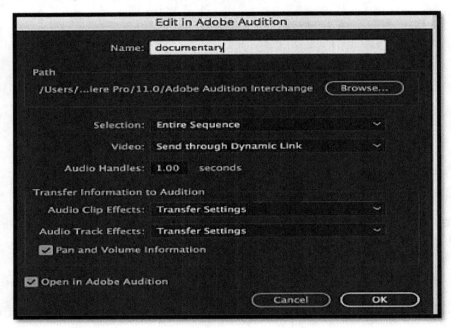

- **Name/Path:** Configure the project information.
- **Selection:** Determine whether the entire sequence or marked In/Out points will be selected.
- **Audio Controls:** Add additional audio beyond the timeline for dynamic editing.
- **Video Preferences**: Choose whether to import the generated video, use Dynamic Link streaming, or nothing

Moving Effects and Presets

Audition can recreate many of the effects within Premiere Pro, so editors never have to re-render them. Effects not moved over are said to be "offline", while VST-compatible plug-ins load automatically.

Options to move over include:

- **Audio Clip Effects:** Select move-over, render, or leave effects.
- **Audio Track Effects:** Determine whether you would like to transfer the track effects or render them out into the audio file.
- **Pan and Volume Information:** Transfer this metadata or bake it into the audio file.

Choose **Open in Audition** to open Audition and immediately load your project. Take full advantage of the advanced audio post with this seamless workflow from Premiere Pro through Audition, driving both casual adjustments and professional-level composition attainable.

Working with Adobe Prelude

Note: As video production requirements have continued to change, Adobe Prelude will no longer be available for download after September 8, 2021.

Simplify Your Workflow with Adobe Prelude

Adobe Prelude has been a great tool for organizing, preparing, and improving video assets in front of the editing in Adobe Premiere Pro. Key features are as follows:

- **Ingest and Transcode Footage**: Prelude facilitates users to ingest raw video clips and perform basic transcoding to prepare the footage for more post-production workflows.
- **Metadata Management**: Prelude's metadata function allows users to manage and annotate efficiently; hence, they can locate and retrieve clips of media with ease during an editing session. Seamless Integration with Adobe Premiere Pro.
- **Creating Subclips, Markers, and Rough Cuts:** Prelude allows users to easily create subclips and markers to tag and label the content. The rough-cut function offers the first assemblage of sequences for effective project assembly.

With your project prepared in Prelude, you can send your sequences, markers, and rough cuts directly to Premiere Pro or export them in a Premiere Pro or FCP XML file. This unified workflow enables fluid movement between Prelude and Premiere Pro, saving time in post by transferring critical metadata and organization information.

Exporting from Adobe Prelude

To finalize and export your project from Prelude:

- Head over to the **File menu** and click on **Export** to open the export dialogue.
- Choose the destination and file type and select either Premiere Pro or Final Cut Pro 7 XML
- From here you can choose whether or not you want the associated media to export.
- Select this option if desired.
- Click **OK** to finish exporting.

CHAPTER THIRTEEN

ORGANIZING AND MANAGING ASSETS

How to work in the Project panel

The Project panel in Adobe Premiere Pro 2025 is your default workspace, where you organize and manage all your media files, sequences, and other assets that relate to your project. This is how you can effectively navigate within it:

1. **Importing Media**

   • **Direct Import:** You can directly drag and drop files from your computer into the Project panel.

   • **Media Browser:** Within the Media Browser panel, you can browse, preview, and import a range of file types from various storage devices without having to leave Premiere.

   • **Import Dialog**: To open the import dialog go to the **File menu** and select **Import** or press Cmd + I (Mac) or Ctrl + I (Windows,) then select your files.

2. **Organizing Assets**

   • **Bins:** Bins are the equivalent of folders. To create a bin, right-click in the Project panel and select **New Bin.** Drag assets into bins to organize them by asset type, by scene, or however, you'd like. You can even create sub-bins inside of bins.

   • **Nested Bins:** Sub-bins are folders within bins. This will allow for more organization, especially in much larger projects.

   • **Labels and Colors:** Right-click any asset to change the label color for easy visual identification.

   • **Metadata Sorting**: Click column headers, like Name, Type, and Media Duration, to sort the assets. Columns to display can be customized by right-clicking the header row and selecting **Metadata Display.**

3. **Previewing Media**

- **Thumbnail and List Views**: The buttons along the bottom left of the panel allow for toggling between **List View** and **Icon View.**

- **Hover Scrub Thumbnails:** With Icon View, hover over the thumbnails to scrub the content of the clip without having to open the clip in the Source Monitor.

- **Previewing Clips**: Double-click to open any clip in the Source Monitor, where you are allowed to view and also mark in and out points.

4. **Creating Sequences**

- **Drag to New Sequence:** You can drag any video clip onto the **New Item icon** at the bottom of the Project panel and create a sequence that automatically matches the settings for that clip.

- **New Sequence Settings:** To create a new sequence by manually choosing settings, go to **File > New > Sequence** or use the **New Item button** and select **Sequence.**

- **Organize Sequences**: Put a number of sequences into the bins and name each with a meaningful name for accessing quickly.

5. **Customizing the Project Panel**

- **Thumbnail Resize:** The bottom slider in **Icon View** sets the size of thumbnails.

- **Filtering and Searching:** Use the search bar at the top of the Project panel to find assets by name or metadata. You can also use the filter icon to show only specific types of media, such as video only or audio only.

- **Adding Metadata Columns:** To show additional metadata, right-click in the header area and choose **Metadata Display** to select and organize columns.

6. **Using the New Features in Premiere Pro 2025**

   - **Auto-tagging:** Adobe Premiere Pro 2025 analyzes the media for the auto-tagging of keywords. This allows for quick searching and saves labor when working on huge projects.

   - **Improved Grouping**: More intuitive grouping and tagging in the Project panel, you can tag several clips and filter them inside Premiere Pro 2025.

7. **Shortcuts and Tips**

   - **Quick Duplicate:** While holding Alt on Windows or Option on Mac drag an asset to make a copy.

   - Toggle Frame Thumbnails: Show or hide the frame thumbnails in List View. In essence, head over to the Project panel settings click the **hamburger icon,** and **toggle Preview Area.**

   - **Expand/Collapse All Bins:** To expand/collapse all bins, hold **Shift** while clicking on the disclosure triangle next to one of the bins.

How to use Creative Cloud Libraries

Creative Cloud Libraries let you capture and organize inspiration wherever you are. They give you access to creative assets across desktop and mobile applications and even from Adobe Stock to elevate any project. In this section, learn how Creative Cloud Libraries can empower your creative workflow in organizing your assets to collaborate with team members.

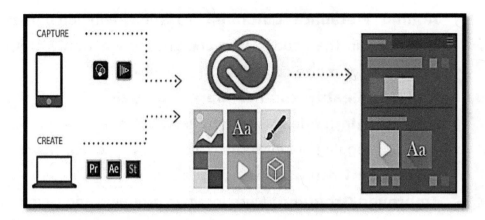

Accessing Libraries in Premiere Pro

In Premiere Pro, Creative Cloud Libraries are easily accessed through the Libraries panel. To access them, do one of the following:

- **Open Premiere Pro:** On the Start screen, click **Libraries** on the top to display the list of your assets.
- **Sync or Download Libraries:** To sync a Library to your desktop, select **Libraries** before inserting the **Library Name**. After that, click **Sync to CC Libraries** on the Library card.
- **Open Libraries Panel:** For quick access, navigate to **Window** and select **Libraries.**

Access on Any Device

Once you've saved Libraries to Creative Cloud, they are accessible:

- **Across Projects:** Reuse your assets easily between Premiere Pro projects.
- **Across Devices:** Access Libraries from any computer that you log into.
- **Across Apps:** Use assets effortlessly across Adobe applications, including After Effects, Photoshop, and Adobe's mobile apps.

Creating Libraries

You can manage your creative assets by creating multiple Libraries:

- Open the Libraries panel.

- After that, click **Create New Library.**
- Name the Library, then click **Create.**

Adding Looks to Libraries

Save color grading effects as "Looks" to be applied to other projects:

- Select the clip in the Timeline panel.
- Make sure the Lumetri Color panel is active.
- Click the **Add Look icon** at the bottom of the Libraries panel. A .look file, named for the clip to which it was applied is added to the Library.

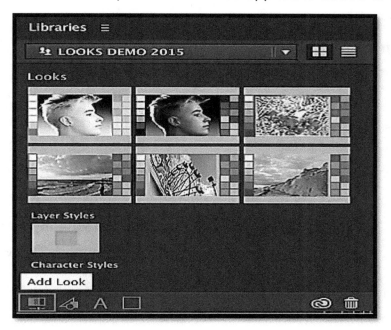

Using Adobe Stock Assets

Find and add high-quality photos, videos, and graphics right within Premiere Pro using Adobe Stock:

- Open the Libraries panel via **Window** and **Libraries.**
- Select how you'd like to refine the search within the Adobe Stock search bar.
- License an asset, or add a watermarked preview to your library to license later.

Note: You might need to sync to refresh the Adobe Stock assets in the Libraries panel.

Locate and Add Adobe Stock Assets

Adobe Stock has millions of royalty-free, high-quality photos, videos, illustrations, and graphics that add creativity to your projects. The following steps walk you through how you can locate and add those assets directly inside Premiere Pro.

1. **Open the Libraries Panel:** Open **Window** and select **Libraries** in Premiere Pro.

2. **Search Adobe Stock:** Type keywords or access your Adobe Stock account by clicking the search icon at the top of the Libraries panel. Results are displayed right within the panel for quick and easy access.

3. **Add to Your Library**: Once you have found an asset, you would want to use:

   - Clicking the **Buy and Save To My Library icon** lets you license and save the asset immediately.

   - Click **Save Preview** to [Library Name] at the top to add it to your Library for later review (Note: this will be a watermarked, unlicensed preview).

Tip: Right-click here for quick actions on assets, or click the **Sync button** in the panel if assets aren't appearing automatically.

Licensing Previews Later: If you save a preview and decide to license it later, right-click the asset in the Library and choose the appropriate option to purchase and replace all linked instances in your projects with the high-quality version.

Apply and Use Assets from Your Library

Adding your Creative Cloud Library assets to your project is easy and flexible:

1. **Graphics**: Drag and drop graphics directly from the Libraries panel into your Project panel or Timeline, or right-click to Add to Project. This imports the graphic as a project item and adds a default-duration still image in the Timeline.

2. **Looks:** Use color grades saved as "Looks" in your Library to enhance clips:

    *   **To apply a Look to the Timeline**, drag a Look from the Libraries panel onto a clip in the Timeline. This adds a **Lumetri Color effect** and updates any existing Lumetri Color effect with the new Look.

    *   **To apply a Look to the Project panel**, drag the Look to a project item to add the effect to the master clip, which will be visible in the Source Monitor.

Note: Looks with the .cube extension populate the Input LUT in the **Basic Correction section** of the Lumetri Color panel, whereas .look files populate the Look field in the Creative section.

Share and Collaborate Using Creative Cloud Libraries

Creative Cloud Libraries make it easy to collaborate on projects with others. By sharing a library, other Creative Cloud users can access the library to view, edit, and use the shared assets in their projects.

*   **To share a library:** From the Libraries panel, select **Collaborat**e, enter the e-mail address of the collaborator and an optional message.

*   **To join a shared library**: Use the Adobe Creative Cloud desktop app to sign in and accept the invitation to collaborate.

For Creative Cloud Library sharing of Motion Graphics templates, ensure you have the latest version of the Creative Cloud desktop application. Keep the application up-to-date to ensure compatibility between Adobe applications.

How to consolidate, transcode, and archive projects

The Project Manager in Premiere Pro is a strong tool that makes project managing, archiving, or transcoding easier. The core functionalities allow you to organize and centralize projects effortlessly for easier sharing, archiving, and editing in the future. Here is a closer look at what it does:

Key Functions and Capabilities

a. Project Media Centralization

- Collates the media files of projects and copies them all to one source for ease of collaboration and sharing.
- Ensures all essential files are kept without conversion, maintaining original file formats.

b. Consolidate and Transcode Media

- Transcode media into a single intermediate or mezzanine codec for optimum archiving and compatibility.
- Trimming of unwanted footage and sequences will save space yet retain important information.

c. Flexible Copy Options

- Copy complete projects, either with or without unused clips. Rename files to a project-named convention to maintain consistency, if desired.

Workflow Details

a. Collecting Files and Copying to a New Location

- Copies the selected sequences, along with all of the associated media, to one storage location. There is no transcoding.
- Excellent option for project sharing if complete editability is to be retained.

Options:

- Exclude unused clips to conserve storage space.

- Include handles (extra frames) for slight edits.
- Keep audio conform files so that audio remains continuous.
- Transcode image sequences into video clips (a single format) for smoother playback
- Include preview files so that rendered effects are preserved

b. **Consolidate and Transcode for Archive**

- Transcode media into one standard format or codec to be stored for a very long period or shared with systems that need compatibility.
- Trim unused footage; retain only those which have been used in any of the sequences.

Transcode Settings:

- **Match Sequence Settings**: The new media would compose settings like your sequence.
- **Match Individual Clips**: Original clip settings are retained during transcoding.
- **Preset-Based Transcoding:** Uniform settings will be applied across all clips, such as DNxHD, GoPro CineForm.

Allows for handles, audio conform files, and trimmed sequences for efficient archiving.

Advanced Options

a. **Dynamic Link and After Effects**

- After Effects compositions that are dynamically linked can be flattened to independent video clips for systems that don't have After Effects.
- Gives you the flexibility in sharing while ensuring compatibility across platforms.

b. **File Naming and Organization**
- Allows renaming of media files to match clip names for consistent organization.
- Updates automatically the file names in the project to make tracking easier.

c. **Destination Management**
- Saves projects and files into named folders, adding numbers to file names if there's already a duplicate.
- Shows the size of files before and after consolidation to better manage disk space.

Practical Applications

a. **Archiving of Big Projects**
- Consolidate complicated projects into an easy-to-handle codec that will reduce the size while only retaining the necessary quality for future use.

b. **Collaboration and Sharing**
- Gather and copy project files in readiness for sharing between teams or transfer to other systems without loss of editability.

c. **Simplified Storage Management**
- Deselect the clips that you don't use, collapse the sequences into smaller file formats, and delete the extra media to free up storage space.

How to Use Project Manager

1. **Opening Project Manager:** Go to the **File menu** and select the **Project Manager**.
2. **Selecting Sequences:** In the Project Manager window, select the sequences where you will apply the process.

3. **Option Selection**
   - **Collect Files and Copy:** This option collects all the files in one location and does not modify them.
   - **Consolidate and Transcode**: This will transcode your media and trim them ready for archiving.
4. **Changing Preferences**
   - Change handles, audio, and preview to whatever suits your needs.
   - Select format, preset, and codec for transcoding.
5. **Defining Destination Path**: Select a destination path to which the new files and project will be saved.
6. **Finalize and Save:** Review file sizes and estimated needs in space for the destination drive. Click **OK** to start to perform.

General Notes and Limitations

- Nesting of sequences or dynamically linked compositions must be specifically selected or, as an alternative, converted.
- P2-compliant MXF file structures are not preserved when copying or consolidating a P2 source media.

How to manage metadata

Improve your workflow and manage your media assets with XMP metadata, a descriptive framework that resides within the files themselves. Metadata defaults to capturing key information about date, duration, and file type for video and audio files. You can improve this metadata further with additional properties such as location, director, and copyright (if needed) based on your requirements of the project.

Metadata within Adobe Applications

The Metadata panel in Adobe video and audio applications allows you to share metadata across applications. Unlike traditional clip properties, which are application-specific to the project, metadata properties written to source files are available across applications, making asset tracking and management much easier. For example, the metadata you create in Adobe Premiere Pro is instantly available for review and use in Adobe Bridge and After Effects.

Schemas and Properties

Metadata properties are collected into schemas, that is, a bundle of properties meaningful to a specific workflow. Some examples are as follows:

- **Dynamic Media Schema:** For video production, this schema includes properties like Scene and Shot Location.
- **Exif Schema:** For photography, this schema supplies properties like Exposure Time and Aperture Value.
- **Dublin Core Schema**: This schema lists general properties like Date and Title.

To display or hide schemas or properties, choose options in the **Metadata Display menu**.

XMP: The Standard for Metadata

XMP, developed by Adobe, is an XML-based platform that allows metadata to be shared across applications without loss of information. Formats like Exif and GPS are automatically imported in XMP and uniformly managed inside the workflows. For the formats that are not supported, metadata is stored in sidecar files.

XMP metadata is often written directly into the source file. However, XMP in Premiere Pro does not always show up for every asset because not all, like Bars and Tone or Transparent Video, have a source file. To take full advantage of metadata, Adobe offers an **XMP Software Development Kit.**

Metadata in Adobe Premiere Pro and After Effects

Each application specializes in how metadata is handled depending on its workflow:

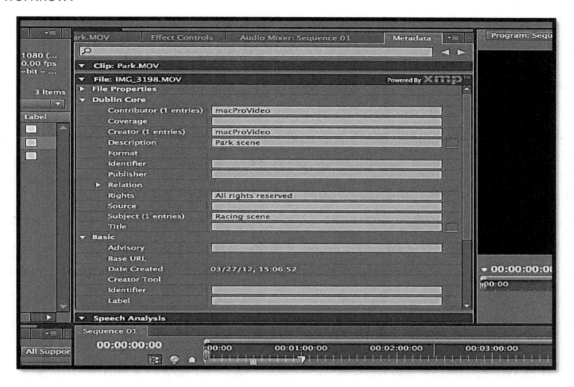

1. **Premiere Pro:** Divides metadata between **Clip** and **File sections.**

    *   **Clip Metadata:** This is stored in the project file and can only be accessed inside Premiere Pro. This is ideal for clip specific details.

    *   **File Metadata:** This is embedded within source files but can be accessed by other applications.

2. **After Effects:** After Effects separates metadata into **Project** and **File categories.**

    *   **Project Metadata**: All metadata that applies to the project as a whole can always be embedded in exported files.

    *   **File Metadata:** All metadata that applies to source files is accessible across platforms.

Metablogging Workspace and Metadata Customization

The Metalogging workspace in Premiere Pro makes metadata entry easier after you import or capture. When you head over to the **Window** to select the **Workspace** and **Metalogging menu option**, it opens the Metadata and Project panels to their full size for efficient data entry.

You can also customize metadata sets:

- Save customized sets that fit your different workflows.
- Create custom schemas and properties for unique project needs.
- Control what metadata is displayed via the Metadata Display menu.

Understanding Clip Metadata and File Metadata

Metadata can be useful when trying to organize, manage, and gain efficiency within the creative workflow of video editing. There are two primary types of metadata that you can expect: XMP file metadata and clip metadata. Each of these pieces of metadata will serve different purposes in both Adobe Premiere Pro and the other video applications from Adobe.

- **XMP File Metadata**

  XMP file metadata refers to information embedded directly within a source file. This metadata remains consistent and applies universally to all instances of that source file, regardless of how it is used in a project. For instance, if a video file is imported into Premiere Pro multiple times or referenced by multiple sub-clips (each with unique In and Out points), the XMP metadata ensures uniformity across all these instances.

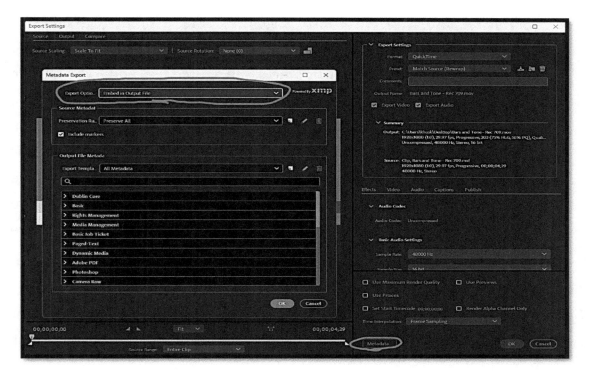

- **Clip Metadata**

  Clip metadata, however, can be thought of as the inherent properties of each discrete, independent clip as it sits within a Premiere Pro project. While multiple clips can reference the same source file, their metadata can differ by capturing information specific only to their context within the project. For instance, two clips that originate from the same source file can have different names, durations, or annotations, all determined by their unique clip metadata.

Working with Metadata in Premiere Pro

- **When to Use XMP Metadata:** Use the XMP metadata fields for information that should always be the same for all instances of a source. Since the XMP metadata is shared among all instances, you know edits you make to XMP metadata in any instance will be visible everywhere, so it is more consistent and reliable.

- **When to Use Clip Metadata:** Clip metadata is great for capturing information about a project or an instance. This will allow the editor to have different clips coming from the same source file, and to be flexible with it.
- **Linking Metadata Fields**: With Adobe Premiere Pro, you can map clip metadata fields to XMP metadata fields. This is useful if you want specific types of information about clips to trickle down to the source file metadata. However, you mustn't map more than one clip metadata field to the same XMP metadata field for clips that share the same source file. Otherwise, you will have conflicts.

Editing XMP Metadata

Some of the video applications from Adobe, such as Premiere Pro, allow for solid editing of XMP metadata. You can edit the metadata of one or many files at once within the Metadata panel:

- **Files or Clips Selection:** Highlight one or several files or clips for which you want to edit the metadata.
- **Metadata Editing**: On the Metadata panel, either edit the text fields directly or click on values to open a popup editor. When multiple items are selected:
    a.   Properties that are in common present their current value.
    b.   Conflicting properties have "<Multiple Values>". You can override them to uniform the information.

Searching Metadata

Quickly locating the metadata you want in the Metadata panel helps you organize better and work more efficiently. Follow these steps:

- From top of the Metadata panel, there is a search box where you can type your search.

- The metadata list dynamically filters with your search string. Only the properties containing the string appear.

The controls at the bottom allow you to find the previous and next items of a search results list, or simply the **Tab key**. Click the **Close button (x)** to clear the search and return to the entire list of metadata.

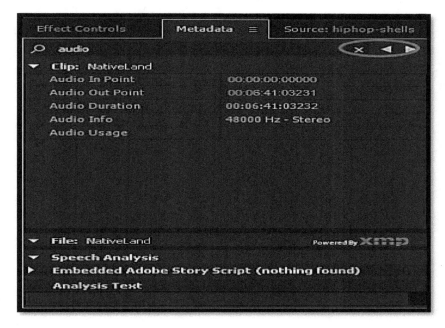

Customizing the Metadata Panel

To customize the Metadata panel for your workflow:

- Click the options menu of the Metadata panel, then select **Metadata Display.**

- To show or hide entire schemas or individual properties, select or deselect items in the list.

Best Practices for Metadata Display and Workflow

Show or hide metadata schemas for simplified display with the following steps:

- To show or hide metadata schemas, use the **Metadata panel options menu**.

- Then, choose **Metadata Display**. Toggle schemas or individual properties.

- Save, switch, or delete custom metadata sets for different projects.

Embracing XMP metadata fully and leveraging its interoperability between applications ensures your production workflows are taking advantage of efficiency, asset organization, and collaboration that's unmatched.

CHAPTER FOURTEEN

LONG-FORM AND EPISODIC WORKFLOWS

How clips work across projects in a Production

To understand how clip referencing works in a production, it is good to consider a workflow involving two main projects: a Media Project containing source clips and a Timeline Project that contains sequences referencing those source clips.

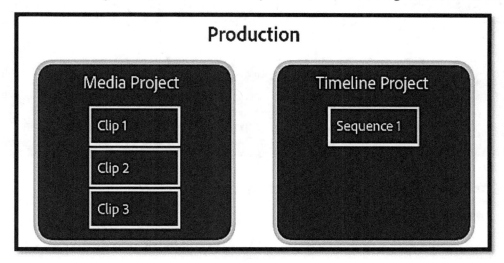

How Production Structure Works

A production involves multiple projects including, but not limited to:

- **Media Project:** This is where all   the source original clips will be housed.

- **Timeline Project:** This contains sequences that reference the source clips of the media project without duplicating them.

In this model, when clips from the Media Project are edited into the sequence within the Timeline Project, no new source clips (as FCP 7 called them, master clips) are added to the Timeline Project. For example, if the Media Project contains 100 clips and all are edited into the sequence, the Timeline Project will still contain only that one sequence, with no duplication of source clips. It will directly refer to source clips from the Media Project in sequences, even when those sequences are transferred between projects in the production.

Key Concepts of Clip Referencing

1. Integration across Projects:

- Clips in the sequences refer to their source in the Media Project.
- When moving sequences between projects, duplicate source clips are not created.

2. Efficient Media Management:

- One reference to a source clip is enough to avoid redundancy among projects.
- This is a simplified structure that only applies to productions. For standalone projects, each sequence clip needs to have a source clip in the same project.

3. Drag and Drop:

- Drag and drop the Production panel can be used to transfer or copy clips and sequences across different projects.

- To copy an item, with the addition symbol appearing next to your cursor, hold **Cmd on** macOS **or Ctrl** on Windows while you drag.
- Items dropped into the root level of the target project automatically bring its Project panel into focus.

Advanced Productions Techniques

1. **Duplicate Clips or Sequences Between Projects:**
   - Select the Edit tab and click on **Duplicate**. You can also choose to copy and paste sequences between projects.
   - Press **Cmd/ Ctrl and** drag the item to duplicate across projects.

2. **Reveal Source Clips:**
   - To Reveal a source clip, right-click the clip in the timeline and choose **Reveal in Project.**
   - If the project of the source clip is closed, Premiere Pro automatically opens it or scans other open projects for re-association of missing clips.

3. **Re-associate Source Clips:**

- If a source clip is missing, use the Edit tab and select **Re-associate Source Clips.** After that, select a project file for Premiere Pro to locate the clip.

Markers, Labels, and Effects in Productions

Markers:

- Adding markers to a clip or sequence updates the corresponding clip instance across open read/write projects.
- Any markers added when one of the projects is closed are local to each project until both projects are opened together

Labels:

- Label colors are shared between source and sequence clips initially, then independent after they have been set

Source Clip Effects:

- Source clip effects can only be modified in the source clip's project when in a read/write state.
- Effects are visible in the Program Monitor but cannot be edited from the timeline clip instance.

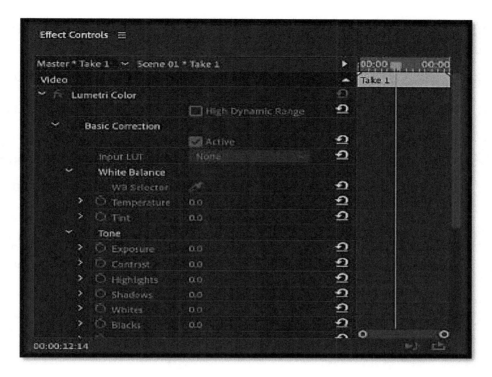

Multi-Camera Sequences:

- Multicam sequences are treated as normal source clips in productions
- To edit open the project that the sequence belongs to in read / write mode and double-click the multicam in the timeline to open it.

How to work with Productions

Productions within Adobe Premiere Pro offer extreme flexibility in saving and managing projects across a variety of storage solutions. Whether you are an independent editor or working in a collaborative team environment, it's very important to know the best configuration option for you related to storage compatibility.

a. Storage Compatibility

Productions are flexible and can work with most storage formats. However, Adobe doesn't pre-approve specific systems for compatibility. If you plan to purchase or rent shared storage between machines, check with the vendor that the system has been tested and is compatible with Premiere Pro Productions.

b. **Shared Storage for Multi-User Collaboration**

A networked shared storage system is necessary for multi-user collaboration on a Production. Here are some key considerations:

1. **Connection Types:** Network-attached storage (NAS) systems often support multiple protocols such as SMB, AFP, or NFS. Always use SMB for maximum compatibility in Premiere Pro.

2. **Cross Operating System Compatibility**: Premiere Pro can handle path differences between macOS and Windows. For consistency:

   - On macOS, make sure that all systems use the same volume name.

   - On Windows, map the shared storage to a uniform drive letter across all workstations.

3. **Proprietary Storage Systems:** Productions can work with shared storage using proprietary file systems or client applications if they provide file system updates compatible with Premiere Pro. It is best to check with your storage provider to confirm.

c. **Optimizing Performance**

1. **Scratch Disks:** Scratch Disks, such as **Auto Save** and **Preview Files,** by default, are kept alongside the Production folder on shared storage. You can change this in Production Settings.

2. **Media Cache:** The Adobe suggestion is to keep the **Media Cache Files** and the **Media Cache Database** locally on the system boot drive or a fast SSD that's directly attached to each workstation.

It is not good to put these files on shared storage since it will harm performance and reliability.

3.   Network Speed:

- Working in a Production requires a minimum of 1Gbps connection speed per workstation.

- For larger productions or projects greater than HD, 10Gbps or faster connections are highly recommended.

- The more users accessing a Production simultaneously, the faster your network and storage system should be.

d.   Best Practices for Collaborative Workflows

1.   **Avoid Consumer File-Syncing Services**: It is fine to store a Production in Dropbox or Google Drive for backup purposes, but it should not be used as a means of emulating shared storage. These services are not designed to support collaborative editing workflows.

2.   **Server Time Synchronization:** Accurate file timestamps are very important for collaboration. Make sure that:

    - The time on the shared storage server matches the time on the editing systems.

    - Whenever possible, the server syncs with an **NTP (Network Time Protocol) server**. If this is not possible, the time is manually set to be as accurate as possible and the time drift is monitored.

    - Even small differences of a few minutes can lead to Premiere Pro behaving unpredictably.

e.   Performance Considerations

Like with regular hard drives, the faster the connection the better the performance. Keep in mind the following:

- It will minimize bottlenecks with high-speed interfaces and storage solutions.
- Optimize the network and workstation setup to handle specific demands for big teams or high-resolution workflows.

By following these extended guidelines, you'll be able to make sure that your Adobe Premiere Pro Productions workflow will be smooth, efficient, and collaborative, whether your project is simple or very complex.

CHAPTER FIFTEEN

COLOR CORRECTION AND GRADING

Overview of color workflows in Premiere Pro

Premiere Pro 2025 provides a professional set of color grading and correction tools that allow content creators to easily elevate their footage from right inside the edit timeline. The tools within the Lumetri Color workspace are designed to provide power to both beginners and seasoned colorists through streamlined workflows.

Overview of Lumetri Color Tools

The Lumetri Color workspace allows for creative and exacting color, contrast, and lighting adjustments. With the integration of editing and grading into one platform, Premiere Pro eliminates the use of external applications, providing a single environment to perfect your visuals. Key features include:

- **Comprehensive Color Tools**: Curves, sliders, color wheels, and other intuitive controls tailored to varying expertise levels.

- **Dynamic Workflow:** Move effortlessly from edit to grade without the need to export or switch software applications.

- **Scopes in Real-time:** Native Lumetri Scopes offer correct luma and chroma analyses for exact adjustments.

  a. **Getting Started with the Color Workspace**

     Premiere Pro comes with a default Color workspace that is set up for ideal grading. To enable it:

     1. Go to Window and select **Workspace**

     2. Also, select **Color**, or select **Color** from the workspace switcher.

     3. This layout includes:

A. **Lumetri Color Panel:** Tools for grading, corrections, and applying creative looks.

B. **Lumetri Scopes Panel:** Real-time waveform displays to evaluate adjustments.

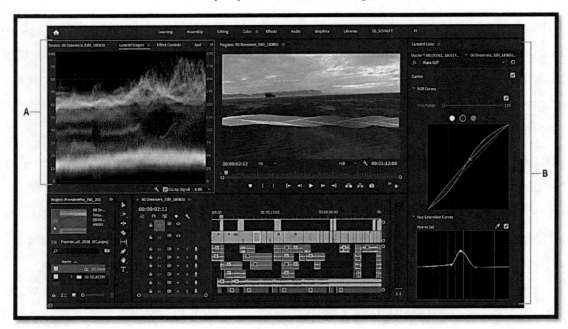

Tip: Use these panels to make quick, intuitive edits from simple color corrections all the way through advanced grading.

b. **Color Correction Workflow**

Step-by-Step Guide to Basic Adjustments

1. **Setup your Workspace:** Check that the Color Workspace is enabled.

2. **Select the Clip:** Position the playhead over your desired clip in a sequence. The **Selection Follows Playhead** feature auto-selects the clip for adjustment.

Tip: To focus only on video clips, disable audio track targeting.

3. **Apply Basic Corrections:**
   - Use **Auto Color** (powered by Adobe Sensei) for intelligent color correction. Refine the results using intensity, color, and light sliders.
   - Adjust exposure, contrast, highlights, shadows, whites, and blacks with sliders or precise value inputs.

c. **Advanced Color Grading Features**
   - **Creative Adjustments:** Add stylized looks using the Creative section and tweak it using adjustment sliders.
   - **Curves**: Expand your grade with fine details using RGB curves and Hue/Saturation curves.
   - **Color Wheels:** Adjust shade, midtone, and highlight to establish an accurate tone.
   - **Color Match:** Match color grade between clips for continuity across shots.

Tip: Use the **Toggle Bypass option** in the Lumetri Color or Effects Control panels to compare changes.

d. **Adding Multiple Lumetri Effects**

Premiere Pro supports multiple Lumetri effects layered on top of one another to extend advanced grading workflows:
   - Add new effects using the "fx" dropdown in Lumetri panel. Each added effect is stackable and independently editable.
   - Rename effects to label them for clarity. Delete effects directly with no confirm dialogs.

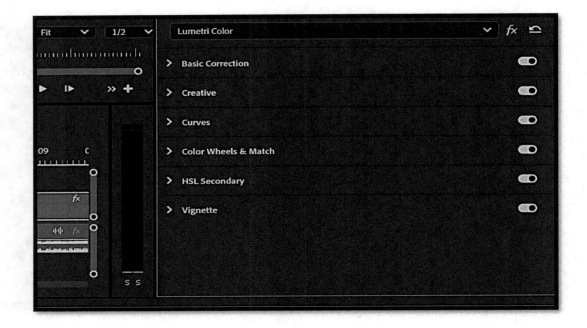

e. **Control Surface Integration**

Improve your accuracy and speed with hardware control surfaces with Lumetri Color. Currently supported devices include **Tangent Elements/Wave/Ripple**.

- Install **Tangent Hub software** and then map Premiere Pro's Lumetri grading controls to the device.

- Each of the Lumetri modes corresponds with basic hardware input for intuitive adjustment: Basic, Creative, Curves, and Wheels.

Tip: Third-party devices also receive support with additional plug-ins.

How to enable DirectX HDR support

Develop your creation and playback of HDR content in Premiere Pro 2025 by enabling DirectX HDR support on Windows. Boasting better stability, performance, and even better color compatibility, DirectX HDR ensures that HDR content will look amazing on displays that can support it.

Why DirectX HDR?

DirectX HDR is based on a modern, efficient codebase, with some key advantages compared to the older standards:

- **Better Stability and Performance**: Optimized for HDR workflows, guaranteeing seamless rendering and playback.
- **Modern Architecture:** State-of-the-art graphics technologies come into play.
- **Deep Color Support:** Starts the advanced color capabilities in Windows 10 on HDR10 capable monitors.

System Requirements of DirectX for HDR Support

1. **Operating System**
   - Windows 10, version 1709 and above
2. **Display**
   - An HDR10-supported monitor. VESA DisplayHDR-certified displays offer optimum performance though they work with all HDR10 monitors
3. **Graphics Processing Unit (GPU)**
   - **Nvidia**: GeForce 1000 series (Pascal) or newer
   - **AMD:** Radeon RX 400 series (Polaris) or newer
   - **Intel**: Select Core 7th Gen (Kaby Lake) or newer

Steps to Enable DirectX HDR

1. **Verify HDR Compatibility:**
   - Right-click on the desktop and select **Display Settings.**
   - Locate the **Play HDR games and apps** toggle. If this option is unavailable, your hardware does not support HDR.

2. **Enable Advanced Color Mode:** Turn on Play HDR games and apps in the Display Settings.

3. **Adjust SDR Brightness:** Navigate to Windows HD Color Settings. After that, use the SDR content appearance slider to fine-tune the brightness of non-HDR content.

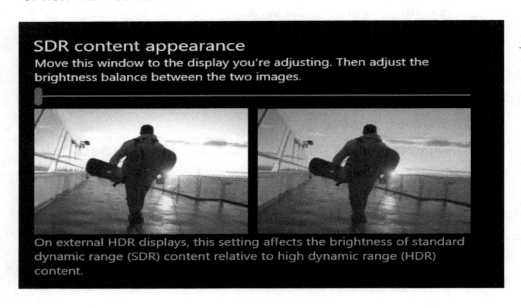

Note: If HDR is enabled, the screen display of non-HDR material will be mute. Only enable HDR settings when working on HDR projects for optimal display quality.

Setting Up Premiere Pro for DirectX HDR

1. **Setting GPU-Accelerated Renderer:** Go to **Project Settings** before clicking on the **General tab**. Then, choose a GPU-accelerated renderer (OpenCL/CUDA).

2. **Enable Display Color Management:** In the General tab, check that **Display Color Management** is enabled under GPU acceleration.

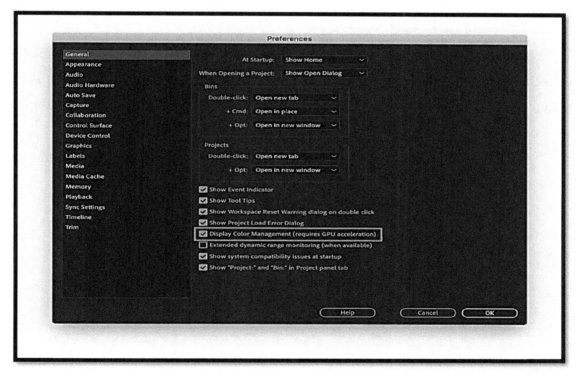

3. **Choose HDR Sequence Working Color Space:** Avoid clipping of HDR data while rendering, by choosing either Rec2100 HLG or Rec2100 PQ from the Sequence Settings.

Views - Supported and Unsupported in Premiere Pro

Supported Views:

- Program Monitor
- Source Monitor
- Export Window
- Transmit

Unsupported Views:

- Legacy Titler

Known Issues and Best Practices

While setting the working color space for the sequence to Rec 709 (SDR), sometimes the preview files might clip into SDR ranges. However, there is no impact on HDR playback for imported clips. To maintain HDR data throughout the workflow:

- Use an HDR working color space (Rec2100 HLG or PQ) in the sequence settings.
- Avoid rendering previews in SDR formats.

Get creative with color using Lumetri looks

The Creative section in the Lumetri Color panel of Premiere Pro hosts an impressive set of tools for adding and refining your footage using professional-level color grading. The tab contains several pre-designed Looks, which are essentially presets performing color improvements in one quick move. You can use these to give your clips an appealing look without much effort. Premiere Pro has a huge library of Creative Looks that will give users enough room to import or create their very own using LUTs, or Lookup Tables. Save them once, and it shows up in the panel for easy access.

Applying Looks

The **Looks Preset Thumbnail Viewer** inside the Lumetri Color panel makes it easy to preview and select different styles;

- You can browse available **Looks** through a dropdown menu or navigate using preview arrows.

- Clicking any of the preview images applies that **Look** directly to your clip.

- These Looks are intended for use either by themselves or in combination with custom color grading at either the base or finishing stage.

- For more choices, check out **Lumetri Presets** in the Effects panel, which offers style options by film stock and camera model.

Fine-Tuning Adjustments

Once a **Look** is applied, several controls can be used to make subtle tweaks to tailor the final result to your creative intention:

- **Intensity:** Determine how intense the applied **Look** should be on your video. Moving the slider to the right increases the intensity and moving the slider to the left reduces it.

- **Faded Film:** Add a retro touch to your video with the faded film effect. Further, improve this feature with the help of a slider for the perfect output.

- **Sharpen:** Accentuate the edges for sharper details. Moving the slider to the right sharpens the edges and enhances the details while moving it to the left softens the video. Sharpness should be handled with care because too much sharpness can make your video look unnatural. Click the slider to **0** for no sharpening at all.

- **Vibrance:** This allows for selective desaturation so that highlights or skin tones do not get over-saturated. It increases the saturation of less saturated colors while maintaining natural skin color.

- **Saturation:** Adjust the master saturation of all colors in the clip. The scale goes from 0 (monochrome) to 200 (double saturation).

- **Tint Wheels:** This first control sets the colors of the shadows and highlights using the **Shadow Tint** and the **Highlight Tint wheels**. Drag within the wheel to apply tints. An empty center indicates no effect has been applied.
- **Tint Balance:** Adjust the balance of the magenta and green tones in your clip to arrive at a pleasing palette.

Taken together, features in the Creative section allow you to boost your projects in video editing and edit the raw footage into professional-looking, cinematic masterpieces.

How to correct and match colors between shots

Color correction is one of the cornerstones in editing video material, keeping your project polished and assuring a cohesive aesthetic. The Lumetri Color panel in Premiere Pro is powered with color wheels and advanced color matching to help you achieve professional, high-quality results with precision and creativity.

Three-Way Color Correction Using the Color Wheels

The Lumetri Color panel introduces three color wheels for adjusting the shadows, midtones, and highlights separately. The wheels will provide fine-tuning of brightness, hue, and saturation for a specific tonal range in a clip, giving you control from subtle corrections to stylistic dramatic changes.

Color Wheel Parts

A. Midtones Color Wheel
B. Cursor or Color Puck
C. Highlights Color Wheel
D. Slider Control
E. Shadows Color Wheel

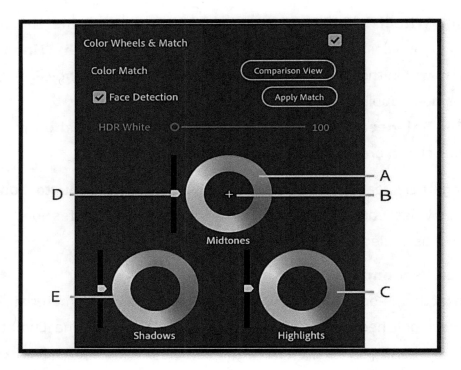

How They Work:

- Refine the **shadow** areas of your shot to add depth or lighten the details.

- Adjust **midtones** to improve overall contrast or emphasize the subject.

- Adjust **highlights** to maintain control over bright areas in your image and prevent them from overpowering it.

Working with Color Wheels and Sliders

- **Wheels:** To apply color, click inside the center of a wheel and drag the cursor to the desired hue. If a wheel center is empty, it indicates no change.

- **Sliders:** Click and drag up or down to adjust brightness levels. For example, you can increase a shadow slider to lighten dark areas or decrease the highlights slider to soften bright highlights.

Color Match between Shots

Matching color in a sequence is one of the important ways of maintaining visual continuity. Color Match in Premiere Pro refines the process of making uniformity among shots.

How to Match Color between Shots:

1. **Switch to Comparison View**

   • Open the Program Monitor or Lumetri Color panel and turn on Comparison View.

   • Show a reference frame concerning the frame you are comparing. This way, you can easily compare differences.

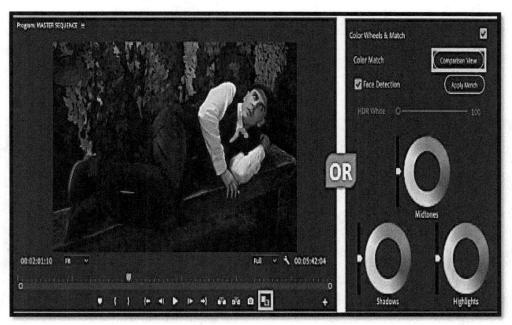

2. **Select a Reference Frame**

   • Locate and select a suitable frame for comparison using the slider, timecode, or edit point arrows.

3. Select the Target Clip

- Position the playhead on top of the clip you want to match and make sure it is highlighted.

4. **Apply Adjustments with Optional Face Detection**
   - Enable Face Detection by default to improve skin tone matching if faces are present.
   - Disable this option to hasten processing or for shots with no faces.
5. **Click Apply Match**
   - Premiere Pro automatically adjusts the **Color Wheels** and **Saturation** in the target clip to better match the reference frame.

Refining the Match:
- If the result isn't satisfactory, select a new reference frame and reapply the match.
- Premiere Pro will clear the old adjustments and then rematch the color based on the new reference.

Why Color Wheels and Matching?

The flexibility afforded by the Lumetri Color tools allows you to address detailed problems in footage and create a unified, visually appealing story. Whether you want to correct inconsistent exposure in sequence shots, match them, or develop your look for your cinematic effort, three-way color correction, and Color Match let you achieve the desired results as accurately, efficiently, and creatively as possible.

How to adjust color using RGB and Hue Saturation Curves

The Curves feature in Premiere Pro represents an advanced color adjustment method that would boost the visual quality of your video projects. Its flexible set of options enables creators to easily and precisely adjust colors, tones, and luminance toward attaining natural, visually pleasant results.

Curves Available in Premiere Pro

Within Premiere Pro, two main kinds of curves are involved in color editing: RGB Curves and Hue Saturation Curves. Each provides a different function and possibility when trying to achieve professional color grading.

1. **RGB Curves**

    The RGB Curves will let you make deep adjustments in the Luma and Tonal Range either across the entire frame or within a specific color channel. You can employ these curves in two ways:

    *   **Lumetri Color Panel:** The Lumetri workspace will provide you with an intuitive, real-time adjustment of this panel.
    *   **Effects Control Panel:** You will have access to the RGB Curves as an effect for point exact editing based on keyframes.

Adjusting Luma and Tonal Ranges

RGB curves add control points to the curve. These allow you to adjust specific tonal values for highlights, shadows, and midtones.

*   **Master Curve:** This changes luminance for the RGB channels. By default, it is a white straight diagonal line. Adjusting this curve will affect the general brightness and contrast of the clip.
*   **Channel Adjustments:** You can independently adjust the Red, Green, and Blue channels to change the tonal values for detailed color grading.

330

Modifying Control Points:

- **Highlights and Shadows:** To adjust the control points to specify highlights, drag them right and up; for shadows, drag them down and left.

- **RGB Colors:** Selectively increase or reduce the tonal values for individual channels.

- **Contrast:** Points can be dragged upward and downward to brighten or darken the tone or horizontally to adjust the contrast.

Keyboard Shortcuts:

- **Delete Control Points**: Hold **Ctrl** on Windows or **Cmd** on macOS and click on a point.

Usage Examples:

- Create S-curves to boost contrast naturally.
- Add warm tones to scenes for a cinematic look.

2. **Hue Saturation Curves**

The Hue Saturation Curves provide detailed adjustments of color relationships in a video. The following curves are included:

- **Hue vs. Saturation:** To adjust the saturation of specific hues.
- **Hue vs. Hue:** To change one hue for another
- **Hue vs. Luma:** To modify luminance for specific hues.
- **Luma vs. Saturation:** To move saturation based on brightness
- **Saturation vs. Saturation:** The fine-tuning of saturation for chosen saturation ranges

Grading Control Points

Take advantage of control points on the curves to isolate and change chosen color ranges. By adjusting these points, the interaction of colors within the video changes.

Adjusting Control Points:

- **Move Points**: Pulling the points upwards and downwards amplifies or lessens the effect within a selected range.
- **Add Points:** To add new points, simply click on the curve itself for more suitable adjustments.
- **Eyedropper Tool:** Sample colors directly from the Program Monitor. This automatically adds three control points: one for the selected color, and two for adjacent hues, luma, or saturation.

Keyboard Shortcuts:

- Hold **Shift** while dragging a point to constrain it either horizontally or vertically for finer tuning.

Sampling Colors:

Work with the Eyedropper to sample specific areas of your video. The tool averages out a 5x5 pixel area, by default, but holding **Ctrl** on Windows or **Cmd** on macOS extends that sample to a 10x10 pixel area.

Processing Order for Hue Saturation Curves

Premiere Pro processes adjustments according to a logical top-down structure in the Lumetri panel:

- Sections like Creative, Basic Correction and RGB Curves are evaluated before Hue Saturation Curves.
- Effects applied before the Lumetri effect will alter the colors being sampled, while those applied after it won't have an impact on color sampling.

- All Hue Saturation Curves process adjustments simultaneously, sampling the color values passed into them from the results of prior sections.

Example of Behavior:

If you change green to blue using Hue vs. Hue and then manipulate Hue vs. Luma, the control points will track in on the same green value. Turning off the Hue vs. Hue adjustment breaks the interaction and allows completely independent manipulations.

How to use HSL Secondary controls in the Lumetri Color panel

The **HSL Secondary tab** in the Lumetri Color panel opens up your creative possibilities, making very precise adjustments possible by fine-tuning certain colors in your footage. Used in conjunction with the other tools in Lumetri, it affords unparalleled flexibility in fine-tuning the shots. Commonly used after primary color correction, the secondary adjustment in HSL is great for the isolation and modification of specific hues without changing the overall image.

Why use HSL Secondary?

HSL Secondary controls are super helpful for the following:

- Dealing with scenarios where general hue and saturation curves have been adjusted as far as possible, many times for broadcast-safe specifications of one sort or another.
- Giving a specific color more life to pop off its background.
- Selectively adjusting local luminance ranges for fine-tuned corrections.

How to Color Correct with HSL Secondary

To use HSL Secondary for accurate color corrections, there exist these three steps: create a key, refine it, and then perform the desired correction.

1. **Create a Key**

   Start by creating an isolation of your target color:

- Open **Color Workspace**, and make sure the Lumetri Color panel can be viewed.

- After that, navigate to the **HSL Secondary tab**.

- Add an Adjustment Layer via the **File menu** and select **New**. Also, select the **Adjustment Layer.**

- Click within the image using the **Set Color Eyedropper Tool** to select a color. Click the plus and minus eyedroppers to add to and exclude pixels from the selection. Alternatively, choose one of the color swatches for a pre-set.

- Check the **Color/Gray** box to isolate (or mask) the affected area by displaying it in grayscale. The Hue, Saturation, and Lightness (H/S/L) sliders can now be used to more precisely set the target range.

Pro Tip: Hold the **Ctrl/Cmd** key while using the eyedropper to sample a larger area for a smoother key.

2. **Refine the Selection**

Once you've set a preliminary key, use the Refine tools to polish it:

- **Denoise:** Smooth out irregularities or noise in the selection for a clean mask.

- **Blur:** Soften the edges of the mask for a natural blend between selected and non-selected regions.

- Refine the transitions of the ranges using the range sliders, where the top triangles set the range boundaries and the bottom triangles soften the transitions.

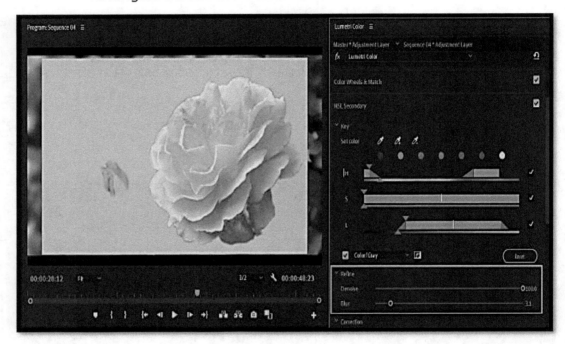

Double-click to reset any slider when necessary, or use the **Reset button.**

3. **Refine the Correction**

   With the key already refined, do a detailed color correction:

   - In the **Correction tab,** use the different grading tools.

   - Work either with the default **Mid-tone Color Wheel** or activate the **3-Way Color Wheel** to individually adjust the colors in the shadows, midtones, and highlights.

- Fine-tune corrections using sliders for Temperature, Tint, Contrast, Sharpen, and Saturation.
- De-select the **Color/Gray checkmark** to view your results in full color.

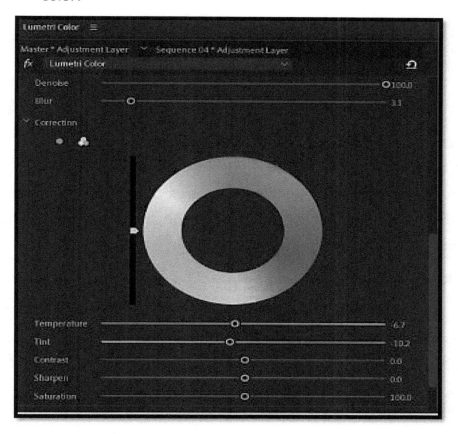

Practical Applications

HSL Secondary controls are very practical to use and have a wide range of creative and technical applications:

- Brighten or improve certain areas of an image
- Correct color on an object or fine-tune skin tones
- Correct ambient lighting problems or color matches between shots.

How to create vignettes

Vignettes are an elegant and versatile tool for visual storytelling. They subtly direct the viewer's gaze to a focal point, be it a person, an object, or a striking landscape. Aesthetically pleasing and beyond, vignettes infuse depth, drama, and atmosphere into any scene, enriching the emotional tone of it.

You can create vignettes in Premiere Pro using various ways, each offering flexibility and creative control for different projects. So, let's take a closer look at these techniques:

How to Create Vignettes in Premiere Pro

1. **The Lumetri Color Panel: Easy Vignette Creation**

   The Lumetri Color panel is the most straightforward and efficient way to create vignettes. You will be able to mold and fine-tune a vignette with just a few adjustments to perfectly frame your subject.

How to Apply a Vignette Using Lumetri Color:

- **Select the Clip**: Highlight the clip you would like to work within the timeline.

- **Go to the Vignette Section**: In the Lumetri Color Panel, open the Vignette Controls.

- **Modify the Settings**:

  a. **Amount:** Controls how much the edges of the frame are lightened or darkened. Negative amounts darken the edges while positive amounts lighten it.

  b. **Midpoint:** This controls the amount the vignette extends toward the center of the frame. Lower values increase the effect outward while higher values contain the vignette to the edges of the frame.

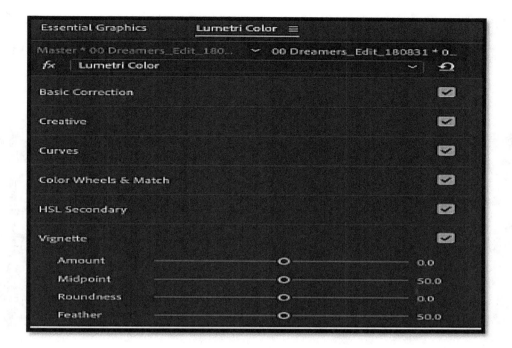

    c.   **Roundness:** Alters the vignette shape. Negative values result in it being more elliptical, whereas positive values deliver a softer, round effect.

    d.   **Feather:** Blurs the vignette edges. The larger the feather, the more it will transition softly, while a smaller feather gives more defined, sharper edges.

This approach is good for quick editing and other general applications, like framing a whole scenery.

2.   Vignettes with Masks: Precision and Drama

Masks provide ultimate control over vignette shape and placement for more artistic and dramatic uses. This method works great in highlighting subjects in interviews or creating cinematic moments.

Steps to Create a Vignette Using Masks:

- **Apply the Effect:** Drag the **Brightness & Contrast effect** from the Effects panel to your clip. Also, lower the brightness and contrast to darken the edges of the frame.

- **Draw the Mask:** Use the **Pen Tool** to create a custom shape, or use one of the **Circle or Square shape masks** available under the Brightness & Contrast section of the Effect Controls panel.

- **Invert the Mask**: Check the Inverted option to darken everything outside the mask, so that your subject remains lit.

- **Refine the Mask:** Adjust Feathering to softly halo the edges for a more natural appearance. **Mask Opacity and Mask Expansion** refine the vignette's intensity and coverage.

- **Track the Subject (if needed): Mask Tracking** automatically keeps the vignette properly aligned with a moving subject so that everything remains consistent throughout the clip.

This technique allows you to create vignettes custom to your scene, which is ideal for when you need extreme accuracy.

Creative Ways of Using Vignettes

- **Focus Attention**: Draw the attention of the viewer to one part of the frame, such as the face of a character or an important background element.
- **Adding Mood:** Subtle darkening of edges can create mystery, intimacy, or nostalgia.
- **Framing Landscapes:** Vignettes may give emphasis to natural contours and draw the viewer's eye into the depth of a scenic shot.

- **Dramatic Highlights:** A custom-shaped vignette can make an object a central focal point, adding drama in a way that progresses the story.

How to display Color Management

Color management is the process that forms the basis of reliably getting consistent and predictable colors across scanners, digital cameras, monitors, and other peripheral devices. Each device has its particular range of colors, or color gamut, over which it expresses its range of reproducing colors. Often, this variability leads to color shifts when moving media from device to device.

This can be demonstrated in an image or video frame that appears on an LCD monitor but may turn out differently on a plasma screen because of their differing color gamuts. This is the rationale for color management, as a translator, to ensure colors are correctly and accurately rendered from one device to the other by mapping them within the specific gamut of a particular device.

Color Transformation between Devices

Color inconsistency can also occur when media is transferred from the camera to monitors and from one device to another. This is due to the fact that all devices interpret colors differently and display them according to their varying abilities.

Color management bridges these gaps by standardizing color translation and ensuring continuity in the visual experience. In video production or graphic design, this alignment is critical to achieving consistent aesthetic intentions across multiple platforms.

Setting Up Color Management in Premiere Pro

Adobe Premiere Pro provides robust tools for managing colors, aiding users to achieve accurate and consistent visuals across monitors and projects. Recent updates in Premiere Pro (Beta) have streamlined access to color management preferences, offering greater flexibility:

1. **Access Preferences:**

    •   Navigate to **Preferences** via the **General menu** or the **Lumetri Color panel.**

    •   Locate settings like **Enable Display Color Management** (requires GPU acceleration) to ensure accurate color representation.

2. **Enable Key Features:**

    •   **Display Color Management:** Ensures color values match on any monitor for fidelity.

    •   **Extended Dynamic Range Monitoring**: Shows out-of-range colors that do not clamp to ensure subtle detail.

3. **Optimizing GPU Settings**:

    If "Enable Display Color Management" is grayed out go to the **File menu** to access the **Project Settings.** Afterward, select **General** and ensure that the Renderer says **Mercury Playback Engine GPU Acceleration.**

    Also, ensure that your GPU is compatible with the following:

    •   At least 1 GB of VRAM

- Updated GPU drivers.
- Clear any warnings that appear in the **System Compatibility Report.**

Effects of Color Management on Projects

Premiere Pro supports both television broadcast standard 2.4 and the macOS standard of gamma 1.96, which provides a great deal of flexibility with various workflows:

- **Gamma Settings:** The Viewer Gamma option, located in the Lumetri Color panel, toggles viewers from broadcast standard to Mac OS standard.
- **Applications:** This feature applies broadly across Premiere Pro:
  a.   Rec.709 video remains consistent between the Source Monitor and Program Monitor.
  b.   Viewer Gamma plays an important role in color-managed footage monitoring in the Program Monitor for correct tone mapping and display.

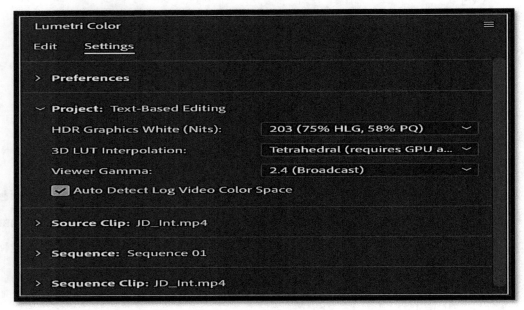

Optimizing for Broadcast and Beyond

By aligning device capabilities with production standards, color management empowers creators to maintain visual integrity across diverse environments. Whether you're crafting native Rec.709 video or working with complex log formats, tools like Lumetri Color ensure that your creative vision remains true from start to finish.

When is Color Management Useful?

Color management is important to ensure that the color of video material is represented correctly when editing, color grading, or playing the clip. It becomes valuable particularly when there is a mismatch between the color space of the timeline and the display color space. This will be an overview of when and why to enable display color management, as well as considerations for different color spaces.

Without color management, the differences between the colors of the timeline and the capability of the display will result in wrong displays of visuals. For example,

- **Color fidelity:** The color played on your screen represents the intended look on various devices.
- **Shadow detail and saturation:** Well-mapped shadow and mid-tones avoid color clipping or crushing.
- **Consistency across workflows:** Correct colors on different screens and under different standards like Rec. 709, sRGB, and P3.

Key Technical Insights

1. **Shadow Compression in sRGB Displays**

   sRGB has less granularity in shadow areas than does Rec. 709. For example, in an 8-bit signal:

   - The 20 lowest Rec. 709 codes are compressed into 7 sRGB codes.
   - This can result in visible loss of shadow detail.

In 10-bit signals, a similar compression occurs:

- The 78 lowest Rec. 709 codes map to just 28 sRGB codes.

2. **Impact on Standard Displays**

- Most consumer displays are sRGB (8-bit) and struggle to represent Rec. 709 content correctly.

- Displays claiming sRGB accuracy ("sRGB-in-name-only") may fail to achieve precise calibration due to sampling limitations during the calibration process.

3. **Wide-Gamut Displays**

- Displays like P3 or HP DreamColor, which support more than one standard, for example, sRGB, Rec. 709, and P3 gain significantly by color management to ensure the proper color profile is used.

Practical use in video editing tools

1. **Premiere Pro Viewer Gamma Settings**

- Switch between different gamma settings: 1.96, 2.2, and 2.4, depending on the environment where the display will be and the device used for playback.

- By default, macOS uses 1.96, but this should be tested on target devices to match best.

2. **Project Settings**

- Change settings in the "Project" section to allow working color spaces; each of these has options to turn off **Auto-Detect Log Video Color Space** to give more detailed control.

Visual Comparison of On/Off Color Management

On an sRGB monitor displaying Rec. 709 content:

- **Without color management:** The shadows are crushed, and colors can appear desaturated or not quite right.

- **With color management:** Shadows and saturation more closely align to the intended Rec. 709 look, though limitations persist thanks to the display's native color space.

Color Settings

The Color workspace in Premiere Pro 2025 unifies color-related options under one roof, for ease of access and manipulation. From adjustments of sequences or clips to display options, tools are intuitively grouped for easy, exacting manipulations.

To get started:
- First and foremost, launch a project.
- From within the main menu, go to **Window** to select the **Workspaces.** Afterwards, select **Color.**

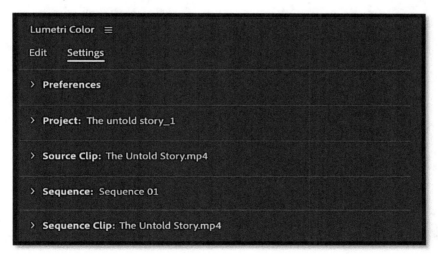

The Lumetri Color interface unifies all the key settings that were previously scattered around the panels and preferences into one efficient area. Now, establish your preferences, your project settings, source and sequence color edits, and even new **Sequence Clip settings** from within Lumetri Color.

Unified Settings Overview

1. **Preferences**

   Launch **Lumetri Color** and unlock global parameters that determine defaults for all projects and clips.

   - Display Color Management: Displays Accurate color on your monitors.
   - Extended Dynamic Range Monitoring: Shows out-of-range color values for expanded HDR workflows.
   - Transmit Device Settings: Shows all connected devices, allows the user to turn video streams on or off, and opens device-specific settings.

   These preference settings apply globally to your Premiere Pro environment.

2. **Project Color Settings**

   Quickly reveal and modify application-level project settings:

   - **Auto Detect Log Video Color Space**: Automates the log color management.
   - **HDR Graphics White (Nits):** Sets the luminance for HDR.

- **3D LUT Interpolation:** Describes how a LUT reads color data.
- **View Gammas:** Select other gammas, depending on your needs.

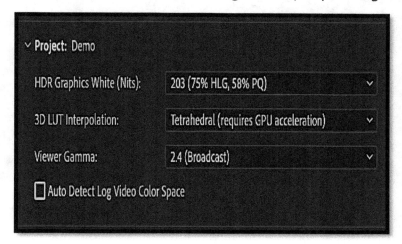

Project Settings provide advanced working color space control that will only apply to the current project.

3. **Source Clip Color Settings**

   Edit color settings for individual media files:

   - **Apply Input LUT:** Allow the use of a LUT to adjust the color profile.

   - **Override Media Color Space**: Specify or change the color space default for the source media.

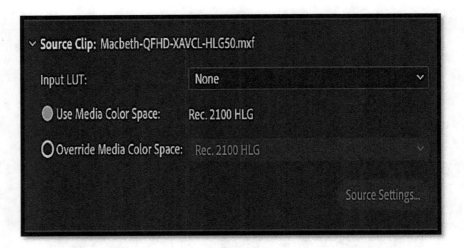

These can be directly set from either the timeline or from the project bin to offer finer control over the source material.

4. **Sequence Color Settings**

    Optimize color management for sequences:

    - **Working Color Space:** Establish the current color space that should be used for the selected sequence.

    - **Auto Tone Map Media:** Enable tone mapping so colors automatically change. This feature was previously limited to Sequence Settings.

Color edits that are specific to the sequence ensure color grading in your timeline matches your creative intent.

5.   Sequence Clip Color Settings

Refine individual timeline clips with Sequence Clip settings:

- **Tone Mapping Method:** Select a method to fine-tune exposure and highlight saturation.

- **Global Adjustments:** Apply settings across all instances of the selected clip in your sequence.

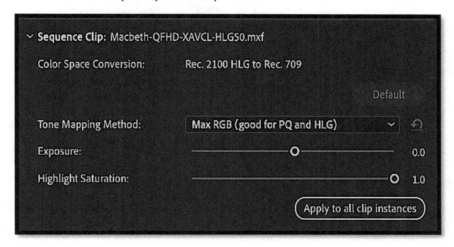

This feature empowers detailed control over specific clips within a sequence.

6.   **Color Settings for Team Projects**

Collaborate impeccably with consistent color workflows:

To edit the HDR Graphics White (Nits), LUT interpolation, and Viewer Gamma on a shared project;

- Select the **File menu.**

- After that, select the **Team Project Settings.**

- Finally, click on **Color.**

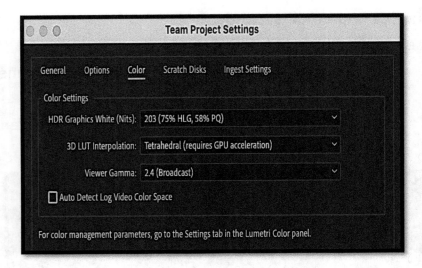

With color settings now synced, team workflows are now sure to be consistent across different contributors.

With the most recent Color Workspace, Premiere Pro gives you a unified, intuitive environment to make fine, exact, and easy adjustments to your media, sequences, and display settings. You will have at your fingertips all the features necessary to master color solo or collaboratively with Team Projects.

CHAPTER SIXTEEN
EXTENSIONS AND PLUGINS

How to install plugins and extensions in Premiere Pro

Premiere Pro supports third-party plugins to a great extent. These add-ons or extensions allow the application to add powerful features, effects, and tools by expanding its competencies for various creative needs and workflows.

a. **Install or Discover Plugins via the Creative Cloud Desktop App**

Creative Cloud allows an intuitive Desktop Application that will enable users to browse and install all plugins managed in Premiere Pro. To begin,

- Download the Creative Cloud desktop application and open it.
- On the left-hand side, click on **Stock & Marketplace** and then on the **Plugins tab,** which would open an enormous library of extensions, vetted and curated for Adobe applications.

For ease, the Creative Cloud interface labels **the Stock & Marketplace** and **Plugins tabs** so you know exactly where to click to find what you need.

b. **Install Plugins in a Snap**

- After searching for a plugin, click **Get** when you find one that fits your project.

- Many plugins are free, but some require a fee. To purchase a paid plugin, click the **price button** below and follow the onscreen prompts to finish installing it.

c. **Simplify Workflows by Creating Custom Panels**

Most of the plugins have been designed to fit into Premiere Pro effortlessly, creating custom panels and tools that boost workflow efficiency. These can save users, typically those with certain editing requirements.

d. **Manage Plugins with ease**

The Creative Cloud desktop app also makes managing your plugins easy. To see all your installed extensions, to update them, or to uninstall any of them, go to the sections labeled **All plugins or Manage plugins.**

By embracing third-party plugins, you will greatly empower Premiere Pro and turn it into a more creative and efficient tool, addressing more particular needs of a single editor.

The latest plugins from third-party developers

Many of these plugins created by innovative third-party developers introduce various capabilities to allow you to improve your editing projects by introducing intricate effects, smooth transitions, broadened workflows, and much more.

Find Plug-ins easily

Find the perfect tools to match your creative vision. Tap into **Adobe's Partner Finder database** to search for plug-ins that boost your Premiere Pro experience. From stunning visual effects to professional-grade audio tools, you'll find everything you need to push your projects to the next level.

Plug-in Categories and Developers

1. **Effects and Transitions**

   Take your storytelling to the next dimension with dynamic effects and flawless transitions. Popular creators include:
   - Yanobox
   - Synthetic Aperture
   - SUGARfx
   - Effects, Inc.
   - RE
   - Red Giant
   - NewBlueFX
   - Film Impact
   - Digital Anarchy
   - ABSoft
   - Boris FX

   With these plug-ins, you can explore stylistic effects, cinematic transitions, and custom visual enhancements to captivate your audience.

2. **Codecs and File Formats**

   Extend the capabilities of supported source formats with the following specialized plug-ins:
   - Minnetonka Audio
   - MediaReactor Workstation
   - fnord software
   - Accusoft Pegasus

These tools will ensure everything operates smoothly and is fully compatible with a broad range of file types, including some of the most advanced codecs: **H.264, Daniel2, and HEVC.**

3. **Audio**

Get studio-grade sound with VST, VST3, and Audio Units format support. Premiere Pro natively supports third-party audio effects written in these formats, ensuring precise control over soundscapes and mixing.

Titles and Closed Captioning

Incorporate polished titles and pro captions using the following plug-ins:

- Noise Industries
- NewBlueFX
- Chyron
- Boris FX

These tools speed up text-based design while meeting broadcast standards for accessibility.

4. **Workflow Tools**

Supercharge your editing workflow by using innovative workflow developments powered by:

- Vision III
- Pond5
- Diaquest
- Intelligent Assistance

Automate repetitive tasks, integrate asset libraries, and extend project management with these workflow plug-ins.

Advanced Tools

1.   **QuickS3D: Revolutionize 3D Editing**

     From Vision III Imaging, Inc., the QuickS3D™ plug-in delivers fully integrated stereoscopic 3D capabilities to Premiere Pro. From Hollywood feature films to mission-critical military applications, QuickS3D expertly aligns 3D imagery for an immersive experience like no other.

2.   **Industry Partnerships for Broadcast Excellence**

     Adobe collaborates with key broadcast players to develop innovative solutions that will meet the demands of modern media. Premiere Pro supports tools, from live broadcasting to post-production, that aid content creators to excel in rapidly changing markets.

CHAPTER SEVENTEEN
IMPROVING PERFORMANCE AND
TROUBLESHOOTING

How to set preferences

Premiere Pro is highly customizable, so you can make it look, work, and behave the way you like. Preferences include everything from setting the default duration when adding a transition to adjusting the brightness and contrast of the user interface.

Most of your changes will persist until you choose to change them again. However, **Scratch disk preferences** are handled differently. In other words, scratch disk preferences are project-based, meaning if you open a project it will open to whatever scratch disk settings have already been defined in that project.

Opening the Preferences

To enter the Preferences menu:

- Windows: Go to the **Edit tab** and select **Preferences.** Also, select a category you'd like to change.

- macOS: Go to Premiere Pro before you select **Settings.** After that, select your category to edit.

Resetting Preferences

If you ever want to return to the default settings for Premiere Pro:

- **Reset Preferences to Default**: Hold Alt (Windows) or Option (macOS) while opening Premiere Pro. Let go of the key when the splash screen shows up.

- **Reset Preferences to Default and Plug-in Cache:** Hold Shift+Alt (Windows) or Shift+Option (macOS) while opening. Let go of the keys when the splash screen shows up.

How to Customize

a. **General Preferences**

In the General tab, advanced settings that you can change include:

- **Startup:** Choose what happens when Premiere Pro starts up.
- **Project Opening:** Choose how projects open by setting preferences.
- **Bins and Organization**: Choose how bins interact.
- **Event Indicators**: Show/Hide visual indicators on specific events.
- **Tool Tips:** Show/Hide helpful tips when hovering over a tool.
- **Display Color Management**: Choose settings to accurately display color.

b. **Appearance Preferences**

The Appearance tab offers several choices to customize the UI to your liking:

- **Themes:** Select one of three themes to best suit your editing environment: Darkest, Dark, and Light.
- **High Contrast/ Low Contrast:** High Contrast makes it easier to see against a light background while Low Contrast provides for impeded elements bringing the majority of content to full view.

To change these options, open Premiere Pro before heading over to **Preferences** and selecting **Appearance. Then,** check off the boxes beside the appropriate choices and click **OK** to apply changes.

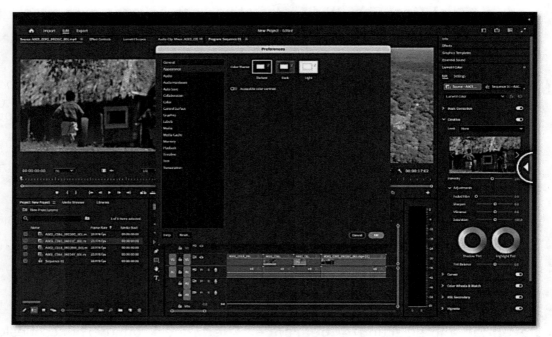

Audio, Control Surface, and Graphics Preferences Setup Overview

a. Audio Hardware Preferences

The Audio Hardware panel can be opened through the **Preferences dialog box** (i.e. select the **Edit tab** to access the **Preferences,** after which you click on the **Audio Hardware** for Windows. For macOS, select **Preferences** and click on **Audio Hardware**. The Audio Hardware panel offers a full range of advanced options to customize and fine-tune your audio configuration. You'll be able to decide here how best to set up playback and recording to work in your production.

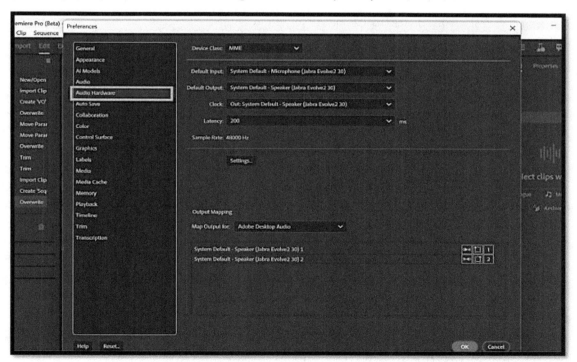

This will include the selection of the appropriate computer audio device and driver type for optimal performance and low latency. Main key hardware configurations, like default input and output, latency, sample rate, and master clock, will be automatically filled in by the panel for correct synchronization and smooth integration with your device.

Key Features and Steps

1. **Inputs / Outputs Setup:** Select which of your audio devices are responsible for playback and recording. By the rule of thumb, professional drivers such as ASIO on Windows operating systems and CoreAudio on macOS will be more desirable.

   - **Windows:** ASIO drivers support professional audio cards, and MME drivers can be used with standard cards.
   - **macOS:** CoreAudio drivers can support both professional and standard audio cards.

2. **Modify Settings:**

   - **Device Class:** Select the appropriate driver for your sound card.
   - **Sample Rate:** Click here to adjust the sample rate of your medium
   - **Master Clock:** Choose a source to synchronize and provide an accurate sample alignment.
   - **Default Input/Output:** Select which devices are to be used as input/output.
   - **Latency or I/O Buffer Size:** This should be adjusted to the lowest value that will not cause dropouts.

3. **Advanced Optimization:**

   Further still, specific hardware settings for further optimization can be found in the documentation for your sound card.

   The **Output Mapping** feature, meanwhile offers a way to route which audio channels go to which computer speakers for extra flexibility.

b.   Auto Save Preferences

Back up and secure your project files with Auto Save preferences. In Premiere Pro, **Auto Save** can be set to a great level of detail in regards to how and where your project backups are saved. You can enable the following:

- **Auto-Save Frequency:** Select the time interval for auto-saving.
- **Maximum Versions:** Put a maximum on how many backup project versions you would like to store. If you don't put a maximum on it, it will get cluttered.
- **Creative Cloud Backup:** Enable it for automatic saving to Creative Cloud in case you need some off-site security.
- **Simultaneous Save:** Allows all opened projects to save simultaneously in case an Auto Save occurs.

c.   Control Surface Preferences

For those working with hardware control devices, the Control Surface preferences provide detailed configuration to effortlessly integrate these tools.

- **Device Class Setup:** Add control surfaces using either EUCON or Mackie protocols or both.
- **MIDI Configuration:** Choose MIDI input and output devices for further compatibility.
- Custom Settings: Customize device functions using the Edit button for maximum productivity.

d.   Graphics Preferences

Graphics Preferences allows the user to set preferences in relation to the **Essential Graphics panel** for a smooth workflow in creating text and shapes.

1. **Typography and Design Features**
   - **Ligatures, Hindi Digits, Smart Quotes:** On/off, depending on the needs of text appeal.
   - **Default Paragraph Direction**: Left-to-right and right-to-left text direction.

2. **Stroke Customization:**
   - **Stroke Line Join**: Choose to join line segments by miter, round, or bevel join.
   - **Stroke Line Cap:** Choose to style line ends as butt cap, round cap, or square cap.

3. **Background Fill Options**:
   Let options indicate text block fill for whole objects or line by line.

4. **Font Management:**
   - **Missing Font Replacement**: Include a default replacement font when fonts are missing in Motion Graphics Templates.
   - **Default Emoji Font**: Assign a preferred emoji font that will be used to render emojis consistently.

Optimizing Media Preferences in Adobe Premiere Pro for Improved Workflow and Performance

1. **Set Media Cache Preferences**

   The Media Cache stores temporary files like peak files (.pek) and conformed audio files (.cfa) to accelerate editing tasks. Clearing out unused media cache files will help avoid performance issues. Cache files that have been deleted automatically will be recreated when needed.

   Key Features:

   - **Cache File Types:** Includes .pek (audio peaks) and .cfa (conformed audio).

   - **Maintenance:** Clearing up the unused files ensures proper storage and performance.

   - **Regeneration:** Cache files are recreated as required by source media.

2. **Set Memory Preferences**

You set the amount of RAM for Premiere Pro using controls in the Memory panel of the Preferences dialog, including the amount of memory available to Premiere Pro for other applications.

Key Features:

- The higher you set in the RAM reserved for other applications, the less that is made available to Premiere Pro.
- The more RAM you have means generally a better editing experience with Premiere Pro and may mean a more responsive editing experience.

3. **Set Playback Preferences**

Playback settings involve setting up Premiere Pro's media playback among multiple monitors and panels.

Key Features:

- **Player Options:** Choose either the default system player or use third-party plug-ins-i.e., capture cards.
- **Preroll/Postroll Settings:** Customize the time length before and after edit points for playback.
- **Playback Functions:** The playback preferences extend to include the following:
  a. Source Monitor
  b. Program Monitor
  c. Project Panel Preview
  d. Trim and Multi-Camera Monitors

Among others, the more detailed options include showing preroll/postroll, enabling step-forward/back controls, pausing the Media Encoder queue during playback, and setting audio/video devices.

- Default transition durations
- User interface brightness
- Label colors
- Audio hardware configurations
- Workspace arrangements such as relocated resized panels

However, the scratch disk preferences remain with a project. If you open a project, Premiere Pro automatically opens to the scratch disk settings you specified when that project was created.

How to Reset Preferences

Backup First!

Before doing a preference reset, you will want to back up your preferences which include customized settings for things such as keyboard shortcuts, workspace, and style. That way you do not lose any valued settings.

How to do a Preference Reset

1. **On Startup, Reset Option**
   - **MacOS:** Hold Command, Option, or Shift (or combinations).
   - **Windows:** Hold Ctrl, Alt, or Shift (or combinations).
   - Open Premiere Pro and continue to hold the key above. A Reset options dialog opens.

     Reset options according to the key combinations are as follows:
   - **Option/Alt:** Application preferences get reset.
   - **Shift:** Plugin loading cache gets reset.
   - **Option/Alt + Shift:** Both app preferences and plugin cache get reset.
   - **Command/Ctrl + 3:** Third-party video plugins get disabled.

Check the options as desired and confirm. The actual reset will happen after Premiere Pro is restarted.

2. **Reset via Preferences Folder**
   - Go to your system and find the Premiere Pro preferences folder.
   - Rename the folder or move it to another location.
   - Open Premiere Pro again; a new preferences folder will automatically be created.

Restoring Preferences

In case you want some setting back, you can retrieve it from the backup. Make sure Premiere Pro is closed during the whole process.

Restoring Based on Reset Method

1. **If Reset via CC Diagnostics (Beta):**
   - The backup folder with the name Profile-<name>_bkp_<timestamp> can be found.
   - To restore individual settings:
     a. **Keyboard shortcuts**: Copy the .kys file.
     b. **General preferences**: Copy the Adobe Premiere Pro Prefs file
     c. **Workspaces**: Copy the Layouts folder.
   - Replace these files in the new preference folder that was just created:

2. **If the Preferences Folder Was Renamed or Relocated:**
   - Rename the folder to its original name [Profile-<name>] or move the folder to its original location.

Cautions and Tips

- Take care to not reinstate any settings that caused your problems in the first place.
- After reinstating any setting, do so one at a time so you know which configuration may cause problems.

- Back up the preferences regularly so that in the future this does not happen.

Resetting and restoring the preferences can immediately solve many Premiere Pro problems, i.e., you could then just go on working efficiently while keeping all of your custom settings within reach.

Recovery Mode

Premiere Pro makes recovering your projects and getting back into editing after an unexpected crash much easier, limiting workflow interruption. Here's how you take advantage of recovery features in it:

a. **Automatic Recovery Mode**

Recovery Mode within Premiere Pro helps you seamlessly restore your project after a crash.

1. **Launch after a Crash**

When you open Premiere Pro again, you get a notification pop-up:

- "Premiere Pro quit unexpectedly while a project was open."
- If there were more projects opened, then the message would adapt accordingly.

2.   Restore Projects

- Click the **Reopen button** to reopen all projects in the last known available state before the crash.

- After restoring your projects, save changes to the main file so that updates may be maintained.

Note: The recovery popup will never show again after being dismissed and after subsequent openings.

3.   Revert to an Earlier Version

- If needed, choose the **File menu** and select **Revert** to return to the last user-saved version of your project.

Pro Tip: If you experience a crash, lower autosave intervals by heading over to the **Preferences tab** and selecting **Auto Save** to reduce data loss.

b. Manual Recovery from Auto-Saves

If the automatic recovery fails, or if a specific version is needed, one might need to do manual recovery. To manually recover your project, follow these steps,

1. **Locate the Auto Save Files**

   - Now, switch to the project folder and open the Auto-Save folder.

2. **Locate Recovery Projects**

   - Inside the Auto-Save folder is a subfolder called **Recovery Projects.** These contain recovery files built during crashes or forced quits.

3. **Access Time-Stamped Versions**

   In opening the Auto-Save folder, access different time-stamped versions of the file. Then, just open whatever file is desired, and it automatically opens in that version.

CONCLUSION

The Premiere Pro 2025 update marks one giant leap in the right direction within Adobe's vows to creators. This release proves Adobe not only listens to user feedback but acts on long-time requests, adding innovative features to further improve editing. Focusing both on practical and creative developments, this update shows that Adobe is refining the tools professionals and enthusiasts of all kinds use to tell their stories.

At the heart of the update is a new dynamic properties panel that intends to make workflows easier by putting important controls in one place. Such an interface instinctively allows users to have quick access to the most-used settings and therefore spend less time looking through menus. The properties panel perfectly epitomizes Adobe's approach to be more efficient, yet with no hit on customization. With this, therefore, editors juggling voluminous projects can be assured of seamless navigation and fluid editing.

Color management also takes a huge leap forward in the update of 2025, where Adobe enhanced tools for precision and consistency in one of the most vital aspects of video production. This gives more power to editors in taking full control over the visual elements to ensure that what ends up as the final output is exactly how they envision it. Be it hue fine-tuning or cinematic consistency across projects, these updates form a strong foundation to produce visually stunning content.

Another powerful feature is the improved function of templates, which revolutionizes the way creators deal with repetitive tasks. Adobe has furthered template personalization and has made integration even easier; editors can make sure their brand is consistent while saving so much precious time. This update ensures an easy workflow so that creators can devote less time to overcoming technical hurdles and more to the artistry of storytelling. All put together, these features make Adobe the clear industry leader in this endless evolution of tools and services.

INDEX